Trig Lane 1974–76: Excavations in progress at Trig Lane in 1975, removing the dumped deposits behind the mid-15th century river wall. To the right are the remains of the 14th-century timber revetments recorded in 1974. Note depth to which archaeological deposits survived. Diesel pump, modern concrete river wall to south, at the top of the picture.

MEDIEVAL WATERFRONT DEVELOPMENT AT TRIG LANE, LONDON

An account of the excavations at Trig Lane, London, 1974–6 and related research

by
GUSTAV and CHRISSIE MILNE

SPECIAL PAPER NO. 5
LONDON AND MIDDLESEX ARCHAEOLOGICAL SOCIETY
1982

The Society is grateful to the Department of the Environment and the Museum of London for grants towards the cost of publishing this report.

Printed by Beric Tempest and Company Limited, St. Ives, Cornwall

ISBN 0 903290 24 3

CONTENTS

Summary

I   The Background
        (a) The Waterfront Project 2
        (b) Documentary Survey by Tony Dyson 4

II   The Excavation
        (a) Excavation method 12
        (b) Post-excavation analysis 13
        (c) The Development of the Medieval Waterfront:
            Descriptions and Discussions 14
            (i)   Period I 14
            (ii)   Period II 14
            (iii)   Period III 17
            (iv)   Period IV 21
            (v)   Period V 29
            (vi)   Period VI 38
            (vii) The Foreshore Features 42

III   Analysis
        (a) Dating 50
        (b) The Revetments:
            (i)   Construction 53
            (ii)   Assessment 55
            (iii)   Reconstruction 57
        (c) The Medieval River Levels 60
        (d) The Development and Use of the Waterfront:
            (i)   Tenement Development 62
            (ii)   Medieval ships and boats 64
            (iii)   The Motivation for Riverfront Reclamation 66
        (e) Conclusions 68
            Acknowledgements 70

IV   Specialist Reports
        (a) Dendrochronology and Carbon 14 Dating by D. W. Brett
            with a contribution by R. L. Otlet 74
        (b) The Finds edited by M. Rhodes
            (i)   Introduction: a discussion of the significance of the
                 waterfront dumps and their contents by M. Rhodes ... 84
            (ii)   Pottery evidence for the dating of the revetments by
                 C. Orton 92

	(iii)	English Official Coinage by J. Clark with additional notes by the late S. Rigold	99
	(iv)	Jettons and Tokens by the late S. Rigold	99
	(v)	Pilgrim Souvenirs and Kindred Objects by B. Spencer	106
		Acknowledgements	108
(c)	Glossary compiled by G. Milne		109
(d)	Bibliography		112

The text of this report was completed in 1980.

MEDIEVAL WATERFRONT DEVELOPMENT AT TRIG LANE, LONDON

An account of the excavations at Trig Lane, London, 1974–6 and related research

Summary

Excavation of the 450sqm waterfront site at Trig Lane in the City of London revealed a series of timber and stone revetments and associated features on the medieval foreshore, sealed beneath medieval and post-medieval occupation deposits. The revetments survived to heights of up to 2.5m and had been erected during the reclamation and subsequent consolidation of the riverfront between the late 13th and mid-15th centuries.

In Part One of this definitive report, the background to the excavation is presented together with a documentary survey of the Trig Lane properties. The revetments, foreshore features and the reclamation process are described in detail in Part Two, but the description of the buildings is not included in this section since it is already published (London Archaeologist, 4 (1981), 31–37). In Part Three the evidence which established the close dating of the sequence is examined, the form and function of the revetments are discussed, and reconstructions attempted. In conclusion, the development of the medieval waterfront and the contemporary river levels are assessed.

In the final section, a general summary of the finds is presented, followed by specialist reports detailing the evidence from which the dating used in this report was derived, on the dendrochronological analysis, radio carbon determinations, Surrey ware pottery, coins, tokens and pilgrim badges. An illustrated glossary of the joinery and timberworking terminology is also included.

PART I

I. THE BACKGROUND

A. THE WATERFRONT PROJECT

In 1973 the Department of Urban Archaeology (DUA) was set up under the auspices of the Guildhall Museum—now the Museum of London—to conduct a programme of excavation and research into various aspects of the City's origins and development. The objectives were basically those set out in *The Future of London's Past*, a document which stressed the importance of large-scale excavation of the London waterfront,[1] where deep archaeological deposits were being destroyed by major redevelopment schemes. A detailed study of this area was obviously needed to understand the growth and layout of the nation's premier port, but before 1972 little detailed work had been possible. Since then the results of several major excavations from Blackfriars to the Tower (Fig. 1(a)) have transformed the picture.[2]

The position of the Roman river bank has been established by excavations at Baynard's Castle,[3] Lambeth Hill and Broken Wharf,[4] Dowgate,[5] Seal House,[6] Billingsgate Buildings,[7] New Fresh Wharf,[8] and Custom House[9] (Fig. 1). In addition timber wharves of 2nd- and 3rd-century date were located on at least four sites east of the mouth of the Walbrook.[10] It is now clear that in the Roman period the Thames flowed some 50m to 100m further north than the modern river. Substantial sections of the Roman defensive riverside wall have also been examined,[11] constructed on dry land which was not at that time subjected to flooding, and demonstrating that the Highest Astronomical Tide (HAT) in the 4th century was below $c.$ +1.5m OD, the approximate level at which the base of the wall was found. By comparison, the present-day HAT is $c.$ +4.5m OD.[12] Part of the southern face of the wall had subsequently been severely eroded by river action by the 12th century, suggesting a rise in river level relative to the land in this period. Evidence of this marine transgression has been observed on sites on both banks of the river,[13] and the implications discussed in a recent paper.[14]

Embankments[15] and river gravels[16] of mid- to late Saxon date have been examined just to the south of what was to become Upper and Lower Thames Street, showing that the Thames continued to flow well to the north of the frontage shown on the earliest accurately surveyed plan of the City's waterfront, drawn in 1671[17] (Fig. 1(b)). The strip of land between the line of the Roman and Saxon waterfront (approximately Thames Street) and the late 17th-century frontage may thus be seen as an artificially created tract of land reclaimed at the expense of the Thames between the 12th and 17th centuries. The excavations at Trig Lane in 1974–6 afforded an opportunity to examine in detail the nature of the medieval development and occupation of the reclaimed land in the west of the City.

The Site

The site is centred on TQ 32078083, lying between Southwark and Blackfriars Bridges on the north bank of the Thames, some 800m upstream of London Bridge but only 100m west of Queenhithe, an important port mentioned in the 9th century.[18] There has been considerable archaeological

Part I—The Background

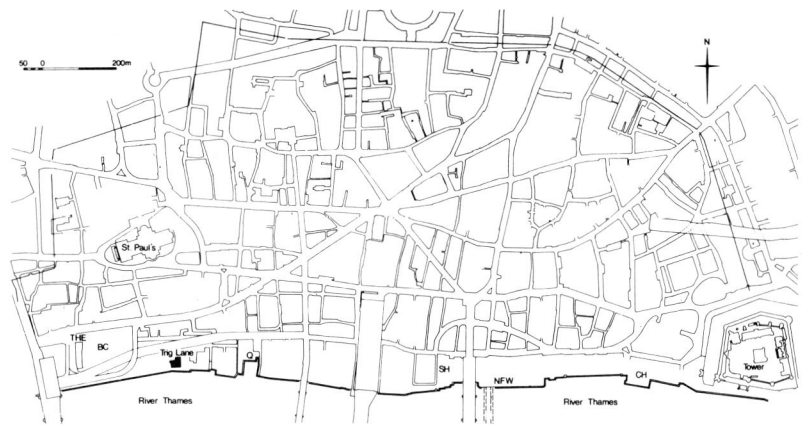

Fig. 1a. Trig Lane 1974–76: City of London, showing site of Trig Lane excavations. Key: THE=Mermaid Theatre; BC=Baynard's Castle; Q=Queenhithe; SH=Seal House; NFW=New Fresh Wharf; CH=Custom House.

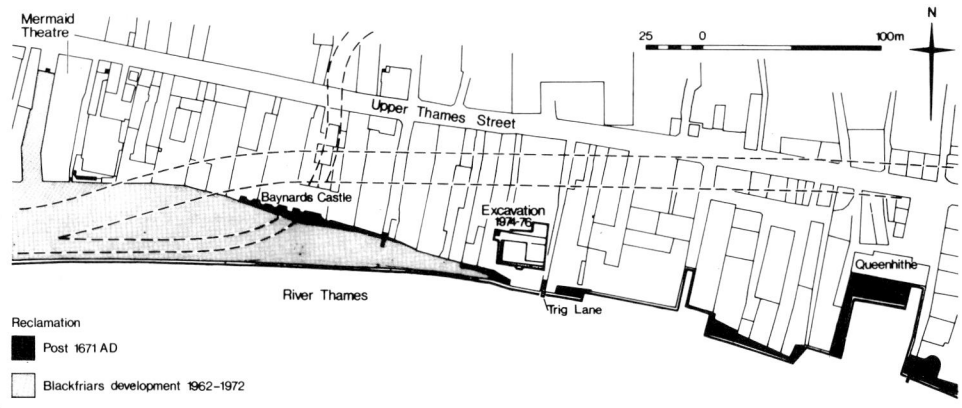

Fig. 1b. Trig Lane 1974–76: Site in relation to river and pre-1970 line of Upper Thames Street. New street alignment shown by broken line. Before work began on Blackfriars Bridgehead Improvement Scheme the line of waterfront had only been subjected to minor modifications since the survey of 1671.

activity to the north, west, and even to the south of the site. Evidence of Roman walls was found below Thames Street in 1841,[19] and the Roman river bank was located by Professor W. F. Grimes to the north of Trig Lane and Thames Street in 1962–3.[20] In 1971–2 a dual carriageway was constructed, changing the line of Thames Street so that it swung south of its historic alignment to run 25m north of the site. Observations by J. Haslam in difficult conditions during these roadworks suggested to him that Trig Lane and its associated properties were not laid out until the late 13th century.[21] However, extensive excavation by P. Marsden on the site of Baynard's Castle in 1972–3 (some 100m west of Trig Lane) showed that the castle was built on land which had already been reclaimed from the river by the mid-13th century.[22] In addition, excavation and observation during the construction of the new river wall on the foreshore to the south-west of Trig Stairs located the remains of three boats,[23] and obtained levels for them and their associated foreshores.

NOTES AND REFERENCES
1. M. Biddle, D. Hudson and C. Heighway *The Future of London's Past* (Worcester 1973) 4.14.
2. G. Milne and C. Milne 'The Making of the London Waterfront' *Current Archaeol*. 66 (1979) 198–204.
3. C. Hill, M. Millet and T. Blagg *The Roman Riverside Wall and Monumental Arch in London* London Middlesex Archaeol. Soc. Special Paper No. 3 (1980).
4. W. F. Grimes *The Excavation of Roman and Medieval London* (London 1968) 57.
5. R. Merrifield *The Roman City of London* (London 1965) 269, gazetteer No. 262.
6. J. Schofield 'Seal House' *Current Archaeol*. 49 (1975) 54–7.
7. D. Jones and M. Rhodes *Excavations at Billingsgate Buildings 'Triangle', Lower Thames Street, 1974* London Middlesex Archaeol. Soc. Special Paper No. 4 (1980).
8. J. Schofield and L. Miller 'New Fresh Wharf: 1, The Roman Waterfront' *London Archaeol*. 2 No. 15 (1976) 390–5.
9. T. Tatton-Brown 'Excavations at the Custom House Site, City of London, 1973' *Trans. London Middlesex Archaeol. Soc*. 25 (1974) 118.
10. Dowgate (P. Marsden 'Excavation of a Roman Palace Site in London, 1961–1972' *Trans. London Middlesex Archaeol. Soc*. 26 (1975) 52–4); Seal House (B. Hobley and J. Schofield 'Excavations in the City of London: First interim report, 1974–75' *Antiq. J*. 57 (1977) 37–8); New Fresh Wharf (J. Schofield and L. Miller *loc. cit*. in note 8); Custom House (T. Tatton-Brown *loc. cit*. in note 9).
11. See, for example, C. Hill *et al., op. cit*. in note 3; G. Parnell 'Excavations at the Tower of London, 1976–7' *London Archaeol*. 3 No. 4 (1977) 97–9.
12. Port of London Authority *Handbook of Tide Tables* (London 1979) 34.
13. See, for example, H. Sheldon 'Excavations at Toppings and Sun Wharves, Southwark, 1970–72' *Trans. London Middlesex Archaeol. Soc*. 25 (1974) 25; T. Tatton-Brown *loc. cit*. in note 9, 128.
14. G. Willcox 'Some problems and possible conclusions related to the history and archaeology of the Thames in the London region' *Trans. London Middlesex Archaeol. Soc*. 26 (1975) 285–92.
15. L. Miller 'New Fresh Wharf: 2 The Saxon and early medieval waterfronts' *London Archaeol*. 3 No. 2 (1977) 40–5.
16. R. Merrifield *op. cit*. in note 5, 269.
17. Corporation of London Records Office, Charter 98.
18. P. H. Sawyer *Anglo Saxon Charters: a handlist* (London 1968) no. 1628; T. Dyson 'Two Saxon land grants for Queenhithe' in J. Bird, H. Chapman and J. Clark (eds.) *Collectanea Londiniensia* London Middlesex Archaeol. Soc. Special Paper No. 2 (1978) 200–15.
19. See R. Merrifield *op. cit*. in note 5, 222; P. Marsden 'The riverside defensive wall of Roman London' *Trans. London Middlesex Archaeol. Soc*. 21 (1967) 149–56; C. Hill *et al., op. cit*. in note 3.
20. W. F. Grimes *op. cit*. in note 4, 57–64.
21. J. Haslam 'Medieval Streets in London' *London Archaeol*. 2 No. 1 (1972) 3–7.
22. L. Webster and J. Cherry 'Medieval Britain in 1972' *Medieval Archaeol*. 17 (1973) 162.
23. P. Marsden 'Archaeological finds in the City of London 1967–70' *Trans. London Middlesex Archaeol. Soc*. 23 (1971) 1–14.

B. DOCUMENTARY SURVEY
by Tony Dyson

The area of the Trig Lane excavation extends over the eastern three of the seven tenements into which the medieval waterfront of the parish of St. Peter the Less was originally divided. Until recent years the site of these three tenements was clearly defined on either side by two lanes which ran south from Thames Street to the river: Trig Lane to the east and Boss Lane, or Alley, to the west. Plot and lanes together may be regarded as a self-contained entity and it is more than possible that, as seems to have been the case with Bread Street Hill and Little Trinity Lane and the intervening land north of Queenhithe in the late 9th century,[1] both were laid out at the same time. No doubt this process occurred considerably later in the parish of St. Peter, but it had certainly come about by the mid-13th century, and in all probability by the late 12th. In any case, the documentary evidence for lanes and tenements is inter-dependent at this early period, and for this reason alone it seems best to consider them together.

Trig Lane was first so named, as *Tryggeslane*, in 1422[2] from the family of fishmongers who had an interest in, and then came to own, most of this property between 1367/90 and 1420. But the name was not firmly established until the end of the 15th century; up to that time 'Fishingwharf lane',

'Freshfishlane', or simply 'Fish lane' had been current from 1346,[3] while the earliest descriptive reference, the periphrastic 'lane by which the Fishwharf is approached', dates from 1291.[4] It is however possible, as will be seen, to identify with this named lane an un-named lane in the same parish which appears in a confirmation of an original deed of 1256.

The term Boss Lane, or Alley, was apparently first used by John Stow in 1598,[5] and does not appear in deeds relating to the adjacent property until 1607.[6] From its earliest mention in 1273, as *Kyngeswatergate*,[7] it continued to be known as *Kingsgate*, *Kingslane* or variants thereof, up to the mid-15th century,[8] except that an alternative of unknown derivation, *Arouneslane*, was also current between 1359 and 1449.[9] The lane first appears, un-named, in 1246, leading from *Kingesgate* past the house of Richard of Beckingham—who was recorded in 1273 as an earlier owner of the tenement on the east side of *Kyngeswatergate*—to the house of Robert le Heyre, 'where the King's wine used to be kept'.[10] From as early as 1205 there exists a series of references to a royal lease of this house, or cellar, one of which indicates that Robert had first received the property from Richard I (1189–99).[11] It therefore appears that Boss Lane originated by at least the late 12th century and probably considerably earlier, as a means by which wine unloaded at the king's landing place or 'gate' (*cf.* Billingsgate, Ebbgate and Dowgate, all recorded by the middle of the 12th century) could be conveyed to his cellar for storage.

It is also clear that, whether or not as a direct result of this early royal interest, this relatively remote sector of the city waterfront was already well developed by the middle of the 13th century. The tripartite division of the land between the two lanes into three separate tenements extending from Thames Street to the river is established by three deeds dating between 1256 and 1275, of which the earliest already shows at least two properties. In 1256 (Deed 1 on Fig. 2) a tenement (C) to the west of an un-named lane was itself bounded to the west by another tenement (B) of Philip of St. Maxentius (S. Maixent),[12] and Deed 2 indicates that in 1273 a Philip le Peytevin (of Poitou) occupied a tenement (B) to the east of another tenement (A) which lay on the east side of *Kingeswatergate* (Boss Lane).[13] Any doubts as to the identity of the two Philips are removed by Deed 4 of 1275 which relates to the central property (B) which John of London received from the executors of Philip of Poitou.[14] To the east of this was the property (C) of William of Beckingham which was also mentioned in Deed 1, lying to the west of the un-named lane of 1256; while to the west of (B) was a tenement once held by the Woxebrigg family who, according to Deed 2, held the tenement (A) to the east of Boss Lane. A similar pattern is evident in the third quarter of the 15th century, when deeds of 1457 and 1475 related to a tenement (B) flanked by two other tenements[15] of which part of the westernmost belonged to the Freke family who held the northern portion of tenement A on King's, or Boss, Lane in 1421 and 1457.[16]

The deed of 1421 (13) which shows the position of the Freke tenement is of especial interest because it is the only medieval document to provide overall measurements for the whole area between the two lanes.[17] It describes a property bounded to the east by Freshfish (i.e. Trig) Lane, and to the west both by King's or 'Arounes' (i.e. Boss) Lane and by the corner tenement of Thomas Freke, woodmonger, and which extended from Thames Street and Freke's corner tenement in the north to the Thames in the south. As was the rule with medieval waterfront properties in London, no north to south measurement was given; but the distance from Freke's tenement to Trig Lane along Thames Street was stated as 59 feet 1 inch, and that from Boss to Trig Lane along the river as 84 feet 7 inches. An intermediate width of 88 feet is also supplied, and, as this was probably closer to the overall distance between the two lanes along Thames Street, it can be seen that the width of the Freke tenement (A) must have been very close to a third of the overall street frontage, and that tenements B and C shared the remaining frontage of 59 feet 1 inch. Moreover, all these measurements conform very closely with the 17th- and 18th-century records of the Armourers' and Brasiers' Company who between 1478 and 1795 gradually acquired the whole of this area. A Company deed of 1668[18] and a plan of 1679[19] both give 60 feet as the Thames Street frontage of a property representing the medieval tenements B and C; the plan shows that tenement A, next to Boss Lane, was 30 feet wide at this point. The plan of 1679 also shows that both the eastern edge of a courtyard leading off from Thames Street and that of a long warehouse on the open area to the south appear to follow an alignment which might well represent an earlier division between the central and eastern tenements (B and C). The partition of this land between the two lanes into three equal parts strongly suggests deliberate planning at the period of earliest occupation which, as has been seen, was earlier than the mid-13th century and may very possibly have begun in the 12th with the development of Kingsgate.

As well as throwing valuable light on the size and disposition of the medieval tenements, the 1421 deed shows that one of the three tenements (A) was subdivided into two, north and south, properties. In fact, tenement A was already partitioned in this fashion by 1273 (Deed 2), while as early as 1256 (Deed 1) the same was true of tenement C. These subdivisions were still apparent in the 16th and 17th centuries, as, in 1457, was the partition of B. No doubt B was partitioned as early as its neighbours, but the fact that all this property, with the exception of the northern part of A, came into common ownership by the late 13th century means that this, and possibly other internal developments of the same kind, was obscured by the practice in subsequent deeds of describing only the external bounds of the whole property. This is the more unfortunate as the evidence of the north-south subdivision of two of the three tenements as early as the third quarter of the 13th century is of potential importance to the question of the successive reclamations which were so characteristic of this site. It implies that by this date there was already sufficient space available south of Thames Street for two separate holdings, and invites the question whether the southern of the two does not represent an early—perhaps the earliest—phase of reclamation.

Although the 1421 deed does not specify how far south the Freke property at the northern end of tenement A extended, its southern limit may be indicated by the Armourers' and Brasiers' survey of 1668 and by their plans of 1679 and 1795[20] which show two kinks in the east and west boundaries of tenement A at a point some 60 feet south of Thames Street. From this point southwards the

Part I—The Background

boundaries deflect noticeably to the west, as also does the boundary between tenement C and Trig Lane, some 60–70 feet south of the street. It is thus possible that these post-medieval kinks and deflections preserve an east-west alignment demarcating the site of the original tenement to the north from a new reclamation phase to the south which made room for a new, and distinct, waterfront property. Whether this hypothetical reclamation is to be identified with the earliest reclamation revetment excavated on site is less than certain; the distance between the two alignments—some 45 ft (15m)—is such that an intermediate phase may well have been involved. Nevertheless, the earliest revetment, like the earliest documentary evidence of subdivision, dates from the mid-13th century, and it is hard to believe that the two phenomena of reclamation and subdivision were not related.

The pattern of single ownership, revealed by the deed of 1421, of all the property between the two lanes—with the exception of the northern portion of tenement A—had been established by the end of the 13th century through the enterprise of John of London, a clerk. In 1275 John had acquired tenement B from the executors of Philip of Poitou (Deed 3),[21] and four years later received the southern half of tenement A from William of Bixle, fishmonger (Deed 5).[22] By 1291 he had also acquired tenement C (Deed 6).[23] This John of London is presumably to be identified with the John le Despencer from whom at some date shortly before 1313 Henry Brian, corndealer, received a house and plot which seems to have formed the middle of the three properties into which tenement C was then, and only then, divided (Deed 7).[24] In 1356 John's son, John le Despencer of Cobham, quitclaimed to William Scote, fishmonger, in a group of four itemised holdings in the parish which apparently comprised all his father's property and which John senior or his wife had previously leased out under various conditions (Deed 8).[25] Two of these lay alongside Freshfish (or Trig) Lane: the northern was then in the possession of Christina, widow of Walter de Berham, baker, for life and was to revert on her death to William Scote. It lay next to Thames Street, 'in the angle' of Freshfish Lane. The southern portion of tenement C was already in William's possession. The two other properties itemised in this deed were not given a specific location, but they were in the hands of Stephen de Stanford, a dyer, for life. Three years later, in 1359, William Scote came to an agreement with Stanford regarding the latter's life interest in his tenement in Arouneslane (Boss Lane)—i.e. in the southern part of tenement A—by which Stanford was to pay Scote seven marks *per annum* for his property until his death, when it would revert to Scote (Deed 9).[26] By the terms of Scote's will of 1367, all his lands and reversions acquired from John le Despencer were bequeathed to Walter de Aldebury, canon of St. Paul's, to John Trig, fishmonger, and to Robert, rector of St. Peter's.[27] Between 1390 and 1412 John Trig, or his widow Emma, received various quitclaims from parties who presumably represented the interests of the other legatees of Scote's will.[28] In 1420 Emma conveyed the property to William atte Stokke, a dyer,[29] who, by the familiar deed of 1421 leased it out to several parties for £20 *p.a.*

From this date, the tidy pattern of single ownership temporarily broke down, and tenements B and C were acquired by the Armourers' and Brasiers'

Company by a complicated process from 1478. For reasons already explained, single ownership reduces the likelihood of reference to any internal structural alterations, and very little information of this kind is available. In 1256 the southern portion of tenement C was said to comprise houses, buildings, a quay and a little chamber above the Thames, while the southern part of tenement A in 1422 featured a messuage and garden with adjacent wharf, 'stairs of the wharf', *le puttyng, pala* and other enclosures of the wharf, as well as *cuvas* and *vasa* for dyeing purposes.[30] The reference to the garden is matched by the mention of a garden and four cottages in the southern portion of tenement C in 1447,[31] and also by a plot of land and a house measuring (superficially?) 15½ ells which lay half-way down tenement C in 1313. Also in tenement C, the two parts into which it was divided in 1447 and 1576[32] each abutted onto neighbours' cellars, and in tenement B in 1475 stood a building called *Le dyehous* adjacent to the wharf, while two chambers over the great gate of the building were also specified.[33] The only direct documentary reference to the extension of the quayside appears in 1481, when the Armourers' and Brasiers' Company, who had acquired tenements B and C three years earlier, successfully petitioned the Court of Common Council for permission to extend their waterfront, at their own expense, ten feet into the river so as to bring it level with neighbouring quaysides.[34]

NOTES AND REFERENCES

1. T. Dyson 'Two Saxon land grants for Queenhithe' in *Collectanea Londiniensia: studies presented to Ralph Merrifield*, ed. J. Bird, H. Chapman and J. Clark (London Middlesex Archaeol. Soc. Special Paper 2 (1978)) 200–15.
2. E. Ekwall *Street Names of the City of London* (Oxford 1954) 143, citing *A Book of London English 1384–1425*, ed. R. W. Chambers & M. Daunt (Oxford 1931) 129. See also *Triglane*, 1485 (Guildhall Library: Armourers' & Brasiers' Deeds, MS 12122/1/39); *Trigge Lane* 1565 (ibid., 2/46); *Tryglane* 1576 (ibid., 2/48).
3. *Fisshyngwharf lane* 1346 (*London Assize of Nuisance 1301–1431*, ed. H. M. Chew & W. Kellaway, London Record Society 10 (1973) no. 396); *Fressihslane*, 1356 (City of London Record Office; Husting Roll 83(72); Armourers' & Brasiers' Deeds, MS 12133/1/1); *venella vocata Fressisshelane*, 1350 (Armourers' & Brasiers' Deeds, MS 12122/1/2); *Fisshelane*, 1392 (Husting Roll 120(123)); *Fysshlane*, 1398 (ibid., 126(149)); *Fresshfisshelane*, 1421 (ibid., 149(9); Armourers' & Brasiers' Deeds, MS 12122/1/12); *Fresshfisshlane*, 1430, 1449 (Husting Roll 177(23)).
4. Husting Roll 20(44). Also *venella . . . versus le Fihswarf*, 1306 (ibid., 34(99)); *venella . . . per quam itur ad kayum . . . vocatum le Fishwarf*, 1313 (ibid., 42(19)); *venella que ducit ad le Fisshwarf*, 1322 (ibid., 60(33)).
5. *Bosse lane* (J. Stow *A Survey of London* ed. C. L. Kingsford (Oxford 1971 ed.) ii.11).
6. *Bosse lane* (Armourers' & Brasiers' Deeds, MS 12122/2/51).
7. Husting Roll 5(5).
8. *Kingesgate (venella)*, 1275 (*Rotuli Hundredorum* i (Record Commission 1812) 433); *Lekynggeslane*, 1343 (*Liber Custumarum*, 452), *Kyngesgate (venella)*, 1363, 1385, 1387 (Husting Rolls 91(29), 114(11), 115(132)); *Kyngeslane*, 1421, 1449 (ibid., 149(9), 177(23)).
9. In 1359 (Armourers' & Brasiers' Deeds, MS 12122/1/1); 1421, 1422 (ibid., 1/12–13); 1449 (Husting Roll 177(23)); cf. Ekwall *op.cit.* in note 2 192.
10. *The London Eyre of 1244* ed. H. M. Chew & M. Weinbaum, London Record Soc., 6 (1970) no. 483.
11. Ibid., no. 217 (1243/4). See also *Rotuli Chartarum*, 151 (1205); *Eyre*, no. 293 (1246–7); *Cal. Charter Rolls 1226–57*, 335 (1248).
12. *Cal. Charter Rolls 1257–1300*, 78.
13. Husting Roll 5(5).
14. Ibid., 7(51). S. Maixent is 45 km south-west of Poitiers.
15. Armourers' & Brasiers' Deeds, MS 12122/1/24, 34.
16. Ibid., 1/12, 24.
17. Ibid., 1/12.
18. Ibid., 2/66.
19. Armourers' & Brasiers' Plan Book (Guildhall Library MS 12104), Plan 4.
20. Armourers' & Brasiers' Deeds, MS 12122/2/76.
21. Husting Roll 7(43).
22. Ibid., 10(15).
23. Ibid., 20(44).
24. Ibid., 42(19).
25. Ibid., 83(22); Armourers' & Brasiers' Deeds, MS 12122/1/1.
26. Armourers' & Brasiers' Deeds, MS 12122/1/2.
27. Husting Roll 96(39).
28. Armourers' & Brasiers' Deeds, MS 12122/1/4–9.
29. Ibid., 10–11.
30. Ibid., 13.
31. Ibid., 19.
32. Ibid., 48.
33. Ibid., 34.
34. City of London Record Office: Journal of Court of Common Council, 8, f. 247^v; *Calendar of Letter Book L*, ed. R. R. Sharpe (London 1912) 180.

Part I—The Background

THAMES STREET

BOSS LANE	A 1273 1363 1385	B 1421	C 1356 1421	TRIG LANE
1273 Kyngesgatelane	1273(2) once Ric de Bekenham; Walter & Wm. de Woxebrigg★ Stephen Passemer	(1273 Philip le Peytevin)	(1256 once Ric. Billing, now Wm. de Beckingham)	1256 'a lane'
	(1275 once Woxebrigg)	1275(3) Execs. of Philip le Peytevyn★ →Jn. de London	(1275 once Wm. de Bekingham)★	
1279 Kingesgate	(1279 once sold by Walt. Woxebrigg to Thos de Seccheville)	1275(4) Jn. de London	(1291 Jn. de London)★	1291 lane leading to la Fywayrve
	1363(10) Hepston→Redyngg 1385(11) Redyngg→Somerton 1387(12) Somerton→Everdone et al.	(1363 1385 1387) once Jn. le Despencer)	1356(8) once Jn. le Despencer, now Christina de Berham; reversion to Wm. Scote★	
	(1421 Thomas Freke)	1421(13) once Emma Trig, now Wm. atte Stokke★	1421(13) once Emma Trig, now Wm. atte Stokke★	
	(1273 Godfrey de Northampton) (1275 once Woxebrigg)★	(1256 once Lambert le Bucher; now Philip de St. Maxentio	1256(1) once Jn. de la Persone; now Ric. Billing →Philip de St. Maxentio	
	1279(5) Wm. de Bixle (who had married the widow of Godfrey of Northampton)→Jn. de London	1275(3) Execs. of Philip le Peytevyn★ →Jn. de London 1275(4) Jn. de London (1279 Jn. de London) (1291 Jn. de London)	(1275 once Wm. de Bekingham)★ 1291(6) John de London (2 messuages)★ 1313(7) Jn. le Despencer →Henry Brian (part only)	
	1356(8) once Jn. le Despencer, now Stephen de Stanford; reversion to Wm. Scote		1356(8) once Jn. le Despencer, now Wm. Scote★	
1359 Arouneslane	1359(9) Stanford & Scote; reversion to Scote			
1363 1385 1387 } Kyngesgate	(1363 1385 1387) once Jn. le Despencer			
1421 Kyngeslane or Arouneslane	1421(13) once Emma Trig, now Wm. atte Stokke	1421(13) once Emma Trig; now Wm. atte Stokke★	1421(13) once Emma Trig, now Wm. atte Stokke★	
	1279 1421	1275(3,4) 1421	1256 1291 1356 1421	

THAMES

Fig. 2. Trig Lane 1974–76: Diagrammatic representation of the ownership of the three tenements between Boss and Trig Lanes up to 1421, as shown by Deeds 1–13. Where a deed relates specifically to one plot, or group of plots, the number of the deed is indicated in bold after the date. Where additional information relating to neighbouring plots is provided, this is included within brackets at the appropriate place. Occasions of common ownership of both parts of an individual tenement are indicated by asterisks.

PART II

II. THE EXCAVATION

A. EXCAVATION METHOD

In April 1974 an area of approximately 160sqm was opened in advance of the proposed development of the site by the Corporation for the City of London Boys' School. The machine used to remove the overburden unfortunately stripped off some of the medieval and post-medieval occupation levels in this area, but the subsequent excavation to September 1974 revealed the well-preserved remains of the medieval timber revetments below them. It was then decided to extend the area by some 170sqm westwards and, in the summer of 1975, by a further 50sqm northwards. During 1976 it became known that the proposed redevelopment of the site would not be taking place so the site was no longer under threat of imminent destruction. Excavation therefore continued until December 1976 when it was felt that the principal problems of the site had been resolved (although the site had not been totally excavated in the time available) and the personnel were needed for more urgent work elsewhere in the City.

Indeed, during the 33 months the site was open, the DUA conducted excavations on at least eleven other sites: the size of the Trig Lane team therefore varied between two and up to fifty persons to meet changing priorities, although a team of between seven and ten was the most usual staffing level. No member of the team—not even the supervisor[1]—worked on the excavation for the full duration, but the authors spent twenty-four months (CM) and nineteen months (GM) on the site.

Although the upper levels were excavated more or less in plan, such a procedure was found to be impractical when dealing with the deeply stratified reclamation dumps below them. These were normally excavated in 'boxes' in a successful attempt to contain the problem of rising water, which had to be pumped from the site daily. The necessarily piecemeal nature of the method of excavation meant that the site was not dug 'in phase', and the sequence shown in Fig. 3 does not therefore reflect the progress of the excavations themselves, for at no time was the whole area opened up. When work in one deep area was completed, it sometimes became the spoil dump for the adjacent area, a process which obviated the time-consuming problem of bucketing and barrowing huge quantities of material to a dump some distance from the site.

No shoring was used in the excavation since the southern and western limits were revetted by solid 15th-century stone walling (Pl. 56), and the northern by 13th- and 14th-century timberwork, while the east was rendered safe by the cutting of a series of off-sets.

Over 3,000 contexts (i.e. layers and features) were recorded, together with over 200 sheets of plans, sections, elevations and detailed timber drawings. This material, together with the site notebooks, 800 black and white photographs and 1,400 colour transparencies, is housed in the DUA archive, where it may be consulted on request.

Part II—The Excavation

The deeply stratified deposits from the lower levels at Trig Lane produced evidence of continuous piecemeal land reclamation on the north bank of the Thames during the medieval period. This process was usually achieved by the erection of a timber or stone revetment upon the foreshore which had formed to the south of the existing frontage, and by infilling the intervening area with refuse (see Fig. 4). Thus an unusual stratigraphic sequence was encountered in which the earliest structures and their associated deposits were found in the northern (inland) part of the site, with the later in the south. This was in contrast to the more normal horizontally bedded deposits that formed the upper levels, in which substantial traces of occupation of the medieval and post-medieval periods were recorded.

B. POST EXCAVATION ANALYSIS

To facilitate the analysis of the excavation record, the contexts were divided into eighteen groups. Groups 1 to 15 comprise the riverfront revetments and associated deposits (the lower levels of the site) and Groups 16 to 18 the evidence for the occupation of the site overlying the previous groups. These may be summarised thus:

Group 1   earliest foreshore features recorded (pre Group 2).
Group 2   revetment and associated deposits (post Group 1; pre Group 3).
Group 3   revetment and associated deposits (post Group 2; pre Group 7).
Group 4   revetment and associated deposits (contemporary with Group 3).
Group 5   revetment repair (post Group 3; pre Group 7).
Group 6   revetment repair (post Group 4; pre Group 10).
Group 7   revetment and associated deposits (post Groups 3 and 5; pre Group 10).
Group 8   river wall and associated deposits (post Group 6; pre Group 10).
Group 9   foreshore features (post Group 7; pre Group 11).
Group 10 revetment and associated deposits (post Group 7; pre Group 11).
Group 11 revetment and associated deposits (post Group 10; pre Group 12).
Group 12 revetment and associated deposits (post Group 11; pre Group 15).
Group 13 foreshore features (post Group 10; pre Group 15).
Group 14 foreshore features (post Group 10; pre Group 15).
Group 15 river wall and associated deposits (post Groups 12 and 13).
Group 16 occupation levels (pre Group 15).
Group 17 occupation levels (contemporary with Group 15).
Group 18 occupation levels (post Group 17).

This report comprises a definitive description and assessment of Groups 1–15 (see pages 14–47), together with a detailed account of the basic evidence required to date the structures (see pages 50–53; 74–83; 92–108). It therefore supersedes all earlier published work on this material.

A detailed summary of Groups 16–18, the occupation levels, has been published,[3] and this includes an illustrated description of the medieval buildings. No further major publication on these topics is currently envisaged by the authors. However, research on the finds from the site is continuing, and it is to be hoped that reports on this work will be appearing at some future date.

The evidence for activity on the site embodied in Groups 1–15 was further subdivided into the six periods outlined below.

PERIOD I   pre mid-13th century
   accumulation of pre Group 1 foreshore
PERIOD II   mid-13th century
   phase i   construction of Group 1 feature
   phase ii   accumulation of foreshore
PERIOD III   late 13th to early 14th century
   phase i   destruction of Group 1 feature. Waterfront advanced with construction of Group 2 revetment and associated deposits
   phase ii   accumulation of foreshore
   phase iii   Group 2 revetment superstructure replaced by Group 3 and 4 revetments
   phase iv   accumulation of foreshore
   phase v   Group 5 and 6 revetment repairs effected
   phase vi   accumulation of foreshore
PERIOD IV   c. 1330 to c. 1380
   phase i   waterfront advanced with construction of Group 7 revetment
   phase ii   accumulation of foreshore; construction of first Group 9 foreshore features; construction of Group 8 river wall
   phase iii   waterfront advanced with construction of Group 10 revetment
   phase iv   accumulation of foreshore; construction of second Group 9 features; construction of first Group 13 features
PERIOD V   c. 1380 to c. 1440
   phase i   waterfront advanced with the construction of the Group 11 revetment
   phase ii   accumulation of foreshore; construction of second Group 13 features
   phase iii   upper level of Group 10 revetment replaced with Group 12 revetment
   phase iv   accumulation of foreshore; repairs to Group 12 revetment; construction of third Group 13 features; construction of Group 14 features
PERIOD VI   c. 1440
   waterfront advanced with construction of Group 15 river wall.

C. THE DEVELOPMENT OF THE MEDIEVAL WATERFRONT: DESCRIPTIONS AND DISCUSSIONS

1.   PERIOD I: Pre mid-13th century

No structural evidence was recovered earlier than the construction of the Group 1 features (Period II, below), since the relevant levels were only recorded in the bottom of the 'box' excavated to examine Structure A (Fig. 5). The only Period I deposits observed were horizontally bedded grey sands and gravels with much organic material, interpreted as a river-laid foreshore accumulation, and demonstrating that the line of the contemporary waterfront lay to the north.

2.   PERIOD II: Group 1 (Figs. 3a; 5; 6); mid-13th century

Two structures, A and B, were built in this period. They stood c. 4.20m apart in the north-east part of the site, and were both sealed beneath the later Group 2 dumping (see Period III, Phase i below).

Structure A (Fig. 5) was fully exposed while a north-south section was being cut through the Group 2 dumped deposits. It comprised a well-secured base-plate into which a vertical post some 2m high had been tenoned and pegged. Traces of a central tenon survived on the head of the post, and a diagonally set brace—broken into two pieces—was pegged to its western edge (Pl. 2). The southern (lower) end of the brace had been severed by a later cut (Period III, Phase

Part II—The Excavation   15

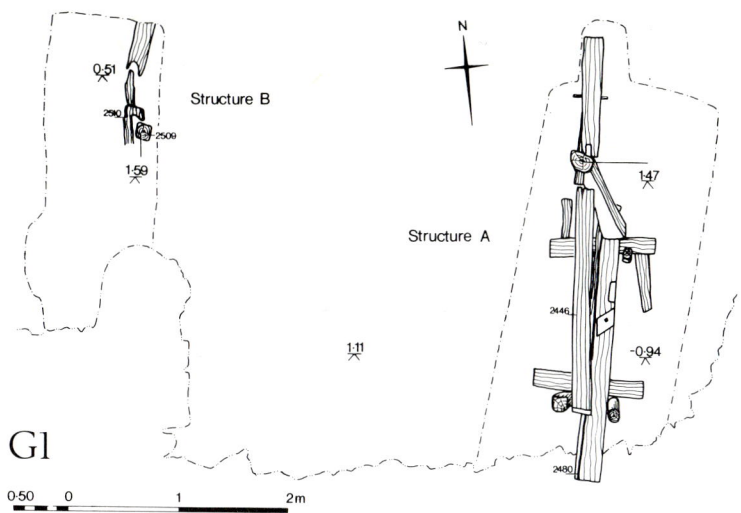

Fig. 5.   Trig Lane 1974–76: PERIOD II. Detailed plan of Group 1 structures (cf. Fig. 3a). Structure B was only partially exposed. Numbered timbers sampled for dendrochronological analysis.

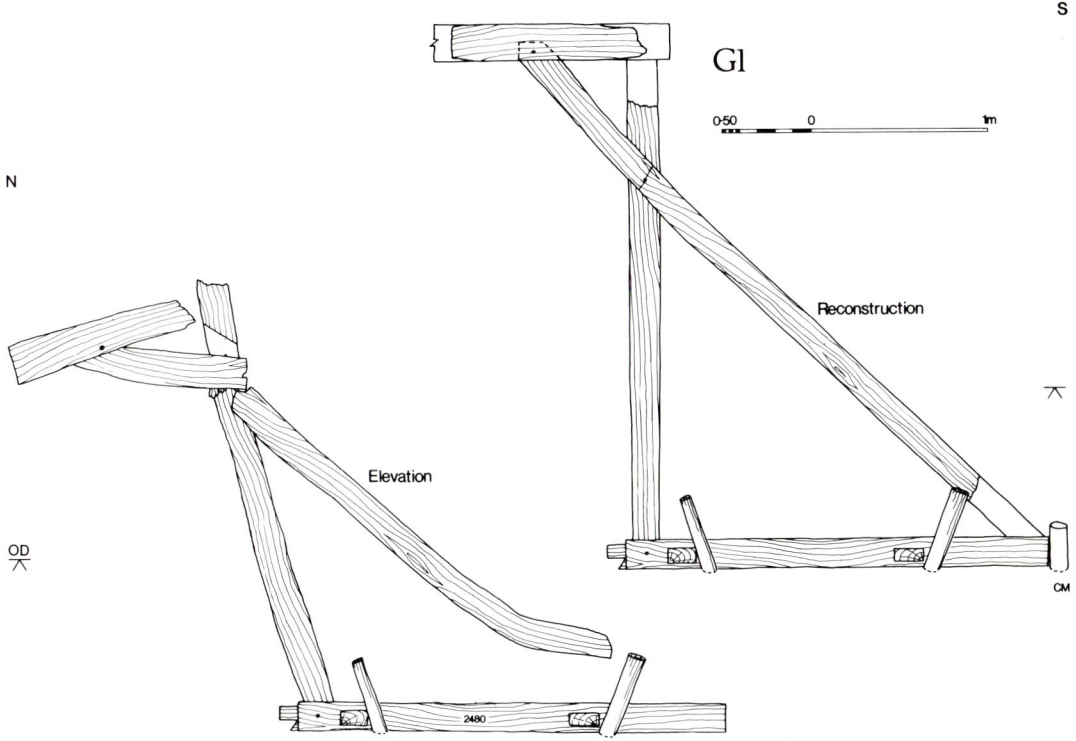

Fig. 6.   Trig Lane 1974–76: Elevation of Group 1 Structure A as found (right); semi-reconstructed (left). For drawing of base-plate see Fig. 7.

iii, see below) through the Group 2 dumping, while the remnants of a fourth principal structural member were chase-tenoned onto its northern end (Fig. 6). The base-plate was laid directly onto the Period I foreshore, and two rectangular holes had been cut into its edges through which two cross-pieces passed. These were retained by beech piles driven in to the south. In addition to the joinery already described, a pair of squint-laps with a shallow semi-circular groove cut along the length of the timber were observed on an adjacent edge and face, as well as a tenon with a spur on the northern end (Pl. 3; Fig. 7; also see glossary, Fig. 66 (e)). These features provide evidence that the timber had at least one former use before it served as a base-plate, and is one of several 'secondary' timbers found reused in later structures on the site. This particular timber may have been a braced corner post in a building with timber cladding on the walls (see Fig. 66 (e)).[4]

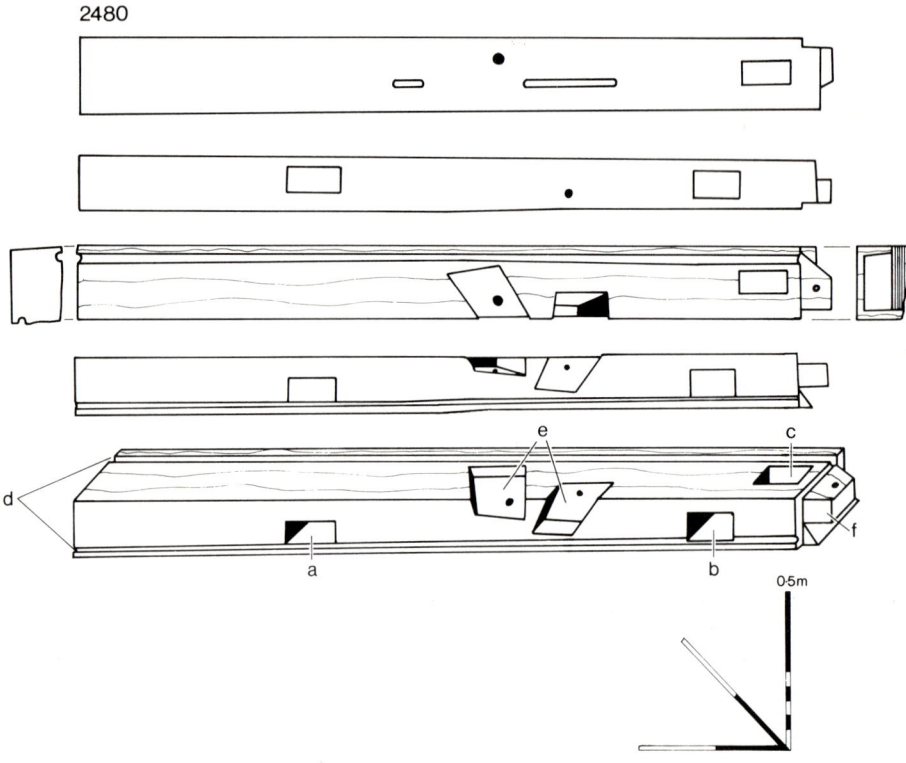

Fig. 7. Trig Lane 1974–76: Group 1, Structure A. Edge, face and end elevations of base-plate 2480 with projection to show a, b, & c: mortises associated with Group 1 feature. The grooves (d); squint laps (e) and tenon with spurred shoulder (f) demonstrate that the timber was reused at least once.

The top of Structure B was located while excavating a post-medieval pit. In the time available, it was only possible to reveal a further 1m of the structure, sealed as Structure A, by the Group 2 dumping. The section that was exposed, although damaged and decayed, indicated that this structure also comprised a vertical member with a pegged diagonal shore (Fig. 5; Pl. 8).

Part II—The Excavation

Reconstruction of Group One Structure A (Fig. 6)

Although Structure A was incomplete, it was possible to make some assessment of its function. It was not part of a planked revetment (*cf.* the Group 3 revetment, Period III, Phase iii, p. 18), since both the brace and the base-plate were aligned in a manner which was inconsistent with such an interpretation, and there was no evidence for any associated contemporary dumping or planking. The dumped deposits which sealed the structure were clearly dumped around it after it had fallen out of use, but before it had completely collapsed. In addition, the angle of the chase mortise-and-tenon which joined the head of the brace to the timber above it indicated that the latter was originally a horizontal member aligned north-south. It had been pegged onto the head of the upright post and traces of a mortise-and-tenon were noted at this juncture (see above, p. 14).

A free-standing structure built onto the foreshore to the south of the contemporary waterfrontage is thus suggested (Fig. 6). This may have been part of a jetty (*cf.* p. 45), but the north-south alignment of its brace and base-plate argues against this interpretation. It may perhaps have served as a support for a platform or as the corner support post for a building built out over the river. The distance of 4.20m between Structures A and B is not inconsistent with this hypothesis, but the very limited nature of the excavations in this particular area must make any such suggestion unproven. Nevertheless, it would seem that the face of the contemporary waterfront itself must have lain at least 3m to the north of the structures—as in Period I—for no trace of it was located in either of the north-south sections cut during the examination of this area.

3. PERIOD III: Late 13th to early 14th century
Phases i and ii: Group 2 (Figs. 3b; 8b)

Traces of a timber base-plate to the south of a series of deposits dumped in quantity and disturbed by east-west and north-south cuts constitute the main features of Phase i, and were located in the north-east area of the excavation (Fig. 8b).

Partial excavation beneath the base-plate of the Group 3 revetment (Period III, Phase iii, below) revealed that it directly overlay an earlier base-plate laid horizontally east-west, and retained to the south by piles, demonstrating that it was therefore still *in situ* (Fig. 8b; Pl. 5). Although 9m apart, these two sections of the Group 2 feature were assumed to be associated as both were of similar size and occupied the same stratigraphic position. However, this feature was not observed in the limited excavation below the later revetment some 3.5m to the west.

A deposit of river-laid material had accumulated against the southern edge of the Group 2 base-plate, and to the north evidence of substantial dumping was recovered. There was insufficient time to excavate these deposits totally, and two attempts at cutting complete sections through them were thwarted by excessive seepage of water from a modern intrusion which had been tunnelled through the medieval deposits. Nevertheless, it was established that the dumping extended over an area of at least 5m north-south and 11m east-west (Fig. 8a), while tiplines indicated that the deposits had been dumped from east to west. Like most of the medieval dumped deposits recorded at Trig Lane and other waterfront sites, this material was principally of an organic nature, dark brown in colour with a distinctive odour, containing much cultural material. These dumped deposits of up to 3m in depth clearly marked, and perhaps caused, the destruction of the Group 1 feature.

A levelling layer of oyster shell up to 0.15m thick and a thicker deposit of brown earth and gravel overlay this organic material, perhaps deliberately laid to seal the smell of rotting vegetation and to provide a well-drained bed for a gravel surface. This metalling was subsequently overlain by a more substantial floor made up from stone chippings of Purbeck marble.[5] The north-south and east-west cuts associated with the construction of the Group 3 revetment (see Phase iii, below) were all cut from this level.

Phases iii and iv: Groups 3 and 4 (Figs 3c; 8a; 8b)

A deep east-west cut in the dumped deposits and surfaces associated with the Group 2 revetment was located (Fig. 8a). It is suggested that this was cut to rob the superstructure of the earlier Group 2 revetment to base-plate level, and was subsequently utilised as a construction trench in which the Group 3 revetment was erected. It was then backfilled to the level of the crushed stone surface described above.

Substantial remains of the Group 3 revetment which replaced the Group 2 structure were recorded in the northern part of the site. It was traced for a distance of 16m (Fig. 8a) and survived in excellent condition to a height of over 2m in the central and eastern areas, where its southern face was fully exposed (Fig. 8b). Between these two areas, the later construction of a chalk building foundation[6] obscured the revetment face, and only the braces were visible (Pl. 4).

The structure comprised a base-plate composed of several timbers joined with edge-halved scarfs with square vertical butts (Fig. 66 (l)), and retained to the south by a series of oak and elm piles (Fig. 9). It was laid directly on top of the Group 2 base-plate (Pl. 5). Squared vertical posts, of about 0.20m in width, and surviving to *c.* 2m high, were set in the upper face of the plate with a central tenon edge-pegged into a mortise. The interval between the posts was just over 0.50m. Five or six levels of horizontal planking were laid edge-to-edge on their northern faces, secured with round or oval-headed nails up to 0.11m long, or, in one instance, set into rebates cut down the north-east and north-west corners of the post (Fig. 10a). Every post had been supported to the south by a shore, to which it had been joined by a chase-mortise-and-tenon. The shore itself ran diagonally southwards, and its foot was cut to form a bird's-mouth abutment (Fig. 10b; Pl. 7), wedged against the northern shoulder of a subsidiary base-plate. The latter ran parallel to the principal plate, but some 1.60m to the south. The northern half of its upper face had been cut back to form the shoulder against which the toe of the shore butted. Dove-tail housings suggested the position of timbers which could have served no structural function in the revetment, and indicated that the timber had been reused from an earlier structure (Pl. 7).

An additional plank 2.20m long had been pegged onto the upper face of the subsidiary base-plate, and two mortises had been cut into it, 0.75m apart. These once housed the pair of squared posts 0.90m high with the remains of tenons on their heads which were found displaced from the vertical position (Pl. 9; marked 'Trestle' on Fig. 8a). Between these posts was a third member, also clearly dislodged. The angle of the lap joint by which its foot was pegged to the subsidiary base-plate showed that this strut had originally run from the plate to the head of the western post. Unfortunately, the head of the strut was not recovered, so the actual method of joining is not known. This feature could be interpreted as a low trestle, perhaps forming part of a stairway or similar structure, rather than mooring or rubbing posts.

Three back-braces were located at intervals of 3.40m (Fig. 8a), cut into the dumped deposits to the north of the planking. Each one comprised a horizontally laid tie-back 3m long, which had originally been centrally tenoned into a vertical post at its southern end, some 1.60m above the base-plate. At the northern end, stability was provided by half-lapping and double pegging a cross-piece over the tie-back (Fig. 9; Pl. 8), and driving retaining piles against its southern edge. An additional strut, chase-tenoned into the face of the tie-back, ran diagonally upwards and southwards, but the junction with the revetment face did not survive in any of the examples recorded.

The Group 4 revetment was only partially examined in the time available to the excavators. It ran west to east for 7.70m (Fig. 8a; 8b) and at its eastern end its planking was clearly married to the Group 3 structure (Pl. 10). The two horizontally planked front-braced revetments therefore functioned together, although it was not possible to determine archaeologically if they were constructed simultaneously. The Group 4 revetment differed in style from the Group 3

Part II—The Excavation

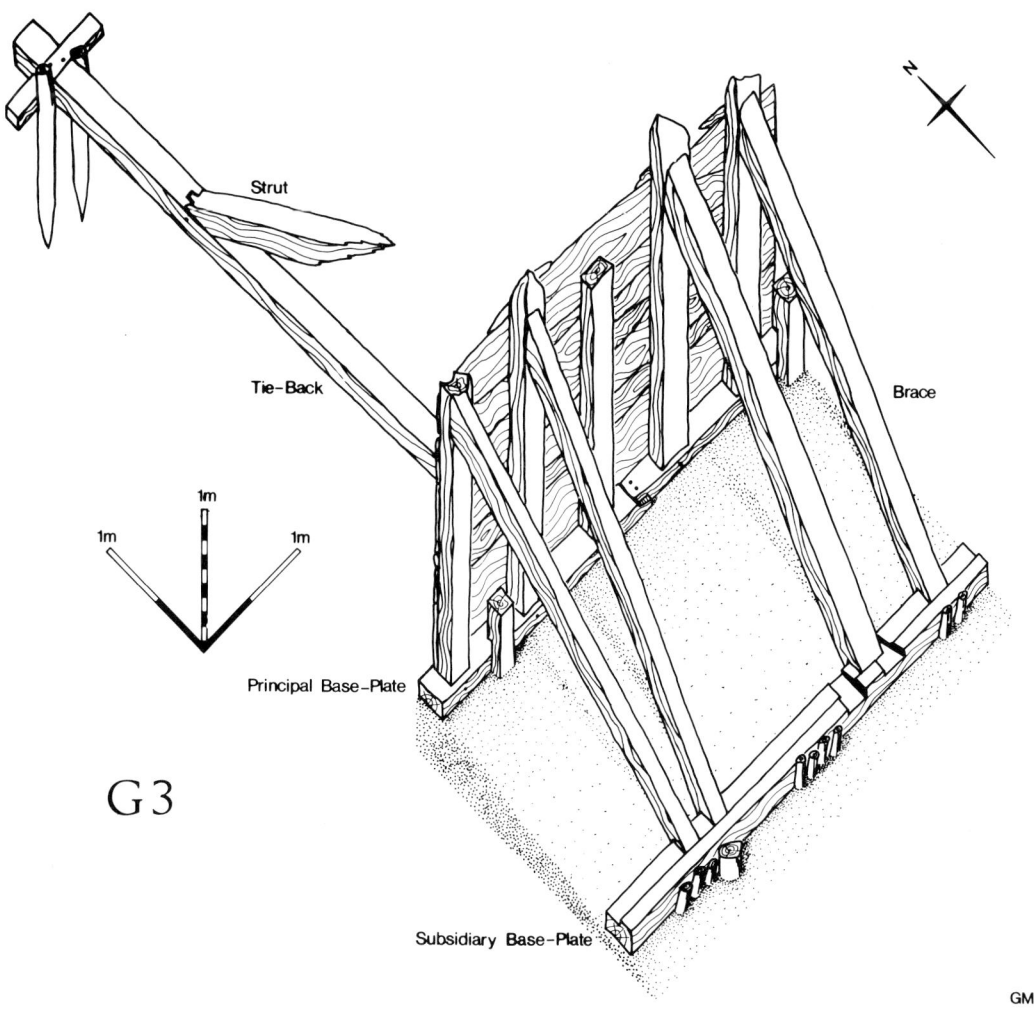

Fig. 9. Trig Lane 1974–76: Axonometric projection of Group 3 revetment, semi-reconstructed. Revetment face as found in centre of site, back-brace modelled on only complete example excavated (see Fig. 8a). River to south.

structure in that its subsidiary base-plate (onto which the feet of the braces butted) had three horizontally laid transverse members joined to it from the north, spaced at 2m intervals (Fig. 8a; Pl. 13): the joint is illustrated in Fig. 66 (f). A similar bracing technique was observed on one of the 14th-century structures from the Custom House site.[7]

Over 0.30m of foreshore material accumulated against the southern face of the Group 3 and Group 4 revetments before the Phase v repairs were effected (see below).

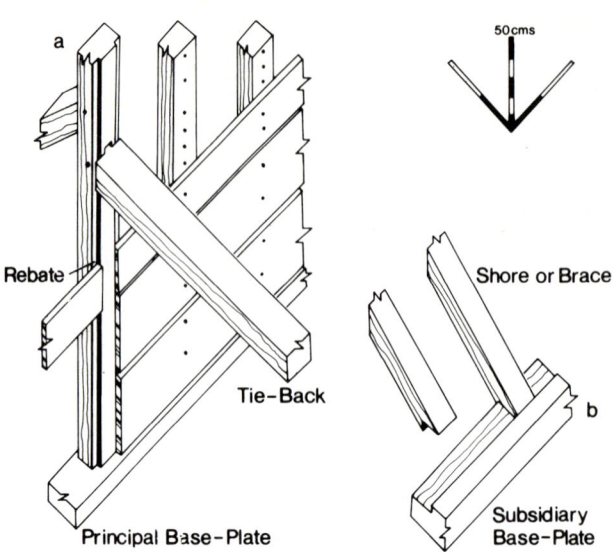

Fig. 10. Trig Lane 1974–76: Axonometric projections of Group 3 revetment to show
a) detail of northern (landward) face: note rebates for planking on post into which tie-back is tenoned;
b) junction of brace and subsidiary base-plate. The bird's mouth abutment used required no tenons or pegs.

Phases v and vi: Groups 5 and 6 (Figs. 3; 11)

Group 5, a minor repair in the east of the site, involved a bracing technique similar to that noted at the Custom House site[8] and at Seal House[9] (see Fig. 11), in which the brace was tenoned into a transverse base-plate. The amount of foreshore which had accumulated over the Group 3 subsidiary base-plate before the Group 5 base-plate was laid (i.e., in Phase iv) suggested that the repair was effected at a relatively late stage in the life of that frontage.

In the west of the site a 5.50m length of the Group 4 revetment had been completely replaced following the removal of the superstructure down to base-plate level. A second revetment, the Group 6 structure, was then superimposed upon the earlier base-plate (Fig. 11; Pl. 12) and comprised a principal base-plate into which were tenoned vertical posts with horizontal planking nailed to their northern faces. Diagonal shores were chase-tenoned into the heads of the posts and ran southwards to abut a subsidiary base-plate parallel to the revetment. An additional member tied the feet of the posts to the shores.

Discussion

The erection of the Group 2 revetment and the contemporary infilling and surfacing of the area to the north is interpreted as an act of land reclamation, while the other four structures ascribed to Period III (Groups 3, 4, 5 and 6) were all associated with the repair and consolidation of the new frontage. Of these, at least two (Groups 3 and 6) involved the total replacement of the earlier revetment above base-plate level.

The surviving base-plate of the Group 2 revetment had a pattern of pegged mortises in its upper face similar to that noted on the subsequent Group 3 revetment, and therefore a similar horizontally planked front-braced superstructure is suggested. This hypothesis is strengthened by the discovery of a timber fragment used as packing in the bedding trench of a Group 3 back-brace,

Part II—The Excavation

which had a well-cut chase-tenon at one end (Pl. 8), suggesting that this member may have been the head of a diagonal shore from the Group 2 revetment removed during its destruction (*cf.* Fig. 9).

It is perhaps significant that the style of revetting used for the waterfront in the Group 3 and Group 4 structures should differ, though they were contemporary and served an identical function. This change may reflect a property boundary dividing owners of different means and inclinations, and the documentary evidence for the site demonstrates that the property was in fact sub-divided from at least 1256 (see above, p. 9).

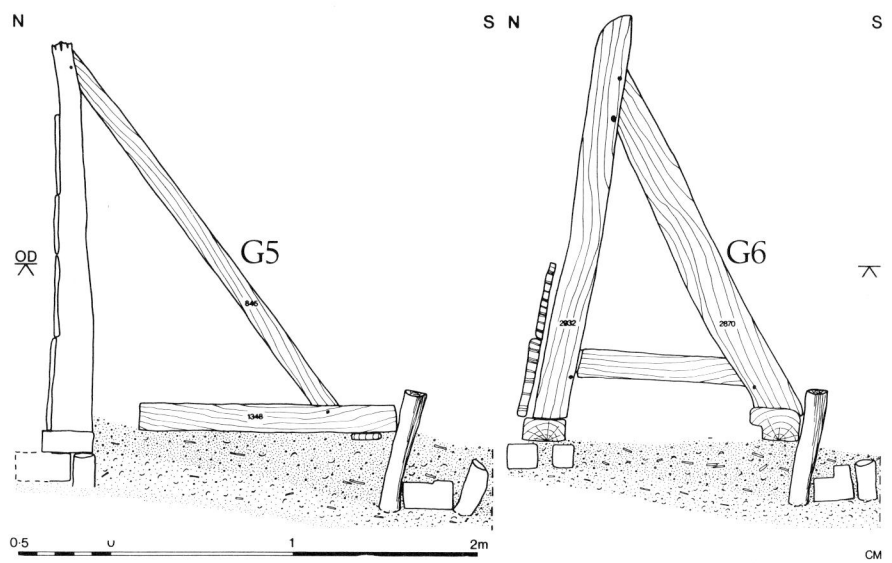

Fig. 11. Trig Lane 1974–76: Side elevations of Group 5 and 6 features, river to south. Numbered timbers sampled for dendrochronological analysis. Note remains of earlier revetments.

4. PERIOD IV

Phases i: Group 7: *c.* 1330–80 (Figs. 3e; 13)

The Group 7 structure was a back-braced, horizontally planked, revetment retaining dumps of contemporary refuse. It ran east-west across the site (Fig. 12a; Pl. 14), and had been built on top of the foreshore which had accumulated against the south face of the Group 3 revetment, *c.* 3m to the north. The western half survived only fragmentarily below the Group 10 structure which sealed it, but the eastern half was found to be virtually intact. It comprised at least two sections of a pile-founded and pile-retained base-plate, joined by an edge-halved scarf with squared vertical butts. Into it, a series of vertical posts with full or half tenons on their feet had been pegged.

The posts were arranged with alternate pairs either coupled or spaced at 0.4m intervals. The adjacent edges of each coupled pair had been trenched to accept the southern end of a tie-back (Fig. 13), and the latter, which was itself edge-trenched, passed between the posts at a height of 1m above the base-plate (Pls. 15; 16). The tie-back was stabilised at its northern end by passing a cross-piece through it, forming a cruciform shape, and driving retaining piles to the south of the arms.

The shores of the earlier Group 3 revetment proved to be an encumbrance for the builders of its successor, especially when the northern ends of the tie-backs were being stabilised (Pls. 17;

G7

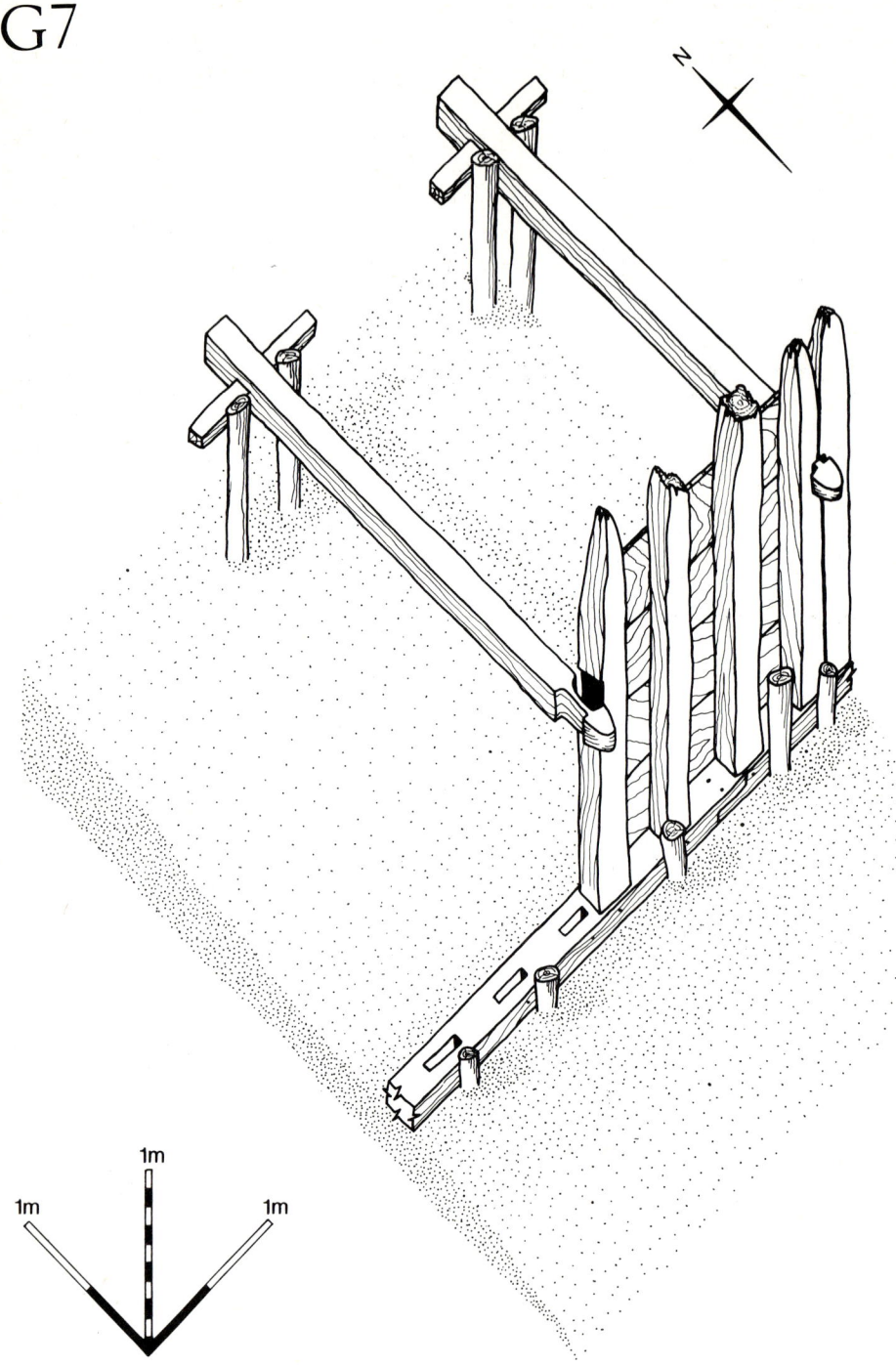

Fig. 12. Trig Lane 1974–76: Axonometric projection of part of Group 7 revetment, river to south. Cf. Fig. 15.

Part II—The Excavation

18; 19). Axes had to be employed on more than one occasion, trimming the shores to accommodate the tie-backs and cross-pieces (Pl. 19).

Evidence of a second series of tie-backs at a higher level was found in the east. Although much disturbed, the remains of two horizontally laid members were observed passing through the revetment face, at which point an east-west member was passed through a mortise cut from edge to edge in the south end of the brace, presumably providing a measure of longitudinal stability for the revetment. Later activity had destroyed much of the evidence concerning the method of securing the tie-back's northern end, but the survival of significantly positioned pile groups (Fig. 13) indicated that a system of cross pieces and piles was employed, as with their lower-level counterparts.

Four or five levels of horizontal planking laid edge to edge were nailed to the northern edge of the posts to retain the dumped material, which a longitudinal section showed had been tipped from east to west (Figs. 14; 15).

To the west the revetment face did not survive, although the base-plate was traced for a further 4.80m, at which point it had been crudely truncated. The severed remains of three more tie-backs were also located (Fig. 13a, with retaining piles still *in situ*), while evidence for a fourth was provided by clear-cut marks on an earlier post and shore (Fig. 8a, similar to the marks seen in association with the eastern tie-backs (see Pl. 19)). Dumping contemporary with the Group 7 revetment—but disturbed by the insertion of the Group 10 revetment and braces—was traced even further west (Fig. 14), suggesting a maximum length of just over 14m for the initial phase of construction.

The remnants of two more upper-level tie-backs were located (Fig. 13a): both had been severed during the construction of the later Group 10 structure, so should be associated with Group 7.

To the south of the revetment and contemporary with it were the remains of further timber features on the foreshore. They included two groups of piles (Fig. 36) and two trestle bases clearly still *in situ* as both were pile-laid. These features are discussed on p. 44.

Discussion

The Group 7 revetment clearly superseded the eastern section of Group 3 revetment by advancing the waterfront some 3m, and its western limit perhaps marked a property boundary.

Apart from the westernmost extent of the dumping, little other evidence of the structure's north-south return wall was seen. No traces of the base-plate or piles which could be associated with it were observed *in situ*, suggesting that it had either collapsed or else been pulled down and then bodily removed from the site. However, at least seventeen fragments of planking were recovered from the area to the west (four are shown on Fig.12a; Pl. 30) and from the deposits associated with the construction of the later Group 10 revetment. The longest was 1.85m, and seven were over 0.90m long. They varied in width from 0.23m to 0.50m, and in thickness from 0.02m to 0.04m, while at least five had nails in them. It is possible that some—if not all—of this planking had originally formed part of the western section of the Group 7 revetment.

Order of assembly (Fig. 15)

It is suggested that a line of piles was driven into the foreshore and levelled. Onto these the sections of the base-plate were laid and scarfed together (Fig. 15a). Although the Group 7 tie-backs could not have been positioned before the dumps on which they were laid had been tipped onto the site, the planking and at least some of the supporting posts must have already been erected before infilling could commence (Fig. 15b). Only then could the most easterly tie-back be laid (Fig. 15c), its southern end pushed through the planking (Pl. 16), and the additional vertical post positioned to accommodate it (Fig. 15d). Its northern end was then stabilized with a cross-piece and piles, after which dumping continued over it (Fig. 15e) in preparation for the laying of the next tie-back to the west (Fig. 15f).

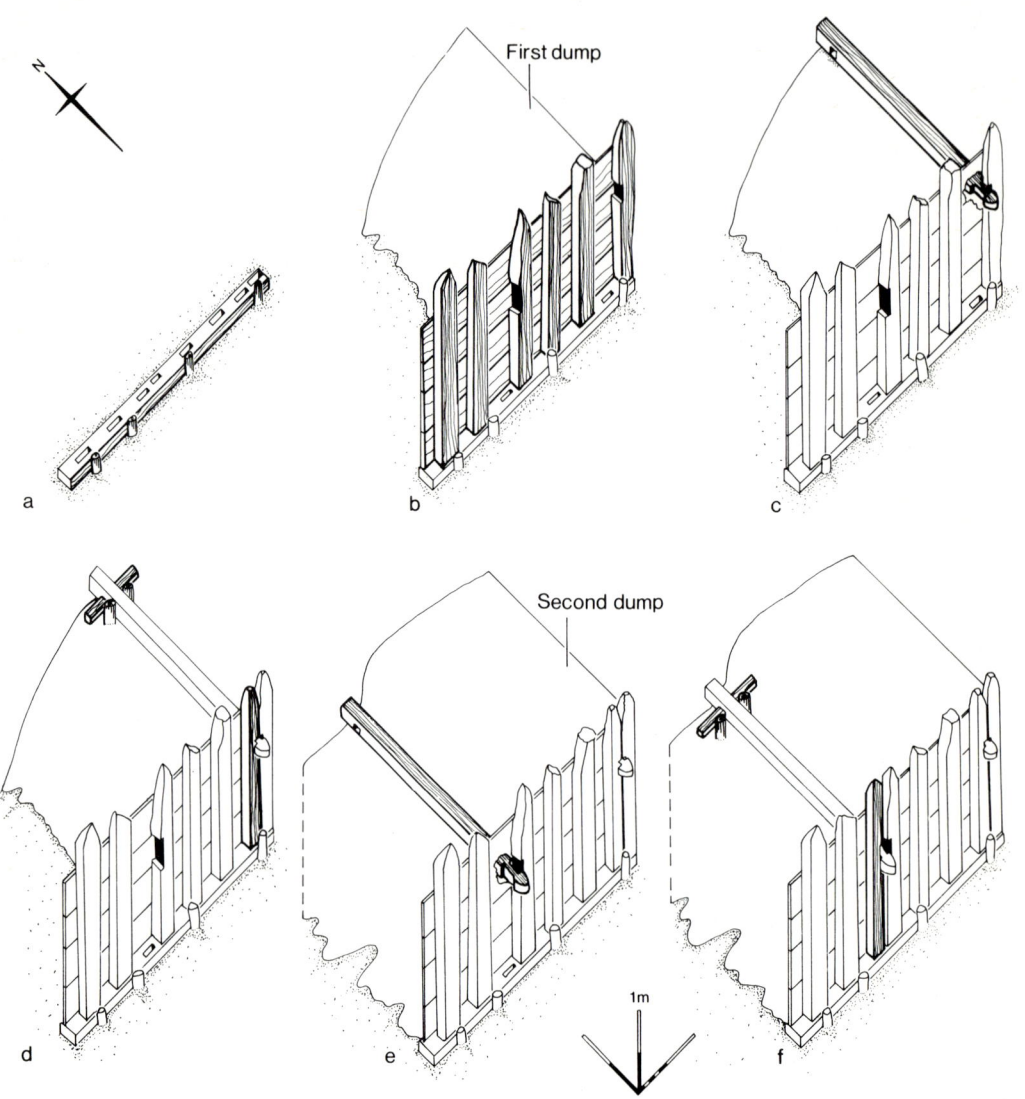

Fig. 15. Trig Lane 1974–76: Suggested order of assembly of Group 7 revetment. The planking had to be nailed to the posts to retain the dumps before the tiebacks could be positioned.

At the same time as the Group 7 revetment was being erected, the deep chalk foundations of the building visible on Pl. 4 were also being laid.

Part II—The Excavation

Phase ii: Group 8 (Fig. 3 (e))

At least 0.3m of foreshore material accumulated against and over the Group 6 subsidiary base-plate before a chalk rubble raft was laid to the west of it. This was part of the foundation preparation for the south-east corner of the Group 8 river wall, whose construction post-dated that of the Group 6 revetment, but pre-dated that of the Group 10 revetment (see Fig. 14).

The Group 8 ragstone wall survived to a height of 2.83m, and 3.05m of the east face and 1.65m of the south face were exposed (Pl. 21). In the north it had been built onto the 0.40m thick rubble raft, and in the south onto substantial timber planks retained by oak and elm piles (Fig. 16). The top of the wall had been disturbed by post-medieval building, but at least eight irregular courses of the original build survived.

The southern face had a 10° batter, but the eastern face on which four mason's marks were observed (see Fig. 16) was vertical. The courses varied from 0.20m to 0.46m in height, and were bonded with a yellow sandy mortar. On the seventh course of the east face one of the blocks projected 0.10m, probably the result of displacement rather than a deliberately laid corbel (*cf.* Group 15, Pl. 62). Oyster shell and tile had been used as occasional levelling agents between blocks.[10] Since the Group 10 revetment's north-south base-plate was laid some 0.50m higher than the base of the Group 8 river wall (Fig. 14), the wall was considered to pre-date that revetment.

The accumulation of up to 0.70m of foreshore material against the south face of the Group 8 wall demonstrates that it functioned specifically as a river wall, a feature paralleled elsewhere (see discussion on Group 15 wall, p. 40).

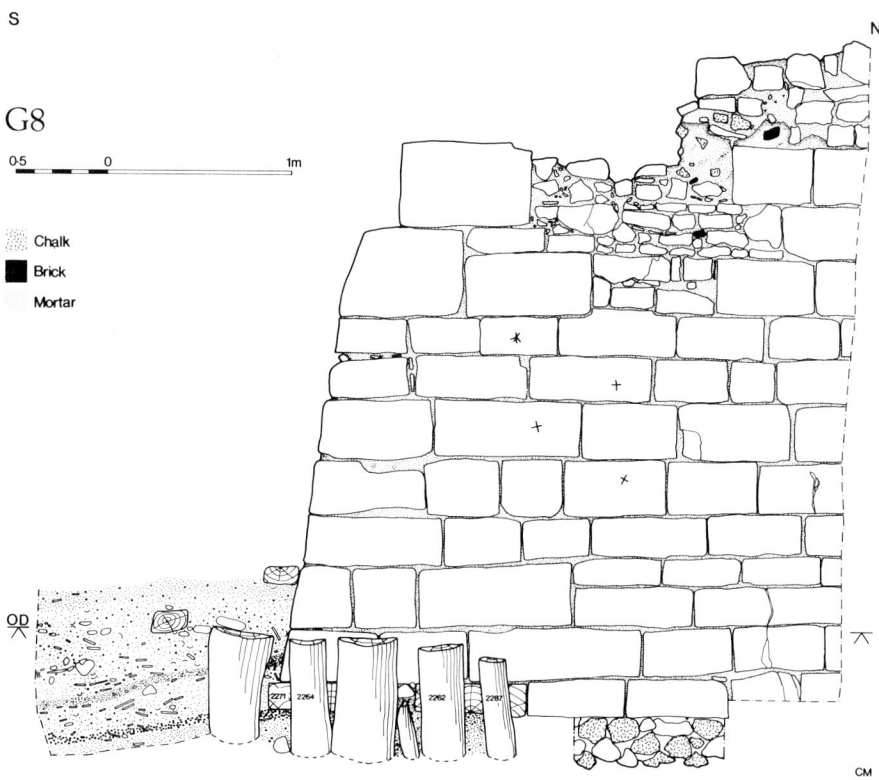

Fig. 16. Trig Lane 1974–76: East facing elevation of Group 8 river wall. Note chalk rubble raft and piled foundation. Numbered timbers sampled for dendrochronological analysis.

Phases iii and iv: Group 10 (Figs. 3 (f); 17)

The dumping associated with the Group 10 revetment completely sealed the Group 6 structure and partially sealed the robbed western end of the Group 7 revetment, demonstrating that these last two features had been in use at the same time, and that both had been constructed earlier than the Group 10 structure.

The Group 10 revetment ran east-west across the site, continuing the same alignment as the Group 7 structure (Period IV, Phase i) for a length of 17.50m (Fig. 17; Pl. 22). The eastern half of the feature was completely excavated, the rest of the revetment face and the southern 1.50m of its back-braces were exposed, and a complete east-west section cut through its associated dumping (Fig. 14; Pl. 23).

The revetment comprised a series of six base-plates joined together with edge-halved scarfs with squared vertical butts, into which forty-five dressed vertical members had been placed. The latter were set into a deep squared groove in the plate, stood c. 1.40m high, and were on average 0.30m by 0.15m in cross section. When first exposed and before considerable shrinkage took place, the edges and southern face of each vertical member were flush with its neighbour, forming an impressive stave wall[11] (Pls. 22; 35). An examination of the southern face of each vertical member revealed twenty-eight examples of incised marking, interpreted as assembly marks. The designs incorporated lines cut parallel to or crossing each other, sometimes with an additional circle or half circle (Fig. 20; Pl. 32), and indicated a west to east direction of construction for the revetment (Fig. 17b).

Support for this structure was provided by five irregularly spaced back-braces up to 2.60m long, laid out north to south behind the revetment (Fig. 18; Pls. 23; 24; 25; 26). Each one comprised a pile-founded base-plate into which two timbers were chase-tenoned at either end, inclined towards each other. The southern strut was similarly tenoned into the underside of the northern brace, forming a triangular shape, but the latter continued to run southwards towards the revetment face itself. Unfortunately, later activity had severed all the braces at this point, so the actual method of joining is unknown. Many of the timbers used to construct the back-braces had additional mortices, half-laps or grooves cut into their edges and faces, suggesting that these members were reused (Figs. 18; 19; Pls. 33; 34).

Four of the brace base-plates had been edge-trenched at their southern ends where they passed between two vertical members of the revetment wall, the relevant pair of staves being similarly edge-trenched to accommodate them. To ensure that the two vertical members did not move apart—and thus allow the base-plate to withdraw—an additional piece of wood 0.20m by 0.20m by 0.03m was completely housed half in each of the paired members' abutting edges, and subsequently pegged. Such extra members are now known as 'free tenons' (Fig. 26).

The fifth back-brace base-plate (1 on Fig. 17) was tenoned directly into a vertical member, to the west of which the revetment face was composed of six plain-sawn timbers c. 0.30m by 0.10m in cross section, but of similar height to the split members to the east.

At the western end of the revetment a return face was recorded, comprising a 1.80m length of pile-founded base-plate into which four vertical posts had been tenoned (Fig. 17; Pl. 71). Against their eastern faces a series of horizontal planks had been laid edge to edge. The only remaining semblance of bracing for this part of the structure was a horizontally laid tie-back 2.65m long aligned east to west, whose western end had been severed, but still just lipped over the returning revetment's base-plate. The eastern end of the tie-back was stabilized by passing a cross member through it, and driving piles to the west.

To the west of the central back-brace (3 on Fig. 17) the back-braces were contemporary with the dumped material, which had been tipped from west to east. East of that brace a different picture emerged, for here the back-braces appeared to have been inserted into north to south cuts in pre-existing dumped deposits associated with the Group 7 revetment. A deep east-west cut running north of but parallel to the Group 10 revetment face also appeared to be associated with its construction (Fig. 17a).

Two small revetments, simple arrangements of planks and piles intended to retain material dumped from the west were also recorded in the eastern area (labelled 'shuttering' on Fig. 17a; Pls. 25; 26; 27), while at the extreme eastern end of the revetment, a 0.50m length of base-plate joined the Group 10 structure to the upstanding section of the Group 7 revetment (Fig 27; Pls. 28; 29). The presence of rivets and caulking on several of the horizontal planks used at this

Plate 1. Trig Lane 1974–76: Medieval riverfront reclamation: general view of Trig Lane excavations in 1974 looking east, river to south. Left of the 4×500mm scale is the early 14th century Group 7 revetment superseded by the Group 11 structure to the right in c. 1380, and the Group 15 river wall in c. 1440. Cf. Fig. 3.

Plate 2. Trig Lane 1974–76: Group 1, Structure A, looking south-west. Note diagonal brace rising from base-plate (left), passing above vertical 10×100mm scale and lapping over the western face of post. To the north it has broken, but is still joined to remains of fourth member which was once tenoned to head of the post.

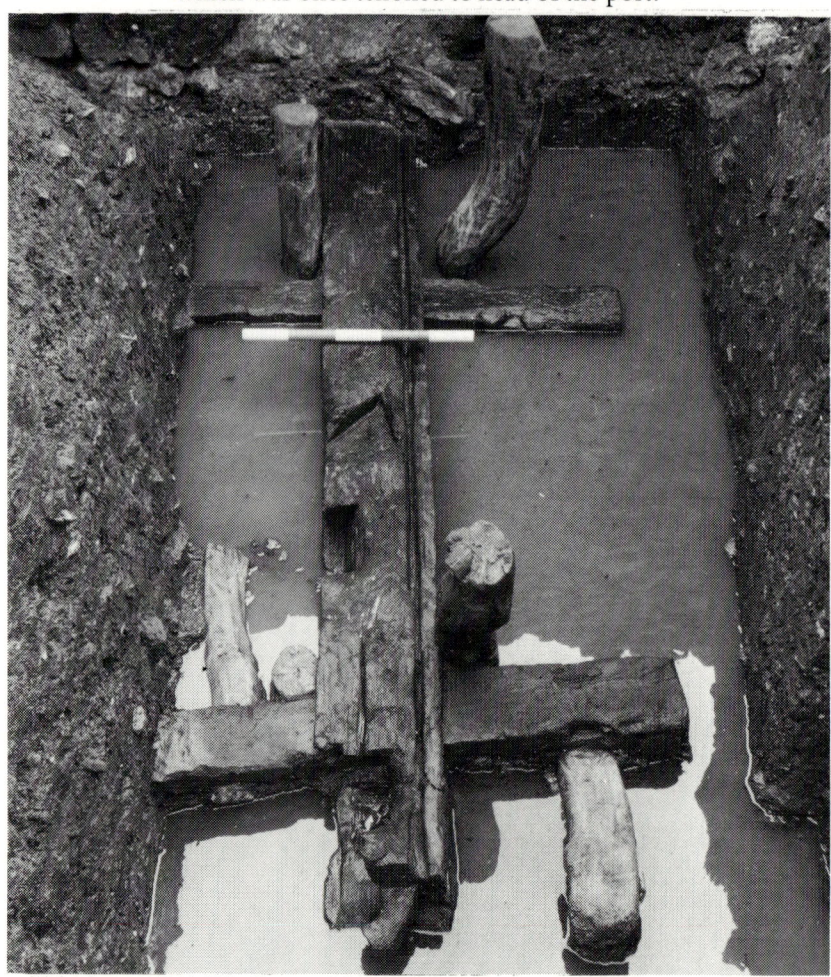

Plate 3. Trig Lane 1974–76: Group 1 base-plate after removal of associated superstructure, looking south. The cross-pieces and piles prevented southern movement. The Group 1 vertical post was tenoned into the broken mortise at northern end of timber. Note squint laps and groove in upper face with tenon in foreground, demonstrating that the timber was reused. 5×100mm scale.

Plate 4. Trig Lane 1974–76: Front-braced Group 3 revetment cut by later chalk foundation, looking north-west, river to south. The subsidiary base-plates are buried beneath the foreshore which accumulated against the revetment's southern face. 4×500mm scale.

Plate 5. Trig Lane 1974–76: Group 3 revetment base-plate with 5×100mm scale overlying the earlier Group 2 base-plate. Both plates utilise different types of retaining pile. Looking north-west, river to south.

Plate 6. Trig Lane 1974–76: Group 3 revetment face showing 2.5m long diagonal brace running from head of post to subsidiary base-plate. Looking north-east, river to south, 5×100mm scale.

Plate 7, a and b. Trig Lane 1974–76: Group 3 subsidiary base-plate with 2×100mm scale looking east, river to south. Note retaining piles and bird's-mouth abutment at foot of braces, a joint which is neither tenoned nor pegged. Traces of dove-tail joint on base-plate show it was reused.

Plate 8.   Trig Lane 1974–76: Group 3 revetment back-brace, looking south towards the river. The revetment face lies beyond intrusive stone wall. The cut into which the partially exposed Group 3 tie-back (with 5×100mm scale) was inserted is clearly visible, packed with timber fragments derived from earlier Group 2 revetment. Decayed remains of Group 1 structure B to east.

Plate 9.   Trig Lane 1974–76: Back-braced Group 10 revetment with 10×100mm scale, looking west, river to south. To right of scale are remains of collapsed trestle tenoned into Group 3 subsidiary base-plate sealed beneath later back-brace.

Plate 10, a (*upper*) and b.   Trig Lane 1974–76: The Group 3 & 4 revetments were of similar though not identical construction, but must have functioned together as planking nailed to head of Group 3 post (to right of 2×100mm scale in a) also nailed to head of Group 4 post to left of scale. The feet of the same braces shown in a) meet different subsidiary base-plates in b), Group 3 with 2×100mm scale. Looking north, river to south.

Plate 11.   Trig Lane 1974–76: Junction of Group 4 & 6 revetments, looking north, river to south. The Group 4 subsidiary base-plate with 5×100mm scale set at lower level than later Group 6 plate. To right of scale is dove-tail which once accommodated the truncated Group 4 member to north.

Plate 12 (*upper right*).   Trig Lane 1974–76: Superimposed base-plates at junction of Group 6 (left) and Group 4 (right) revetments. Looking north, river to south, 2×100mm scale.

Plate 13.   Trig Lane 1974–76: Dovetail joint on Group 4 subsidiary base-plate, looking north. To north of 10×10mm scale is broken mortise which once accommodated foot of Group 4 diagonal brace.

Plate 14. Trig Lane 1974–76: Group 7 revetment to left, looking north-west, river to south. Stone-founded building to north (with 10×100mm scale) contemporary with it. Close spacing of Group 3 revetment front-braces (centre, right) made positioning of Group 7 back-braces difficult.

Plate 15. Trig Lane 1974–76: Internal face of Group 7 revetment, looking south towards the river. 10×100mm scale.

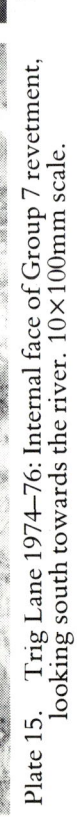

Plate 16. Trig Lane 1974–76: Group 7 tie-back pushed through crudely made hole in revetment planking. Looking south-west, river to south, 10×10mm scale.

Plate 17. Trig Lane 1974–76: Relationship between northern end of horizontally laid Group 7 tie-backs (centre and left) and front-braced Group 3 revetment. Looking north, river to south, 5×100mm scale.

Plate 18. Trig Lane 1974–76: Group 7 revetment tie-back, cross-piece and earlier Group 3 revetment front braces partially encased in the stone foundation. Looking north-east, river to south, 5×100mm scale.

Plate 19. Trig Lane 1974–76: Group 3 revetment brace cut to accommodate later Group 7 revetment tie-back and pile retained cross-piece. Axe marks clearly visible to right of 5×100mm scale. Northern end of tie-back broken off. Looking north, river to south.

Plate 20. Trig Lane 1974–76: Internal face of Group 7 revetment showing rivetted overlapping strakes from clinker-built boat reused as cladding. Looking south towards river, 2×100mm scale.

Plate 21. Trig Lane 1974–76: South-east corner of Group 8 river wall looking north-west, river to south and east. 5×100mm scale rests on timber capping beam, with offset foundation to north on chalk rubble raft shown half-sectioned. South face of wall partially obscured by foreshore which developed against it.

Part II—The Excavation

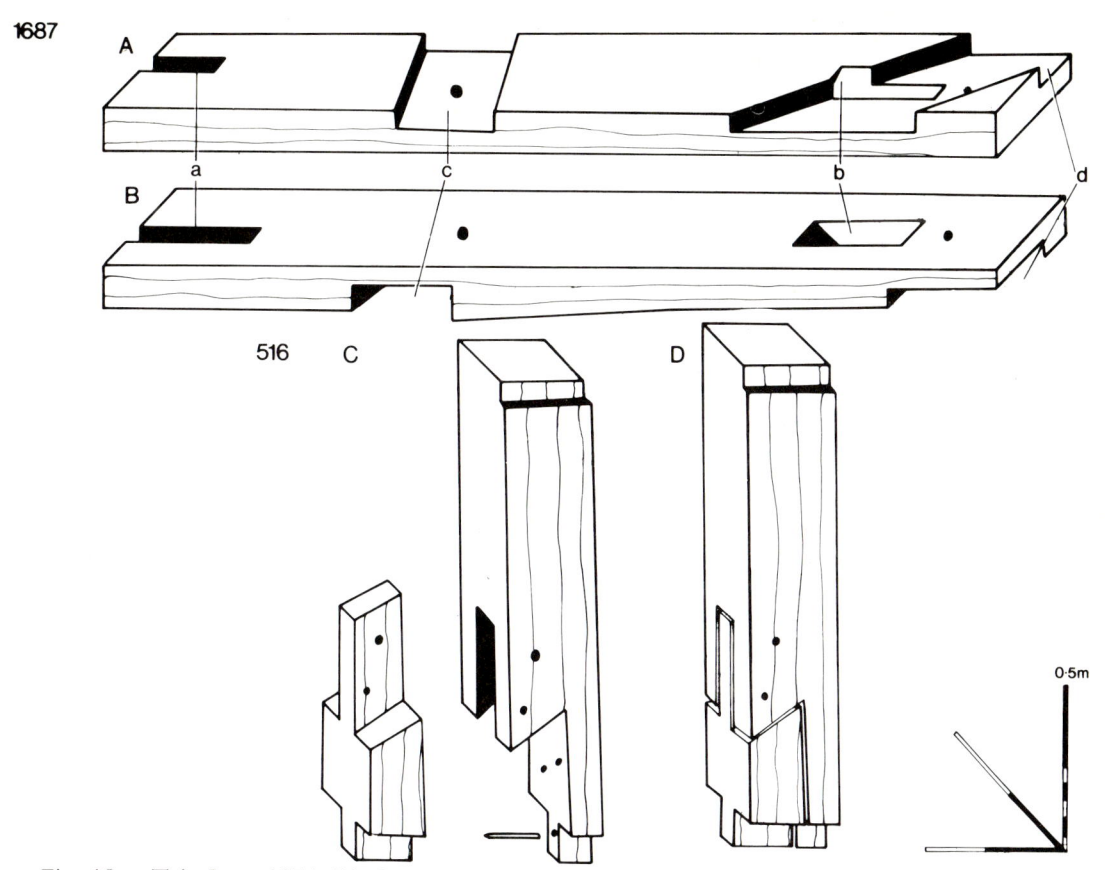

Fig. 19. Trig Lane 1974–76: Group 10 revetment members. Back-brace base-plate 1687: A lower face; B upper face, showing a and b mortises associated with Group 10 back-brace; c and d diagonal lap-joints indicating a former use. Stave member 516: C exploded view of repaired stave; D stave as found.

juncture (Pl. 20) suggests that they may have been the reused strakes of a clinker-built boat.[12] Just to the south of this point (Fig. 17a) was a timber base-plate running north to south, with a retaining pile driven into the foreshore at its southern end. A chase mortise in its upper face suggests that it once held the foot of a brace whose head supported the junction of the Group 7 and Group 10 revetments.

The Group 13 features, which included a pile group, postholes and a possible platform base, were recorded on and within the foreshore which developed against the south face of the revetment (see Fig. 36): they are discussed on p. 45.

Discussion
Assembly marks

The marks incised on the southern face of the Group 10 revetment wall were apparently confined to the irregularly shaped split members east of Brace 1 (Figs. 17b; 20): no trace of such marks was observed on the more regularly dressed sawn members west of this point. The section of the revetment east of Brace 5 was exposed during the earliest stage of the excavation: the apparent absence of marks here may be the result of inadequate cleaning, for it was not appreciated at that time that such marks might survive. Where they were

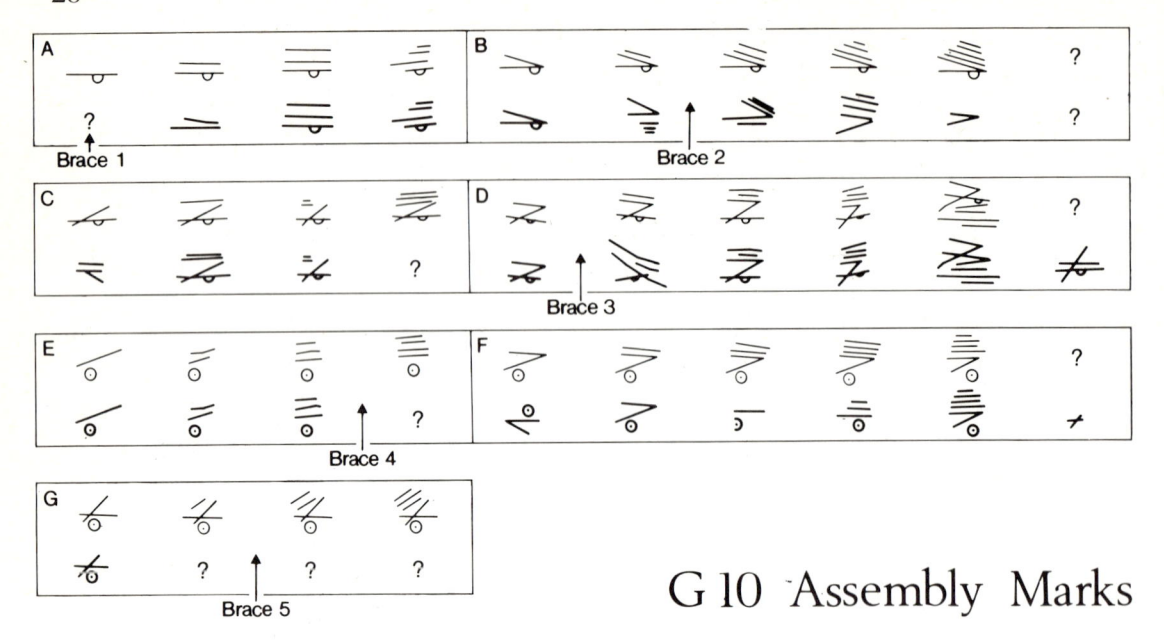

Fig. 20. Trig Lane 1974–76: Marks incised on the Group 10 revetment face drawn as found in the heavier lines. Above them, the lighter line drawing shows the hypothetical numbering sequence which the marks may have represented.

recorded, the quality of the surviving marks was variable. Several of the examples were only identified after the closest scrutiny. Some parts of the motifs seemed to have been worn away while other lines which were visible may not be directly associated with the marks. Nevertheless, the overall pattern which emerged seems to involve a simple accumulative sequence developing from west to east with no special marks indicating the positions of the five braces. Seven base motifs were identified (Fig. 20):

A   horizontal line and half circle;
B   horizontal line with diagonal line descending left to right and half circle;
C   horizontal line with diagonal line descending right to left and half circle;
D   two parallel horizontal lines with diagonal line descending right to left between them and half circle.

E, F and G repeat the design used for A, B and C respectively, but with a full circle replacing the half circle. The A, C, E and G motifs seem to appear in runs of four, the B, D and F motifs in runs of six. However, the form of the final mark in the latter group is not known, so this particular point was not established. No other significance for these possible groupings can be determined other than the obvious one that a run of four and six timbers forms a unit of ten. Fig. 20 shows that twelve of the surviving marks tally exactly with the hypothetical sequence shown above them, and a further ten incorporate a substantial element of the conjectured motif. The remainder were, with one or two exceptions, too worn to be cited as evidence for or against the hypothetical sequence. Nevertheless, in spite of the poor survival and recording of the marks, there was sufficient correlation of the surviving marks with the hypothetical sequence to at least suggest that the latter was broadly correct, although it cannot be proved to be so. If this assumption is valid, then it follows that the marks are most likely to be contemporary with the Group 10 revetment, as they do not reflect the random assembly of marked timbers derived from an earlier structure.

The marks may therefore have served as assembly marks denoting a pre-arranged order of assembly for a prefabricated structure, rather than, for example, as a method of deducing how many timbers had been ordered. The spacing of the back braces was determined by the positioning of the staves through which the back-brace base-plates passed (marked on Fig. 20), so the correct assembly of the staves was essential for the successful erection of the revetment.

This method of numbering therefore facilitated the correct assembly of some forty timbers by the matching of the developing motifs. Marks similar to these have been recorded on many English medieval buildings.[13]

In the west, the construction of the Group 10 revetment can be seen as an act of reclamation, pushing the waterfront southwards by 3m, but in the east it served a different function: here it replaced the western 8.40m of the Group 7 revetment before being married to the surviving remnant. It would seem likely that this action was to remedy a collapse, imminent or actual, of the frontage at this point, there being little point in removing and replacing a complete section of a perfectly sound revetment.

A detailed examination of the structure and the east-west section cut longitudinally through its associated dumping (Fig. 14) enabled the order of assembly to be elucidated. The tip lines observed in the dumping and the assembly marks both demonstrate that work began in the west and moved east, while the mortise pattern in the principal base-plates, together with the two small internal revetments, shows that the Group 10 feature was constructed in discrete sections. The section to the west of Brace 1 (Fig. 17a) was erected first, and was infilled. The revetment was then extended westwards beyond Brace 3 and infilled up to the western shuttering. Brace 4 and its associated staves were then positioned, and further infilling as far as the eastern shuttering preceded the erection of Brace 5 and the subsequent marrying of the Groups 7 and 10 revetments.

The structural variety exhibited by the Period IV revetments is further evidence of the piecemeal nature of waterfront development in this part of the City.

5. PERIOD V

Phases i and ii: Group 11 (Figs. 21; 23): *c.* 1380–*c.* 1440

The first phase of Period V was marked by the construction of the vertically timbered back-braced Group 11 revetment (Pls. 36; 37), behind which over 70 cubic metres of rubbish were dumped. The revetment cut the Group 10 structure (Fig. 27) and projected some 6m to the south, at which point it turned to run east for at least a further 6m (Fig. 21). The structure survived to a height of *c.* 1.70m and was supported by four large triangular back-braces. The remains of a substantial timber platform were recorded in the south-west corner (Pl. 38).

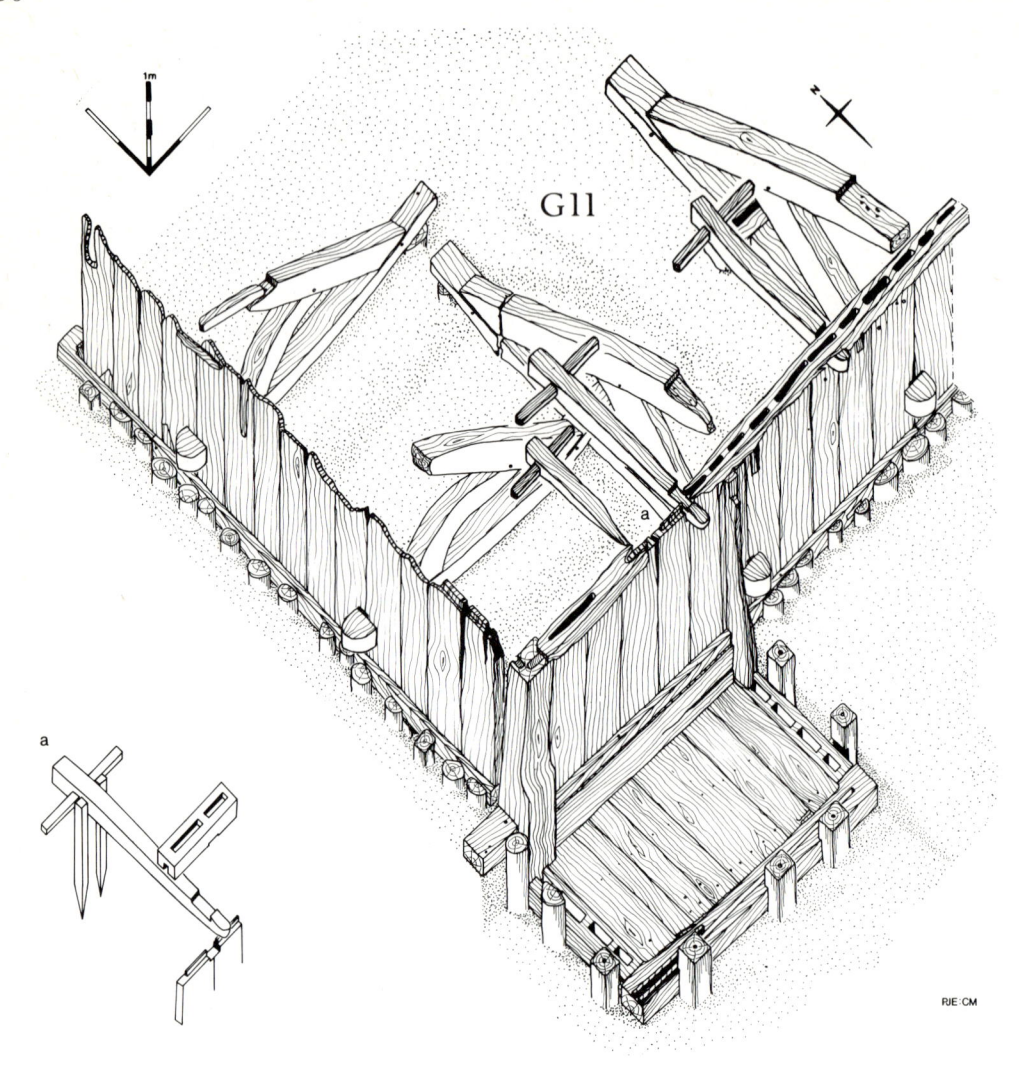

Fig. 23. Trig Lane 1974–76: Axonometric projection of back-braced Group 11 revetment, with base of (?) water tank in south-west corner. River to south and west. Inset: detail of junction of tie-back, plate and revetment face, semi-reconstructed.

The two timbers which formed the base-plate of the western wall were joined with an edge-halved bridle-butted scarf (Fig. 25). They were laid on a levelled row of piles, while a second row of piles (also elm) had been driven into the foreshore deposits to the west of the plate to retain it (Pls. 43; 44; 45). At its northern end, the Group 11 base-plate passed some 0.50m over the top of the earlier Group 10 base-plate (establishing the relative chronology of the two revetments) and a rough wedge separated them (Fig. 27). The base-plate had been laid level, and did not therefore conform to the southerly slope of the foreshore, which it directly overlay only at its northern end. A series of dumps had been spread over the area to raise the level of the construction surface in the south.

The mortise pattern cut into the upper face of the base-plates comprised a series of up to five short mortises *c.* 0.40m long, interspersed with single longer mortises up to 0.90m long (Fig.

Part II—The Excavation

21a; Pl. 45). Into these the tenons on the feet of the plain-sawn vertical members had been set. There were fourteen members in the west wall and at least twelve in the south. On average they were 0.45m by 0.07m in cross section and stood up to 1.60m high. Each one was joined to its neighbour by a 0.03m square dowel 0.15m long, set into circular holes bored into the adjacent edges of the vertical members, which were then butted flush (Fig. 26). Tenons on their heads

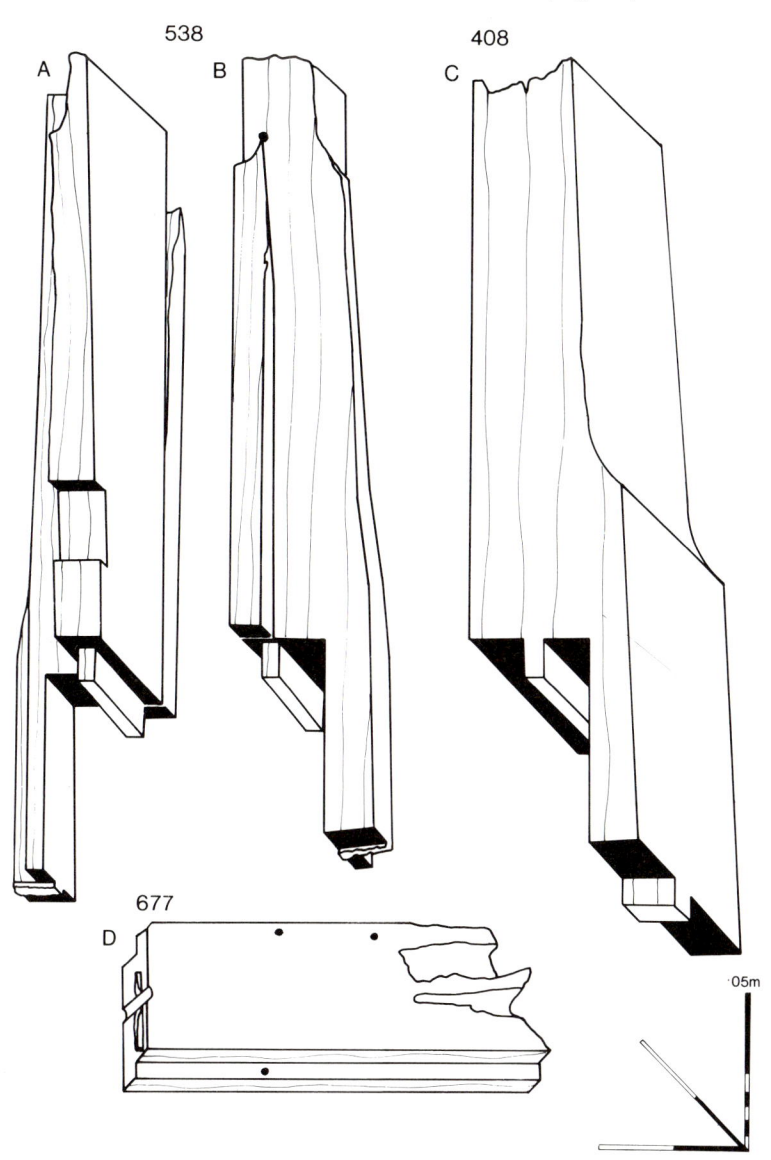

Fig. 24. Trig Lane 1974–76: Group 11 revetment members, positions indicated on Fig. 21.
A and B: east and west edge of stave 538.
C: west edge of corner post 408. The tenons on extended feet of these members were mortised into platform to south of Group 11 revetment; tenons on base of staves mortised into Group 11 revetment base-plate (cf. Fig. 28).
D: timber 677 found discarded on foreshore, but possibly part of Group 11 platform superstructure (cf. Fig. 28).

accepted a plate which also had mortises in its upper face (visible in Pl. 42), suggesting that the structure originally carried a second level of vertical planking, none of which survived.

A complete record of four of the back-braces which supported the structure was made (Fig. 22), and a base-plate of a possible fifth brace extended beyond the limit of excavation (Fig. 21; Brace 5). They were similar in type to those already described for the Group 10 revetment (p. 25), but exhibited a higher standard of workmanship and utilised only new timber. The head of the brace, the longer of the two diagonal members, was cut back to form an edge-halved scarf joint above the level of the upper plate (Figs. 22; 23).

Joined to the revetment and extending 2m south of it was a platform 3.40m wide. It consisted of three squared pile-laid frame members mortised and tenoned together at their south-east and south-west corners (Pls. 38; 39; 40), and retained externally by piles. The frame was not a later

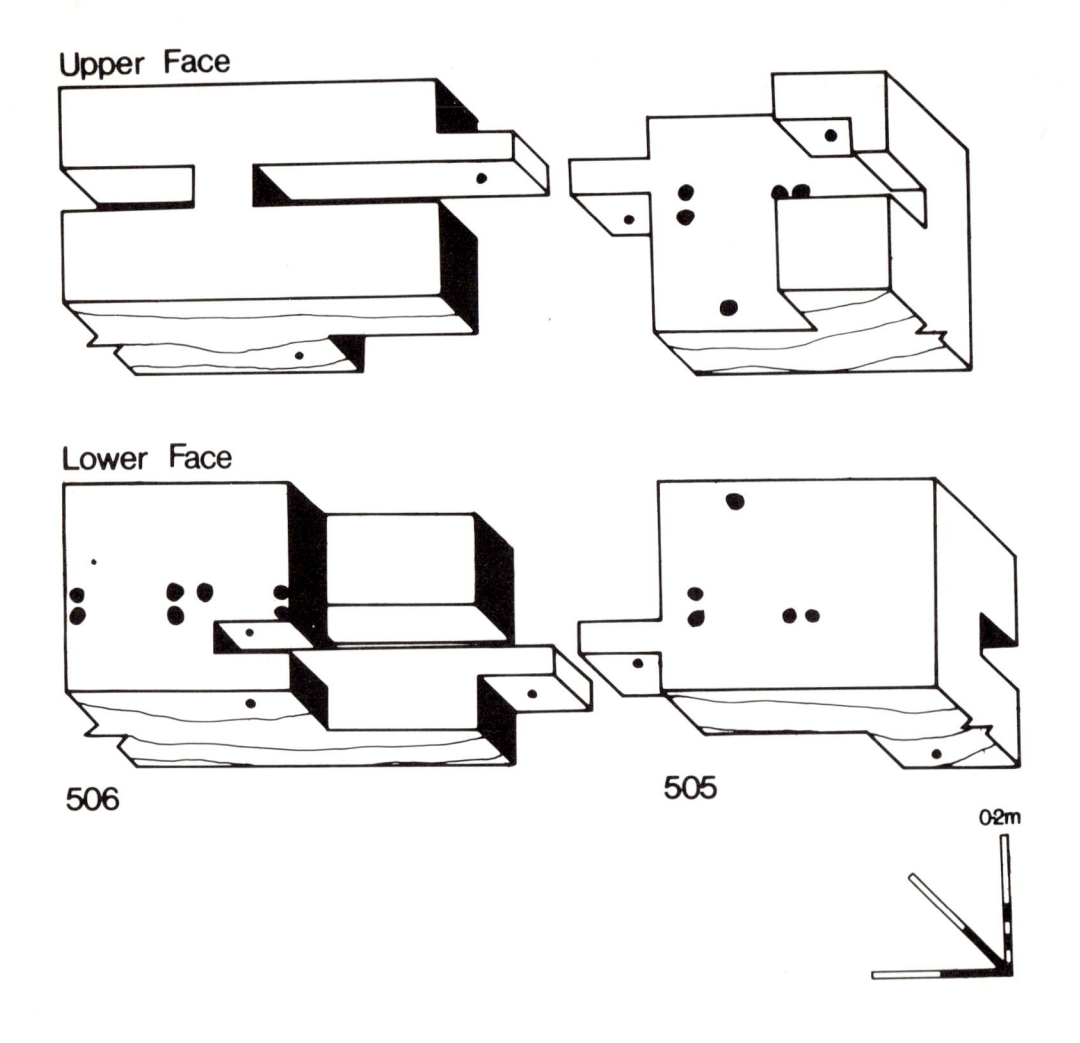

Fig. 25. Trig Lane 1974–76: Projection of edge-halved bridle-butted scarf with two edge pegs joining two sections of the Group 11 base-plates shown on Fig. 21. Mortises cut in upper face housed tenons on feet of staves: dowel holes in face contained pegs driven into foundation piles.

Part II—The Excavation

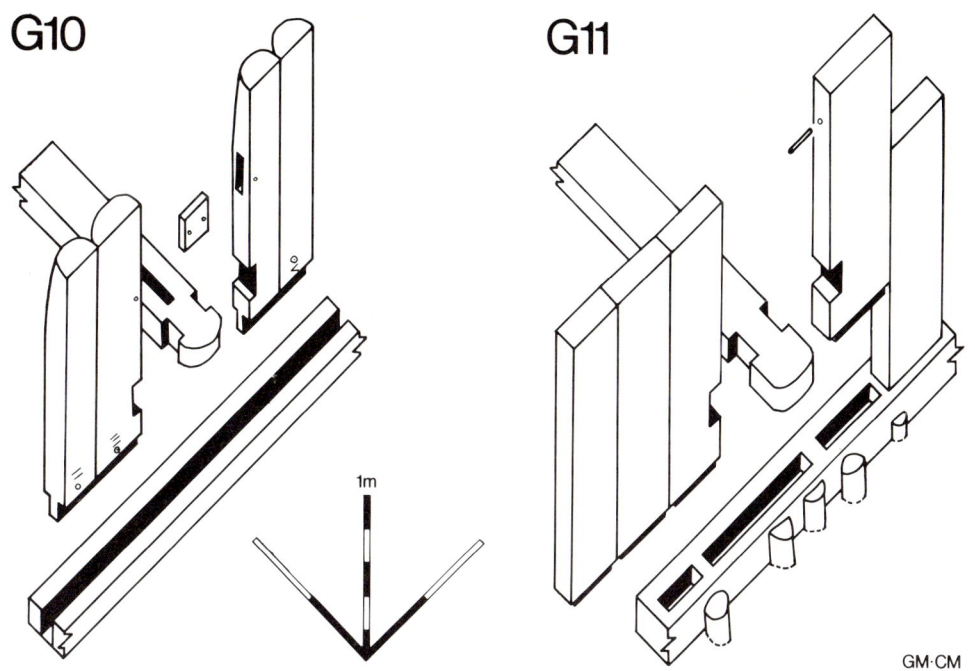

Fig. 26. Trig Lane 1974–76: Axonometric projections of part of Group 10 and 11 revetments to show similar method of construction. River to right.

addition to the revetment, but an integral part of it, as both the eastern and western frame members were joined to well-carpentered tenons cut on the feet of vertical revetment timbers (408 and 538 on Fig. 21), some 0.60m below the revetment base-plate (Figs. 23; 24; 28). Three regularly spaced joists were centrally tenoned into the internal edges of the opposed frame members, and well-fitted planking up to 0.04m thick was nailed to them, with edges set into rebates cut on the upper face of the frame (Pls. 38; 39). Individual mortises in the upper face of the eastern and western frame members and a groove cut for almost the entire length of the southern member suggested that it had once supported a tank-like superstructure.

Six braces had been laid at about the level of the upper plate, within the dumping behind the revetment (Fig. 21b; Pl. 42). Although much decayed, they were clearly of cruciform type, that is to say, aligned at right angles to the revetment wall with a cross member passed directly through the northern end, and retained to the south by piles. The lower group of three tie-backs passed through the revetment face just below the upper plate (Fig. 23), while the southern ends of the upper three (some 0.30m higher) had suffered badly from decay and subsequent disturbance (the latter are not shown on Fig. 23). Traces of a possible cut line suggest that these horizontally laid braces were a later addition to the revetment.

Further evidence for later modification of the main structure was recovered to the south of the revetment, where two small base-plates were found (Fig. 23) pile-founded onto the foreshore which had accumulated against the revetment. They were *c.* 1m long and *c.* 1.20m apart, with chase mortises in their upper faces and retaining piles to the south. These piles and the angle of the mortises indicate that the plates had once secured the feet of braces which ran diagonally northwards to butt against the revetment face, a suggestion which is consistent with the shallow mortises cut into the facing at exactly the point the hypothetical shores would have reached (Fig. 23).

Also within the foreshore deposits was a vertical plank pressed up against the revetment's southern base-plate, and, in a clearly residual deposit, a plain-sawn plank some 1.40m long. Traces of a tenon were visible on its foot, while both edges had been cut back to form rebates on opposed faces (No. 677, see Fig. 24). This member may once have formed part of the platform's superstructure (Fig. 28).

34 Gustav and Chrissie Milne

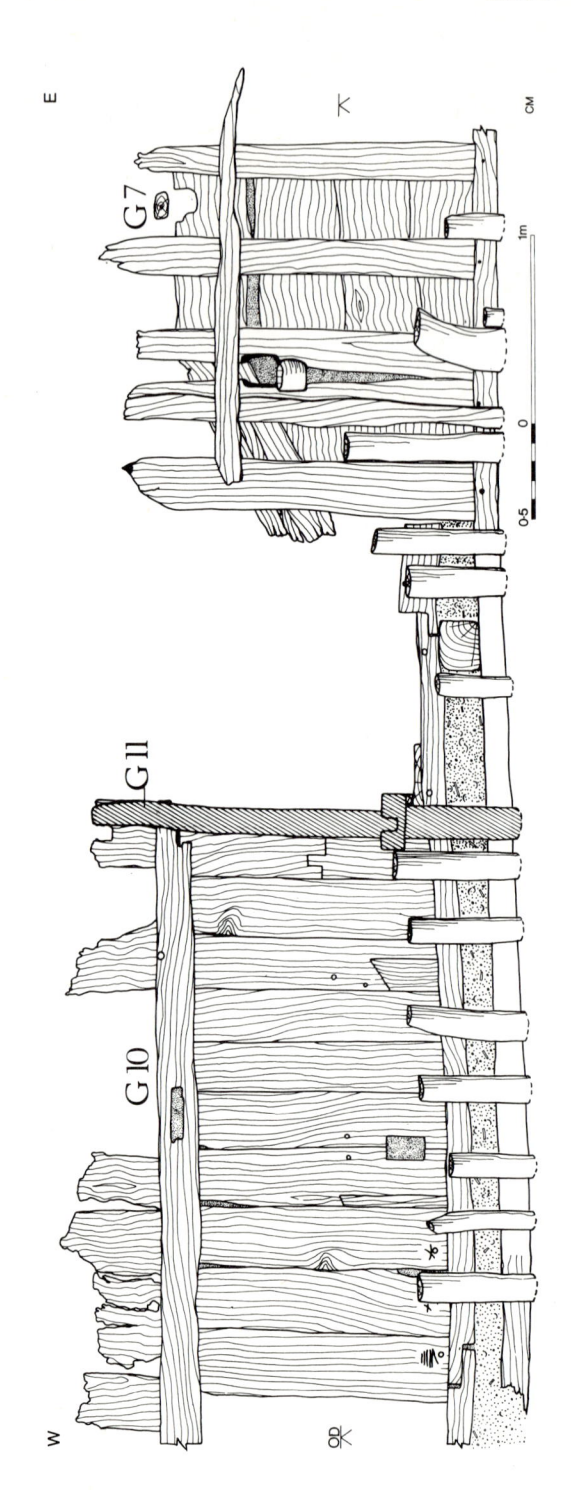

Fig. 27. Trig Lane 1974–76: Elevation of junction of Group 7, 10, 11 and 12 revetments.

Part II—The Excavation

Discussion

The Group 11 revetment superseded the fragment of the Group 7 structure which survived the major waterfront modification in Period IV, Phase iii, as well as the easternmost 2m section of the Group 10 revetment (Fig. 27). However, the western 16m of the latter structure subsequently functioned with the Group 11 revetment to form a timber-faced frontage that continued in use until both sections were sealed within the dumping associated with the construction of the Group 15 river wall, in Period VI.

The construction of the Group 11 revetment is interpreted as an act of reclamation which advanced part of the waterfront by *c.* 6m. The width of the area involved in this action, which was greater than that exposed during the excavation, precludes the possibility that the feature was a jetty.

If the base-plate which extended beyond the eastern limit of excavation (Fig. 21, Brace 5) is interpreted as part of a back-brace dismantled during the construction of the sump above it (Fig. 4), and if it is assumed to be the same size and type as the other Group 11 braces, then the possible eastern extent of the reclamation may be taken as lying along the line of Trig Lane itself (Fig. 21). Because no evidence of a more northerly base-plate was found on the eastern side of the revetment, its outline was probably asymmetrical, suggesting that the waterfront to the east of Trig Lane had already been advanced south of the Groups 7 and 10 alignment before the Group 11 feature was built.

The order of assembly for the Group 11 revetment was established. First, the seating and retaining piles from the principal base-plates were driven into the foreshore, and their tops were then sawn off level with the contemporary foreshore in the north. In the south, however, because the foreshore sloped southwards, the piles stood proud of the surface. The principal base-plates were then laid and scarfed together, and the initial dumps were introduced to level up the area inside this frame. Within the south-west corner, the Brace 2 base-plate overlay the Brace 3 base-plate (Fig. 21a), demonstrating that the south wall was constructed before the western.

The edge-trenching used to join the back-braces to the revetment members necessitated a single direction of construction, in which a run of planks and a brace were erected alternately, as the brace base-plate could not be passed between its associated vertical planks if both of the latter were already finally positioned. It was noted that the mortises for the western wall were cut for individual vertical members, with the exception of the double length ones: in each case the larger mortises were aligned to the north of the junction with the back-braces. Thus the southern four vertical planks were positioned first (Pl. 47), and then the back-brace base-plate was fitted into the associated edge trench on the last vertical member (Pl. 48). The next plank, with its edge trench, was then slid into position (Pls. 49; 50) from the north utilising the long mortise. It can thus be shown that the erection of the western wall proceeded from south to north (Pls. 43–51), after the southern wall had been completed from west to east. The position of the platform, an integral part of the revetment, accounts for the direction of construction of the latter wall. The platform itself was laid on the contemporary foreshore, at a predetermined depth below the revetment base-plate. Such an elaborate sequence suggests that the structure was planned in advance, and was totally prefabricated. This complex work must have involved measured scale drawings, known to have been used for the building of major structures in the medieval period.[14]

Phase iii: Group 12 (Figs. 3h; 29)

The principal phase iii feature, the Group 12 structure, was constructed in two similar but distinct sections comprising a plate laid directly onto the Group 10 revetment staves, into which a wall of vertical planks had been set, braced from the north by a series of six tie-backs.

In the west (Fig. 29g) the three braces were horizontally laid between 2m and 2.40m apart, and stabilized at their northern ends by cross members retained to the south by piles (Fig. 30 west). The braces were tenoned into mortises cut in the edge of the plate. All three sealed an east to west cut line which ran to the north of the revetment wall through the Group 10 dumping, down to the base-plate.

A further series of three braces was recorded in the west of the area within the dumping associated with the Group 12 structure, but some 0.30m to 0.40m higher than the tie-backs already described (Fig. 29a).

The plate had a squared groove running the length of its lower face, in which the tenons on the heads of the Group 10 revetment staves were housed. A similar groove in its upper face accepted the tenons on the feet of the vertical planking which formed the upper portion of the revetment (Pl. 54). These members were on average 0.30m wide, but did not survive to heights of more than 0.50m.

A scarf with vertical bridled butts and two edge pegs joined the western plate to the eastern, but the latter was not joined directly to the underlying flat-topped stave wall. Northward movement was prevented by cutting back part of the northern edge to form a pronounced shoulder. Bare-faced tenons on the feet of the vertical planking were set into individual mortises in the plate's upper face in this eastern section (Pl. 54).

Three braces of a complex type were recorded in the east, spaced at intervals of 2.40m (Fig. 29a). Each one comprised a tie-back some 3m long, laid horizontally north to south, level with the plate (Fig. 30 east; Pls. 52; 53). A face-tenon at the southern end was passed through a mortise in the plate's northern edge and secured to the south with a vertical peg. Such a joint is now known as a 'tusk tenon'.

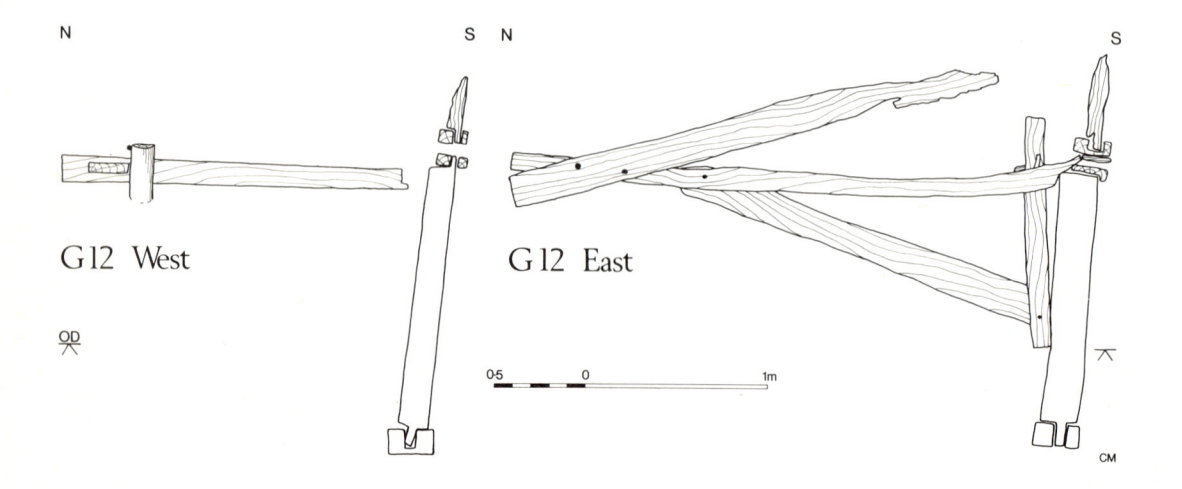

Fig. 30.   Trig Lane 1974–76: Side elevations of eastern and western Group 12 back-braces.

Part II—The Excavation 37

A vertical member 1m long had been passed through a mortise in the face of the tie-back just north of the junction with the revetment itself: to prevent this member slipping completely through, an east to west retaining piece had been inserted horizontally through its head. At its foot, it was pegged to a diagonal strut which ran northwards to be halved and pegged to the tie-back's eastern edge, forming the hypotenuse of a right-angled triangle with the vertical and horizontal members already described. A second diagonal strut was similarly lapped and pegged to the western edge of the tie-back, but ran southwards and upwards. Its junction with the revetment face did not survive, since this end of the timber had decayed. All three of these braces had been inserted into narrow cuts though the dumped deposits associated with the Group 10 revetment (Fig. 14). The fill of the cut sealed the severed ends of the earlier Group 10 back-braces.

Discussion

As the heads of the shores of the Group 10 back-braces passed over the top of their associated stave wall, it is clear that this revetment formerly supported a second level of timberwork (*cf.* Fig. 18). The Group 12 feature is therefore seen as a replacement of the original upper storey, rather than an act of reclamation or a heightening of the earlier structure.

The division between the eastern and western Group 12 structures was on the same alignment as the division between the contemporary Groups 3 and 4 revetments (*cf.* Fig. 3c and Fig. 3h), and suggests either that the property boundary postulated in Period III was still extant in Period V, or that the two sections of the Group 12 revetment were erected at different times (although both ultimately functioned together). These interpretations are not, of course, mutually exclusive.

Post-excavation examination of the north to south sections cut through the deposits behind the Group 10/12 revetment indicated the following sequence of events (Fig. 44). After the two-storeyed Group 10 revetment had been erected and the associated deposits dumped behind it, the revetment face itself began to collapse southwards. The strain on the back-braces may have been too much for the timber components, many of which were already weakened by former use (Pl. 34). As a result of the movement of the retaining wall, the dumped deposits also began to slip forward, producing the irregular 'cut-line' found by the excavators and traced with much difficulty. Repair work necessitated the removal of the original upper plate and planking, which involved the physical severing of the back-braces from the revetment, wherever this had not already occurred.

The Group 12 plate, planking and back-braces were then positioned, the revetment stabilized, and the area between the Group 10 staves and the original dumping infilled. The corner post (context 1284 on Fig. 17a) was also added at this stage (p. 80).

The complex braces which replaced the Group 10 back-braces in the eastern area (Fig. 30 east) embodied an as yet unparalleled bracing technique, but cannot be seen as the chance assembly of random timbers, since the three recorded examples were identical. An examination of these braces indicated that they only supported the revetment's second storey, and were not in fact relieving the pressure exerted on the stave wall from the north by the dumped material. Presumably it was considered that the pressure exerted from the south by the accumulating foreshore deposits would be sufficient to prevent a second collapse of the revetment face. The row of piles which ran parallel to, but south of, the Group 10 stave wall may best be interpreted as an attempt to consolidate the foreshore and may thus be associated with the Group 12 repair phase (Fig. 44). Assuming that these piles were driven until their heads were level with the contemporary surface, it would appear that c. 0.50m of foreshore had already developed against the Group 10 stave wall before their presence was required.

Phase iv

A number of features can be shown to post-date the construction of the Group 10/12 revetment, and predate the Period VI river wall. Those which were recorded on the foreshore to the south of the revetment (Group 13) are described and discussed on p. 44, the others are assessed here.

About 4m from the eastern end of the Group 12 revetment was a group of nine vertical planks varying in height from 0.44m to 0.94m, and on average 0.10m wide by 0.03m thick (Fig. 29). They had been inserted into a cut in the dumping immediately north of the plate, and are interpreted as a repair to the original Group 12 structure, a situation paralleled in the west by a similarly placed plank group (Pl. 54).

The Group 14 revetment

To the west of the Group 12 revetment was a timber set horizontally on the foreshore, retained by four piles to the south. Three holes up to 0.05m wide had been drilled into its upper face. Fourteen timbers of irregular size had been roughly driven into the foreshore against its northern edge to form a crude revetment c. 1.30m high. Part of the western side of the northern face bore the addition of several strips of horizontal planking up to 0.20m wide (Fig. 3h; Pls. 70; 71). Some of the 'vertical' members—they actually inclined southwards, up to 20° from the perpendicular—were round in cross-section, others squared, while traces of joinery indicated the reused nature of many of them. None of the timbers appeared to be joined in any way to the others in the revetment. To the north, a 0.70m thick deposit of dark brown organic matter had been dumped into the area bounded by the Group 8 wall to the west, the Group 10 revetment to the east, and the Group 14 revetment just described to the south.

This feature is clearly quite different from the reclamation revetments previously described (e.g. Groups 3, 7, 11), and is seen as a revetted rubbish dump.[15] The especial interest here is that it appears to be blocking the river-end of Bosse Alley (see p. 00), the alley which once divided the properties in the west from those on Trig Wharf. The revetment's construction must predate that of the Period VI river wall but, as both were sealed by the same reclamation dumps, it is clear that the Group 14 feature was visible—and therefore presumably operative—for a considerable time. However, a plan of 1679 suggests that the alley was still a thoroughfare at that time, although the earliest documentary evidence for the blocking of Bosse Alley apparently dates from 1607 (information from T. Dyson).

6. PERIOD VI: c. 1440, Group 15 (Figs. 3i; 31)

All the Period V features were sealed beneath the dumping associated with the construction of a substantial faced stone wall, which survived to a height of 2.50m, and had a total length of 35.80m (Pls. 55; 59). The wall ran the 24m length of the southern edge of the excavation (Fig. 31) returning north-south for 10.55m along what became the western limit of excavation. It survived virtually to its full height for most of its length, and proved substantial enough to act as vertical shoring for the deep area excavation conducted behind it. The internal offset face of the wall was therefore fully exposed, but it was only possible to examine one cross-section and one 2m portion of the external face completely, although limited investigations of the upper courses took place at a number of points. This was considered sufficient to establish the main features of its construction.

Part II—The Excavation

The western half of the north-south return wall was seated on a timber raft 0.20m thick pegged to and retained by substantial elm piles up to 0.35m in diameter (Fig. 35). The piles driven into the foreshore beneath the eastern half of the wall were slighter, 0.10m to 0.15m in diameter and between 0.60m and 0.70m long.

The external face (Figs. 33; 34) comprised at least ten courses of dressed ragstone blocks, varying in depth from 0.15m to 0.20m, and in width from 0.22m to 0.65m, bonded with a yellow sandy mortar. The vertical face of the stones had been dressed with a ¼ inch (6mm) punch, and ten masons' marks were recorded (Pls. 63; 64). The core of the wall, which varied from 1.40m to 1.70m wide at the base, was principally of uncoursed chalk rubble, although some flint and ragstone were included. The internal offset face was stepped in a series of three offsets, causing the wall to diminish to a width of 1m at the surviving top. The offsets were built mainly from dressed chalk rubble brought to courses, but again, flint and ragstone were also used. The uppermost courses were, however, wholly ragstone like the facing, as these were exposed to the elements, a situation for which chalk was not suitable. A major intrusion, a Victorian well (Fig. 32), had cut away part of the wall to the rubble core 3m from the junction with the east-west running wall, and part of the highest wall level had been disturbed by the insertion of a stone-built foundation.

Beneath the corner itself was a chalk rubble raft (Pl. 56) similar to that observed below the Group 8 wall (Fig. 16). To the south, the upper levels of the corner had been robbed of their facing stones to a depth of 1m, while further robbing and other disturbances (also post-medieval) were noted at various points along the top of the east-west wall. By far the largest intrusion was a 4m wide by 1.70m deep cut which had removed the stones down to the level of the first offset (Fig. 32). In contrast to the return wall already described, the offsets themselves did not run the complete length of the southern wall's internal face: in the centre the stonework was carried straight up to the level of the second offset and, in the west, to the level of the third.

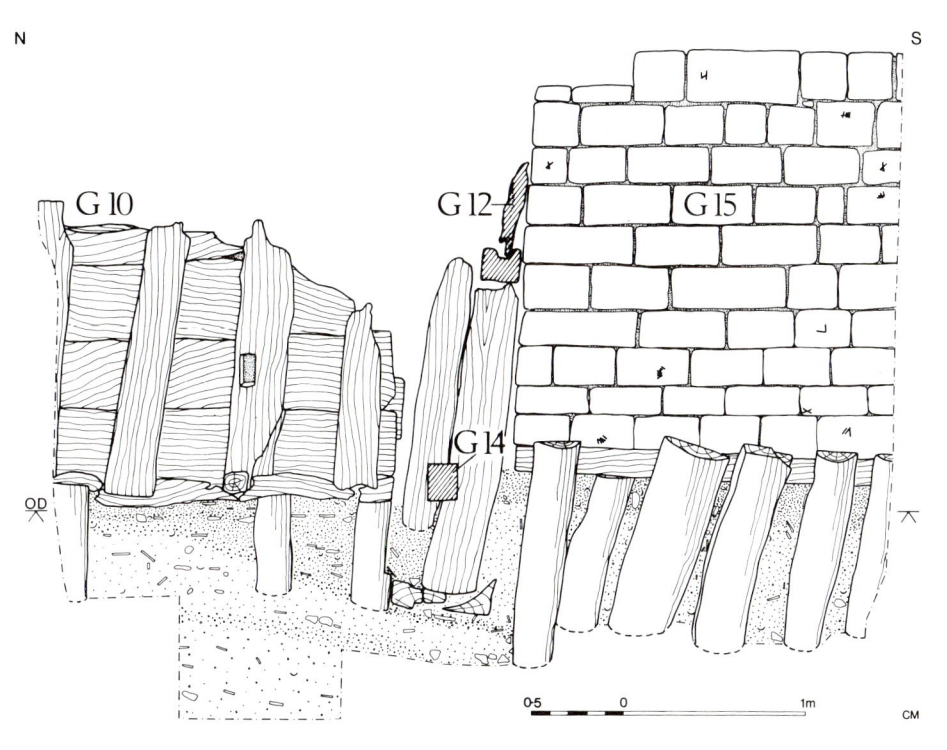

Fig. 33. Trig Lane 1974–76: Front elevation of Group 10 revetment and Group 15 river wall.

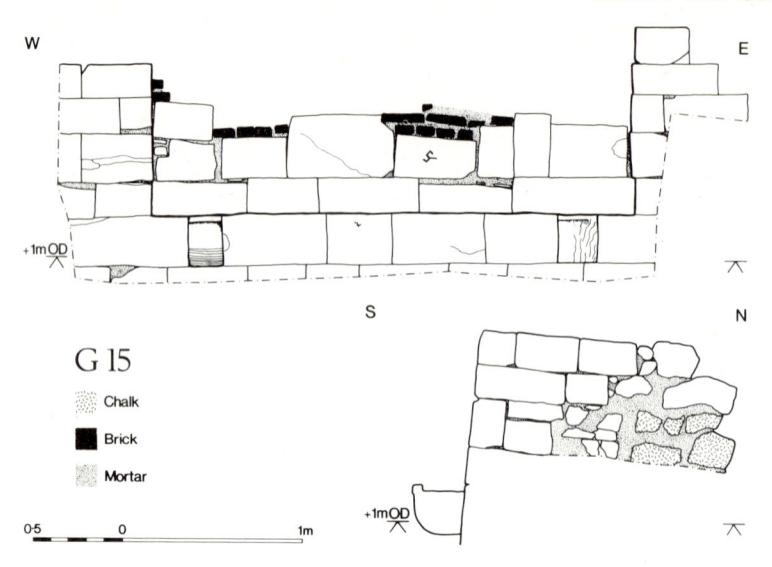

Fig. 34. Trig Lane 1974–76: Front elevations of Group 15 river wall. Positions of sections shown on Fig. 31.

A feature of especial interest was the access point (Fig. 34; Pls. 60; 61). It comprised two sets of opposed faced blocks 2.65m apart, built into the thickness of the wall top. The space between had evidently been blocked off at a later period using irregularly coursed ragstone blocks and brickwork (Fig. 34). On the external wall face 0.20m below the opening, a corbel projected 0.25m southwards, with a 0.30m lip on its southern edge and a rounded base. The rusted remains of an iron bolt were observed in the northern half of the level top of the corbel (Pls. 60; 62). 1.82m to the east were the remains of a second corbel which had been broken off close to the wall face.

North-south and east-west sections were cut through the material which had been dumped behind the wall, to examine the method of tipping, and it was noted that the major tiplines appeared to respect each offset (Fig. 44). The infill material was similar to the mixed dumped deposits from the Groups 2, 7, 10 and 11 structures, in that a considerable percentage was of a dark brown organic nature, containing large quantities of domestic refuse.

At the western end of the Group 10/12 revetment, it was observed that the revetment was leaning some 15° from the vertical when the Group 15 river wall was built up against it (Fig. 33). The fact that dressed stone was not used to face this northern abutment suggests that the Group 12 planking probably extended at least 0.80m above the plate, and that the wall rubble was simply packed against it (Pl. 59).

Discussion

The accumulation of foreshore deposits against the external face of the wall indicates that it functioned as a river wall. The use of stone in such structures is suggested as early as the 12th century in York, and is well known from at least 1220 at Westminster.[16] It was, of course, evident in the early 14th century in London, when the Group 8 wall at Trig Lane, and those of the abbots of Chertsey to the west, were built. The Group 8 wall was still operative when the Group 15 wall was constructed, and they functioned together thereafter.

The construction of the stone wharf at the Tower of London in 1389 by Henry Yevele under the direction of one Geoffrey Chaucer, both men better

Part II—The Excavation 41

G 15

Mortar

Ragstone

Chalk

Tooling

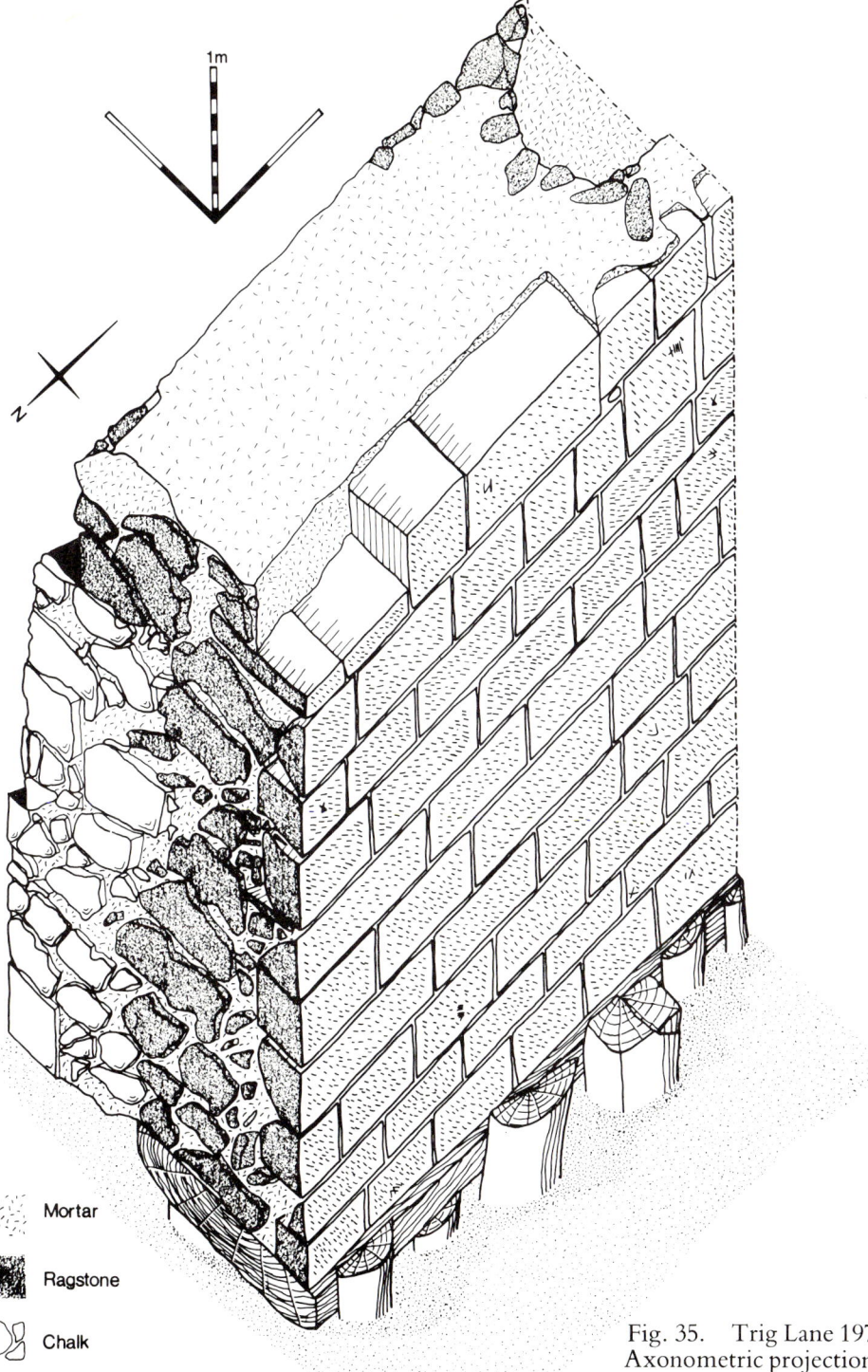

Fig. 35. Trig Lane 1974–76: Axonometric projection of northern end of Group 15 river wall showing off-set internal face, dressed external face, rubble core and piled foundation.

known for their Canterbury connections, also affords an interesting parallel. The wall was to be 8ft. thick at the base, diminishing to 5ft. at the top, and 16ft. 6ins. in height (c. 2.40m by 1.55m by 5m), with a facing of ragstone, the remainder of chalk.[17]

Timber-planked foundations would appear to be a well-tried method of wall construction on unstable land such as the foreshore, observed on several London sites such as Brickhill Lane, Dowgate,[18] New Hibernia Wharf in Southwark[19] and the Jewel Tower at Westminster.[20] Documentary references to this practice include mention of the City Quay at Norwich, built on a '. . . foundation with piles and planks of oak . . .'[21] and the post-Great Fire walls of London's Fleet Canal whose piles, Sir Christopher Wren decreed, were to be '. . . given the extra protection of a covering of good planks securely pinned down to them . . .'.[22]

The use of an offset wall with a vertical face laid on a piled raft is further paralleled in an early 20th-century riverwork construction manual, but with precast concrete blocks substituted for ragstone.[23] The dressing of the faced stones would have been a time-consuming task: Mr. William Smart, a stone mason working at the Tower of London, has suggested that it could have taken one man a day to punch each block. Assuming there were thirty dressed stones per metre of wall, a total of 1,000 man-days may have been expended on this labour alone.

An examination of the associated dumps and the coursing on the wall enabled its order of construction to be established. In the south-west corner, the lower two north-south offsets had been built onto, and therefore after, the lowest two east-west offsets, but the third east-west offset was butted against the north-south wall (Pl. 56). Construction would appear to have started from the corner eastwards and the irregularities in the east-west wall's alignment and offsets were perhaps the result of gang-working from opposite directions (Fig. 31).

The major tiplines that were seen to relate to the offsets suggest a construction sequence which involved the laying of the lower wall courses, dumping behind them, laying the middle courses, dumping behind them and so forth, rather than building the entire wall first, and then introducing the dumps. The former method ensured that the working surface was clear of the damp foreshore, as well as obviating the need for scaffolding on the internal face. Further confirmation of this building method was provided by a chalk and mortar layer which overlay the second offset on the east-west wall and continued southwards into the body of the wall below the third offset, while also spreading northwards horizontally over the dumped deposits. These must therefore have been dumped before the third offset was built (Pl. 57). Again, the Tower Wharf contract quoted above offers a parallel, since the king was to provide for the filling of earth and rubble 'as the work proceeds'.[24]

7. THE FORESHORE FEATURES: Groups 9; 13; (Fig. 36)

A number of pile-laid base-plates (some with vertical posts set in them), pile groups, a planked platform and several displaced timbers were recorded on or within the foreshore deposits to the south of the Group 7/10 revetment (Pls. 66;

Plate 22. Trig Lane 1974–76: 16m length of the back-braced Group 10 revetment looking south-east, river to south and west. Piles which supported the north-south return wall in foreground. Two back-braces which supported the section beyond the vertical 10×100mm scale have been removed.

Plate 23. Trig Lane 1974–76: Group 10 back-braces laid on dumped deposits overlying foreshore sealing earlier Group 3 & 4 subsidiary base-plates. Looking north-east, river to south, 5×100mm scale.

Plate 24. Trig Lane 1974–76: Group 10 revetment back-brace with 5×100mm scale supported by piles and cross-piece wedged against earlier Group 3 brace. Group 7 tie-back to east with southern end severed when associated revetment face replaced by stave wall to right. Looking north-east, river to south.

Plate 25. Trig Lane 1974–76: Group 10 revetment Brace 4, looking south-west towards river. The stave-built revetment replaced the Group 7 revetment. Right of the 10×100mm scale is a Group 7 tie-back *in situ* severed at its southern end by cut which removed its associated revetment. To its right is 2m wide cut through the Group 7 dumps in which Group 10 brace was erected. Note shuttering to east & west of brace enclosing an area which had to be backfilled before construction work could progress eastwards.

Plate 26. Trig Lane 1974–76: Group 10 back-brace with 5×100mm scale erected in deep cut through Group 7 dumped deposits (top centre). Note shuttering to left and fragments of Group 7 revetment planking on floor of cut. Looking north-west, river to south.

Plate 27. Trig Lane 1974–76: Shuttering behind the Group 10 stave wall, looking south-east. Baulk of Group 7 dumping with 5×100mm scale cut on southern and western sides. Shuttering probably comprised timbers removed from Group 7 revetment: post in south with tenon and groove may have been corner post.

Plate 28. Trig Lane 1974–76: Junction of Group 7 and 10 (with 5×100mm scale) revetments looking south-east. Later Group 11 revetment to west, cutting Group 10 stave wall running south towards river. To east are posts, planks and tie-backs of Group 7 revetment.

Plate 29. Trig Lane 1974–76: Junction of Group 7 & Group 10 revetments, looking north, river to south. Later Group 11 revetment visible in extreme left of picture. Group 10 base-plate (with 2×100mm scale) did not butt flush with Group 7 structure on right, so crudely scarfed timber used to fill gap. Note groove in Group 10 base-plate (and therefore associated stave wall) stops short of Group 7 revetment post. This gap was covered by reused boat timbers, just visible above plate.

Plate 30.　Trig Lane 1974–76: Planking presumably derived from the Group 7 revetment (with 5×100mm scale) reused as walk boards facilitating the construction of the Group 10 revetment, the internal face of which is visible at top of picture. Looking south.

Plate 31.　Trig Lane 1974–76: Internal face of Group 10 revetment looking south, showing three scarfed sections of principal base-plate. The revetment was constructed from west to east (right to left) but abutment at western end of eastern section was wrongly cut, so short central section (with 2×100mm scale) added to rectify mistake.

Plate 32.　Trig Lane 1974–76: Carpenter's assembly mark, four horizontal lines above a crossed line over a half circle, incised upon the southern face of the Group 10 revetment. Looking north 10×10mm scale.

Trig Lane 1974–76: Group 10 back-brace members looking west, showing timbers reused from earlier buildings.
Plate 33 (*upper*).   Chase mortises. 10×10mm scale.
Plate 34.   Base-plate (with 2×100mm scale) splitting across diagonal half lap on its lower face.

Plate 35.   Trig Lane 1974–76: Internal face of Group 10 revetment, looking west. Note subsidiary base-plate of earlier Group 3 revetment (5×100mm scale) set at lower level.

Plates 36 and 37. Trig Lane 1974–76: South and west walls of stave-built Group 11 revetment with infill material removed. River to south and west, 4×500mm scales.
a) looking north
b) looking north-east.

Plate 38. Trig Lane 1974–76: Platform feature on south-west corner of Group 11 revetment, looking north-west, with planking removed to reveal joists. Note mortises in frame members for a tank-like superstructure, and revetment stave on right tenoned into platform frame. 10×100mm scale.

Plate 39. Trig Lane 1974–76: South-east corner of Group 11 platform feature, showing well-butted corner tenoned and pegged; mortises for superstructure; rebates to accommodate planking. 10×10mm scale.

Plate 40. Trig Lane 1974–76: South-west corner of Group 11 platform feature, with peg for tenon to left of 10×10mm scale and additional slats (? sluice) to south.

Plate 41. Trig Lane 1974–76: Internal face of Group 11 revetment's southern wall, looking south towards the river. 4×500mm scale.

Plate 42. Trig Lane 1974–76: Upper level of Group 11 revetment's south wall, looking east. The heads of two large back-braces can be seen, with two levels of horizontally laid tie-backs. 4×500mm scale.

Plate 43. Trig Lane 1974–76: Western wall of Group 11 revetment as found in 1974, looking east. The section shown reconstructed in Plates 44 to 51 is to the right of the 4×500mm scale.

Trig Lane 1974–76: Construction of the Group 11 revetment (Pls. 44–51).
Plate 44 (*left*). Seating piles to left, retaining piles to right, 2×100mm scale.
Plate 45. Base-plate *in situ*, looking south, river to right. Note double-length mortise at northern end of 10×100mm scale.

Plate 46. Group 11 revetment. First vertical member *in situ*, looking south-east. 10×100mm scale.

Plate 47. Group 11 revetment. Second vertical member *in situ*, looking south-east. Note trench on northern edge. 10×100mm scale.

Plate 48. Group 11 revetment. Brace base-plate *in situ*, set in edge trench, looking south-east. 10×100mm scale.

Plate 49. Group 11 revetment. Utilising the double-length mortise, the 3rd vertical member trenched on its southern edge, is slid into position. Looking south-east. 10×100mm scale.

Plate 50. Group 11 revetment. 3rd vertical member in position. Looking south-east. 10×100mm scale.

Plate 51. the fourth vertical member inserted into the northern end of the double-length mortise. Looking south-east. 10×100mm scale.

Plate 52.   Trig Lane 1974–76: Group 12 revetment back-brace looking west, river to south. Note pegged squint lap. 10×100mm scale.

Plate 53.   Trig Lane 1974–76: Internal face of Group 10 stave wall, with 10×100mm scale, overlain by Group 12 plate into which back-brace is tenoned. Looking south towards river.

Plate 54.   Trig Lane 1974–76: Group 12 revetment second-storey members in west of site. Note groove in upper face of plate; bare-faced tenons on vertical members; repair timbers set behind plate. Looking north-west, river to south, 2×100mm scale.

Plate 55. Trig Lane 1974–76: Internal face of Group 15 river wall, looking south, river to south and west. Note remains of river stairs on foreshore behind wall. 10×100mm scale.

Plate 56. Trig Lane 1974–76: Internal face of Group 15 wall, showing construction of south-west corner. Looking south-west. 10×100mm scale.

Plate 57. Trig Lane 1974–76: Massive dumps of refuse covered the internal face of the lower ⅔ of the Group 15 river wall before this chalk and mortar surface associated with the construction of the uppermost courses of the wall could spread horizontally northwards. Looking south-east, river to south, 5×100mm scale.

Plate 58.   Trig Lane 1974–76: Internal face of Group 15 river wall, looking south-west, river to south. Note exclusive use of ragstone on upper courses; half sectioned dumps sealing chalk rubble raft. 10×100mm scale.

Plate 59.   Trig Lane 1974–76: Dressed ragstone on external face of Group 15 river wall, looking south-east, river to west. The wall is built on foreshore which accumulated against Group 10 revetment, with 5×100mm scale.

Plate 60. Trig Lane 1974–76: Partially exposed external face of Group 15 river wall showing blocked stair head above corbel. Looking north, river to south, 10×100mm scale.

Plate 61. Trig Lane 1974–76: West face of Group 15 wall stair head, looking west, river to south. Ghost of stair clearly visible. 5×100mm scale.

Plate 62.   Trig Lane 1974–76: Corbel from Group 15 river wall which supported timber stair to foreshore. Note (?) bolt to north of 10×10mm scale. Looking west, river to south.

Plates 63 and 64.   Mason's marks incised on external face of Group 15 river wall. Approx. 50mm across.

Plate 65. Trig Lane 1974–76: Detail of London waterfront between Queenhithe and London Bridge in mid-17th century, showing variety of river and jetty stairs.

Trig Lane 1974–76: Timber features *in situ* on the foreshore, looking north-west towards the land:

Plate 66.   pile-laid platform, visible between two mooring posts on left, would have been set at the foot of a river stair to the north. 5×100mm scale.

Plate 67.   to the right of the 10×100mm scale are remains of trestles which once supported a jetty.

Plate 68 (*left*).   Trig Lane 1974–76: External face of Group 10 revetment left of 10×100mm scale, looking east, river to south. Note post holes associated with contemporary river stair cut into foreshore to south.

Plate 69.   Trig Lane 1974–76: One of a pair of levelled timbers found *in situ* on the foreshore to south of Group 10 revetment. Part of base of river stair. Looking north-west towards the land, 2×100mm scale.

Plate 70 (*left*).   Trig Lane 1974–76: Inlet between Group 8 river wall (left) and Group 15 wall (right), looking north, river to south. The top of the Group 14 rubbish dump (with 5×100mm scale) is clearly visible.

Plate 71.   Trig Lane 1974–76: The Group 14 revetment after removal of refuse dumped behind it, looking north, river to south, 5×100mm scale.

Part II—The Excavation

jetty, they might have been associated with it, and can be interpreted as mooring posts.

At a lower level, sealed beneath the foreshore which had accumulated against the face of the Group 10 stave wall, were two timbers, aligned north-south *c.* 3.20m apart (1 on Fig. 36). Although not piled, they had been deliberately laid on timber wedges and were therefore still *in situ*. Below them (and not directly associated with them), two rows of postholes *c.* 2m apart ran north-south from the Group 10 revetment (Pls. 68; 69). These features are interpreted as evidence of earlier landing stage or river stair structures on a similar alignment to the feature illustrated in Fig. 37.

To the south-west of the Group 11 revetment, sealed within the foreshore deposit, was an east-west base-plate with the severed feet of two pairs of posts still tenoned into it at either end (17 on Fig. 36). The outer post of each pair was vertically set, the inner ones inclined inwards (Fig. 38). Although not set on piles, the plate was considered to be *in situ*, as the planked floor which it overlay (see p. 00) had been noticeably depressed at that point. This indicated that the trestle was laid after the planked floor's superstructure had been dismantled (and a thin layer of silt accumulated over the floor itself) and had originally supported a structure bearing a considerable load. The replacement of the conjectured tank feature by the trestle structure suggests a change of use or ownership of the eastern property, which may relate to the termination of the Trig family interest in *c.* 1420 (see p. 7).

No specific interpretations are offered for the partially exposed base-plate (1 on Fig. 36), the post and plank feature (5 on Fig. 36), or the two base-plates with vertical members abutting the Group 11 revetment (11 and 12 on Fig. 36). However, all were pile-laid, and therefore *in situ*, and could not be regarded as displaced timbers, many of which were also found on the foreshore.

Discussion

Foreshore deposits have rarely been archaeologically excavated, but, when they have been, structures of great interest have often been revealed. The discovery of boat fragments[25] in the Thames, the landing stage at the Tower of London,[26] the wattle breakwater at Westminster,[27] and the fish weirs on the Trent[28] are recent examples. It is therefore regrettable that there was insufficient time to excavate the sealed pre-1440 foreshore at Trig Lane in the detail it deserved. Nevertheless, the complex nature of this type of deposit was clearly evident, and a vivid picture of the continued importance of gaining access to the river emerged.

The analysis of the construction of the revetments and the documentary evidence both demonstrate that the property between Boss Alley and Trig Lane was subdivided from the 13th century. It would appear that the eastern, central and western plots (marked A, B and C on Fig. 36) each had its own river stair. Three main types of stair were noted:

A PARALLEL STAIR—a landing stage or platform laid horizontally against the frontage, presumably incorporating a stair descending parallel to the frontage (e.g. 1 on Fig. 36).

B TANGENTIAL STAIR—an extended stair descending at right angles to the frontage, to a landing stage or platform at its foot (*cf.* Pl. 65).

C JETTY STAIR—a horizontally planked walkway extending at right angles to the frontage, terminating in a stair descending to the foreshore (e.g. 3 and 4; 14 and 15 on Fig. 36. See Fig. 37).

The access point already noted in the centre of the Group 15 stone wall would have been of Type B, a flight of wooden stairs bolted to the corbel at the head and descending to the foreshore at right angles to the wall, possibly terminating in a platform similar to the pegged planking recorded in the foreshore to the north (4 on Fig. 36).

Documentary evidence for Type C is known from Broken Wharf (directly east of Trig Lane), where a contract dated to 1347 and referring to the rebuilding of a wharf stipulates that there was to be a '. . . bridge with steps leading down to the water . . .' in the middle.[29]

At Trig Lane, an attempt was made to reconstruct the original form of the best-preserved trestle (17 on Fig. 36; see Fig. 38). It was assumed that the converging shores were lapped and pegged at their point of convergence (dictated by the angle of the chase tenon), and then continued upwards to meet the top-plate to which both they and the vertical posts would have been joined with the same joints as were used at their feet. This basic scissor-braced trestle would have been one of a series supporting a planked top jetty extending out into the Thames. This conforms to Rigold's 'TYPE II' trestle, '. . . by far the commonest and more persistent type of support in English moat-bridges, producing an evolving series from the late 11th century to the late 16th'.[30] It is of interest to note that the 1347 contract from Broken Wharf (see above) describes the river stair as a bridge (*pontem*), and the style of construction used for moat bridges is not perhaps therefore an inappropriate parallel. In function, the Trig Lane scissor-braced structure is paralleled by the less robust structure from the London Custom House site,[31] while evidence for a frame-based jetty stair was also found on the same site,[32] and at Toppings Wharf, Southwark.[33]

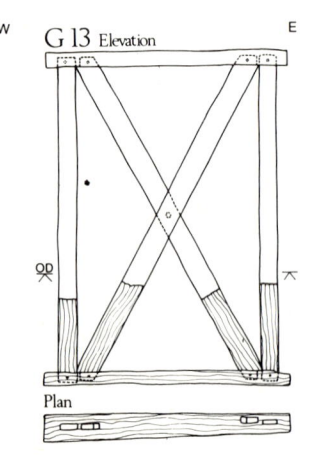

Fig. 38. Trig Lane 1974–76: Reconstructed front elevation of trestle feature (cf. Fig. 37, C2).

Part II—The Excavation

NOTES AND REFERENCES

1. The site was initially supervised by M. E. Harrison.
2. The principal reports in question are M. Harrison 'Trig Lane' *Current Archaeol.* 49 (1975) 57–9; G. Milne 'Trig Lane' in B. Hobley and J. Schofield 'Excavations in the City of London: First interim report 1974–1975' *Antiq. J.* 57 (1977) 39–43; G. Milne and C. Milne 'Excavations on the Thames Waterfront at Trig Lane, London 1974–6' *Medieval Archaeol.* 22 (1978) 84–104. Further detailed analysis has now refined the dating suggested in the last paper, which was written in 1977. The descriptions and discussions are still valid.
3. G. Milne & C. Milne 'Medieval Buildings at Trig Lane' *London Archaeol.* 4 No. 2 (1981) 31–37.
4. *Cf.* P. Marsden 'Excavations on the site of St. Mildred's Church, Bread Street, London, 1973–4' *Trans. London Middlesex Archaeol. Soc.* 26 (1975) 188, Fig. 8.
5. Identified by the Geology Dept., Bedford College, University of London.
6. The foundation was part of 'Building C', a feature contemporary with the Group 7 revetment. See note 3.
7. T. Tatton-Brown 'Excavations at the Custom House site, City of London, 1973' *Trans. London Middlesex Archaeol. Soc.* 25 (1974) 136, Fig. 18.
8. T. Tatton-Brown *loc. cit.* in note 7, 130, Fig. 12.
9. J. Schofield 'Seal House' *Current Archaeol.* 49 (1975) 56.
10. The use of oyster shell 'for the setting of stone' is known at Westminster, for example, where in 1532 masons had 25 bushels delivered to them for that purpose. L. F. Salzman *Building in England down to 1540* (Oxford 1952) 89.
11. For discussion of the use of the stave building technique, see G. Milne and C. Milne *loc. cit.* in note 2.
12. Report by P. Marsden (Museum of London) in preparation. Boat timbers have been found reused in revetments at the Custom House (T. Tatton-Brown *loc. cit.* in note 7) and Bridewell Place (supervised by D. Gadd, Museum of London) in London, and also at Dickinson's Mill in Lincoln, see *Med. Archaeol.* 18 (1974) 201.
13. R. Harris *Discovering Timber Framed Buildings* (Princes Risborough 1978) 15, Fig. 11.
14. See L. F. Salzman *op. cit.* in note 10, 15–22 and J. Harvey *The Master Builders* (London 1971) 30–38.
15. City legislation states that 'all the lanes leading unto the Thames, between Castle Baynard and the Tower, shall be cleansed of all dung and rubbish'; see, for example, *Munimenta Gildhallae Londoniensis: Liber Custumarum,* 204.
16. Report on Coney Street, York by P. V. Addyman (forthcoming): J. M. Green 'Excavations of the Palace Defences and Abbey precinct wall at Abingdon Street, Westminster' *J. Brit. Archaeol. Assoc.* 129 (1976) 59–76. Concerning the choice of timber or stone to face a waterfront, the contract for the rebuilding of Broken Wharf, London, in 1347, is of interest. See L. F. Salzman *op. cit.* in note 10, 434. It shows that John of Oxford, one of the richest merchants in London (see G. A. Williams *Medieval London* (London 1963) 126) and therefore able to afford the best in mercantile wharf and revetment design, had faced his wharf with timber, rather than stone.
17. L. F. Salzman *op. cit.* in note 10, 501.
18. Guildhall Museum Excavation Register VII, 51–2.
19. H. Sheldon 'Excavations at New Hibernia Wharf' *London Archaeol.* 2 No. 5 (1973) 103.
20. J. M. Green *loc. cit.* in note 16.
21. L. F. Salzman *op. cit.* in note 10, 501.
22. T. F. Reddaway *The Rebuilding of London after the Great Fire* (London 1940) 212.
23. H. Shenton and F. Shenton *Riverwork construction details* (London 1935) 46, Fig. 32.
24. L. F. Salzman *op. cit.* in note 10, 501.
25. P. Marsden 'Archaeological Finds in the City of London 1967–70' *Trans. London Middlesex Archaeol. Soc.* 23 (1971) 1–14.
26. G. Parnell, pers. comm.
27. J. M. Green, *loc. cit.* in note 16.
28. Forthcoming report on recent work in the Trent Valley by Dr. C. P. Salisbury in *East Midlands Archaeological Bulletin* No. 12.
29. L. F. Salzman *op. cit.* in note 10, 434.
30. S. E. Rigold 'Structural aspects of medieval timber bridges' *Med. Archaeol.* 19 (1975) 56–7.
31. T. Tatton-Brown *loc. cit.* in note 7, 133, Figs. 14 and 15.
32. T. Tatton-Brown *loc. cit.* in note 7, Trench IV, Figs. 14 and 18.
33. H. Sheldon 'Excavations at Toppings & Sun Wharves, Southwark, 1970–1972' *Trans. London Middlesex Archaeol. Soc.* 25 (1974) 27.

PART III

III. ANALYSIS

A. DATING

Figure 39 shows how the dating used in this report was determined. The depth of foreshore which accumulated against each revetment is shown diagrammatically by the 50mm graduations on the scale on the left. The depth of foreshore which accumulated after the construction of the Group 1 structure, but before the erection of the Group 2 revetment, is shown at the foot of the table, with the depth of the post-Group 2 pre-Group 3 foreshore shown above that, the post-Group 3 pre-Group 7 foreshore above that, and so forth. Average values were calculated in cases where the deposited material was deeper in the east than in the west, as for example with the Group 10 revetment. By tabulating in this way the depth of the accumulation between each successive phase of construction, it was possible to suggest a theoretical total accumulative depth of foreshore which would have developed against the earliest structure by the end of the period in question, given a consistent rate of deposition.

Approximate dates for the beginning, middle and end of this sequence were then established, principally from independently datable artefacts. Cecil Hewett suggests that the squint laps and the spur tenon on a reused timber from the Group 1 structure (Fig. 7) could be dated to the early or mid-13th century,[1] while an ampulla from the Group 2 dumps must post-date 1170 since it depicts the martyrdom of Thomas Beckett: Brian Spencer has suggested a date of c. 1225–50 for its manufacture. This item and another ampulla from the same deposit may have been discarded in the third quarter of the 13th century (p. 106). Such a dating also consistent with Clive Orton's suggestion that the Group 2 pottery assemblage is post-1250 (p. 98), and with Stuart Rigold's identification of an associated lead token of D1 type, datable to the mid- to late 13th-century (No. 61, p. 103).

The pottery evidence suggests that the Group 7 revetment predates c. 1350, and that the Group 10 structure should be later than 1350 (p. 98), while the two worn English Sterling jettons presumably derived from the dumps behind the Group 10 revetment (Nos. 29 and 30, p. 99) show that it must have been built after 1330 at the earliest. Of the two coins from the foreshore deposit which accumulated after the construction of the Group 10 revetment, one was dated to 1363–9, while the other was thought to have been discarded in the last quarter of the 14th century (p. 99, Nos. 23 and 24).

The dumps behind the Group 11 revetment contained three late 14th-century English 'Post-Sterling' jettons, a French official jetton of the 1370s–1380s, and a French unofficial jetton in good condition datable to c. 1380 (p. 99, Nos. 32, 33, 34, 41 and 50). The foreshore which developed between the construction of the Group 11 revetment and that of the Group 15 river wall contained two worn jettons of the mid- to late 14th-century (pp. 99, 101, Nos. 35 and 42), two late 14th-century to early 15th-century lead tokens of D5 type (p. 106, Nos. 97 and 98), and a late official French jetton of the 1430s–1440s (p. 102, No. 45).

The deposits dumped behind the Group 15 wall also contained coins. Two

Part III—Analysis

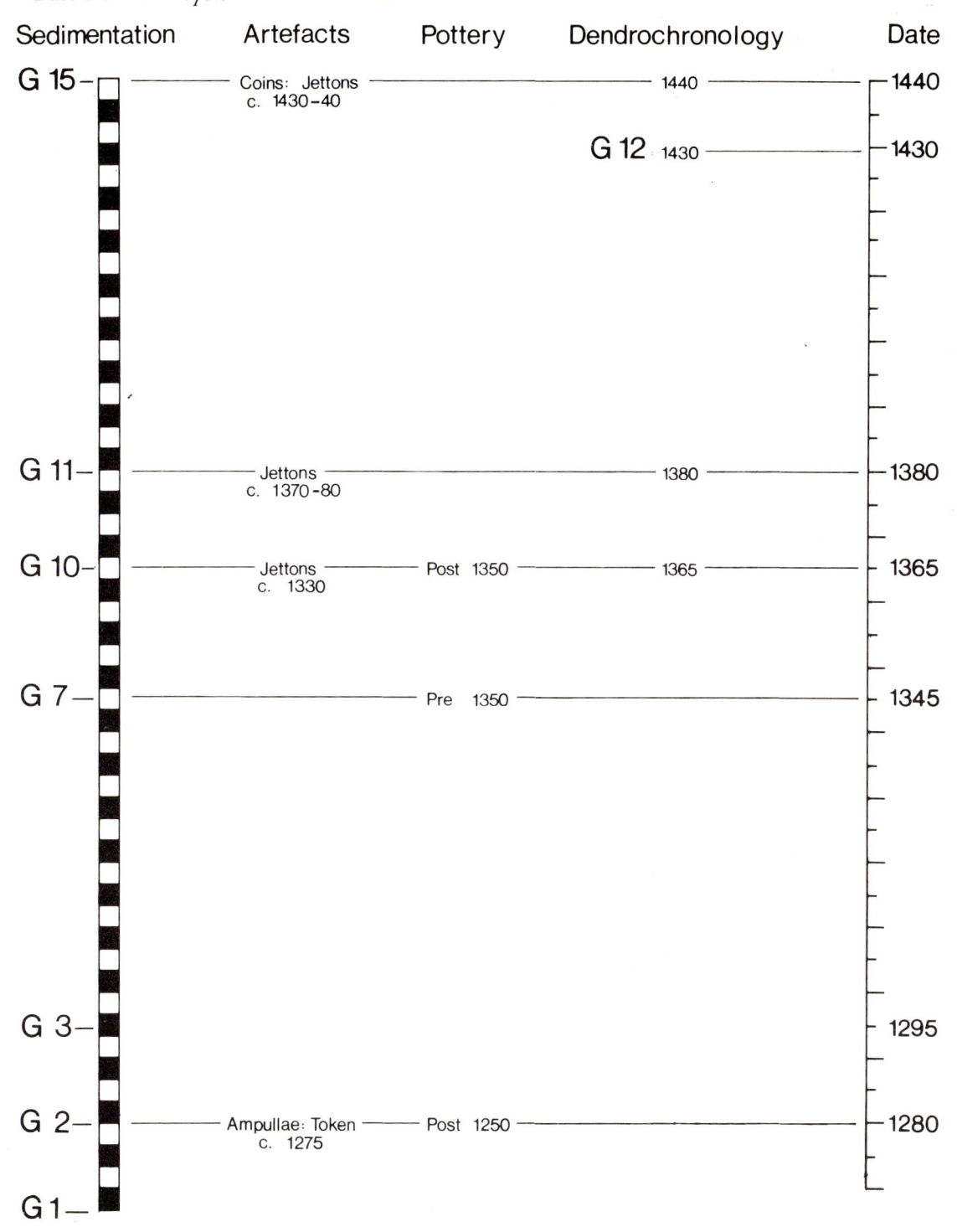

Sedimentation	Artefacts	Pottery	Dendrochronology	Date
G 15	Coins: Jettons c. 1430–40		1440	1440
			G 12 1430	1430
G 11	Jettons c. 1370–80		1380	1380
G 10	Jettons c. 1330	Post 1350	1365	1365
G 7		Pre 1350		1345
G 3				1295
G 2	Ampullae: Token c. 1275	Post 1250		1280
G 1				

Fig. 39. Trig Lane 1974–76: The dating evidence: sedimentation scale in 50mm graduations.

were moderately worn and dated to 1413–22 (p. 99, Nos. 26 and 25) while the third, dated to 1427–30 (p. 99, No. 27), showed very little wear, suggesting a date of *c.* 1440 for the dumping. It is worth emphasising that the medieval dumps found at Trig Lane contained a very high proportion of organic peaty material, in which straw and other plant matter was readily identifiable with the naked eye. This indicates that the refuse heaps from which the waterfront dumps were presumably derived were still relatively fresh at that stage since the plant matter had not decomposed. Thus, the possibility of finding artefacts of a substantially greater age than the associated organic dumps is reduced.

Dates for five of the groups were therefore suggested as: Group 2, *c.* 1250–75; Group 7, pre-1350; Group 10, *c.* 1360; Group 11, *c.* 1380; Group 15, *c.* 1440.

The sequence therefore spanned a period of between 165 and 190 years, during which time a total depth of *c.* 2.40m of material gradually accumulated against the face of the revetments. If it is assumed that these foreshore deposits built up at a consistent rate, then the annual accumulation may be calculated by dividing 2.40m by the total number of years. The resulting figure of 15mm *per annum* can only serve as a guide rather than an absolute standard, but it provides a useful method of approximating calendar dates for each phase of construction.

According to Donald Brett, the dendrochronological dates cited in Fig. 39 could not be established with certainty *on statistical grounds alone* (p. 81). However, the dating of the artefacts provides considerable support for the dendrochronological results and enables them to be viewed with more confidence than the '*t*' values on their own would allow.

Working from a match with the Central German Chronology, Donald Brett's dendrochronological analysis suggested that the felling dates for the Group 11 and Group 15 timbers could be *c.* 1380 and *c.* 1440 respectively. These results are supported by the coin evidence, so the earlier match based on the Belfast Index Chronology may be safely rejected (p. 81). Accepting the dating derived from the Central German Chronology, the most likely date for the construction of the Group 10 revetment is *c.* 1365 (which again is in accord with the coin and pottery evidence), with the Group 12 phase at *c.* 1430. In addition, the *c.* 0.85m of foreshore which separates the Group 11 and Group 15 structures can be shown to have accumulated over a period of *c.* 60 years, supporting the suggestion of a foreshore development of *c.* 15mm *per annum*. The dates shown for Groups 2, 3 and 7 in the right-hand column of Fig. 39 were calculated on this assumption, and are also independently supported by the finds evidence.

The radiocarbon determinations for the Group 11 and 12 samples shown in Fig. 59[2] support the 14th and 15th felling dates for the timbers calculated by Donald Brett working with the Germans chronologies (p. 81), rather than, for example, the Belfast Index chronology. These results not only confirm the late medieval dating of the timbers but arguably enable the tentative results of the dendrochronological analysis to be viewed with more confidence.

In conclusion, the Group 10, 11, 12 and 15 features may be considered to have been dated to the decade (± 5 years from the central date quoted in Fig. 39), while the suggested dates for the Group 2, 3, 4 and 7 structures, although

Part III—Analysis

open to modification in the light of future research, are viewed with considerable confidence, and should be correct to within twenty years, i.e., ± 10 years from the central dates quoted.

The close dating of the sequence at Trig Lane is obviously important for a full understanding of the reclamation process and for any assessment of the durability of the medieval revetments themselves. In addition it provides those working on the associated artefacts and environmental research with good groups of dated material, a situation not often encountered in medieval archaeology.[3]

B. THE REVETMENTS

1. Construction

The majority of the wood used in the excavated revetments was oak, presumably derived from the formerly extensively wooded counties of south-east England. In contrast to the 200- to 300-year-old timbers selected for the Roman quays in London,[4] the medieval timbers were cut from young trees. Over 80% of the samples examined were from trees between 40 and 80 years old (Fig. 49) and this suggests that the timber was not derived from the clearance of primary woodland, but from a managed woodland in which trees were regularly cropped.[5]

Although the Group 11 revetment contained many new timbers cut specifically for that structure (p. 79), most of the members used for the Group 10 back-braces were obviously reused (Fig. 18; Pls. 33; 34), and must have been obtained from timbers derived from earlier structures dismantled by the carpenter elsewhere. There are many documentary references to this practice. In 1310, for example, Richard de Rothinge was allowed to retain as much of the old timber from the development at St. Michael le Querne as could not be readily reused in the new building.[6]

Tools known to have been used to cut and dress timber in the medieval period[7] include cross-cut saws,[8] bow saws,[9] frame-saws,[10] axes[11] and adzes.[12] Although the Trig Lane revetment timbers had been cut down from larger timbers, the marks left by the tools used did not always survive. The external face of the structures had been exposed to the elements and to the abrasive action of river-borne grits which removed virtually all evidence of working. However, it was possible to show that the Group 3 revetment posts had been roughly squared with adzes, that the tenons on the feet of the Group 10 staves had been cut with axes, and that the Group 11 vertical members had definitely been sawn from substantial trees.[13] In addition, chisels must presumably have been used for the intricate joinery on the Group 11 scarf joint illustrated in Fig. 25, for example, and augers or bits 1 inch (250mm) in diameter were used to bore the peg-holes in the timbers. The planking on the Group 3 and Group 7 revetments was assumed to have been split from larger timbers with wedges, and subsequently trimmed with adzes or axes.

The dressing of the timberwork need not have been done on the waterfront itself, as the revetments could have been prefabricated in the more congenial conditions of a carpenter's yard. The general principle of prefabrication is well attested. For example, from 1394 onwards, oak from Hampshire, Hertfordshire and Northamptonshire for the hammer-beam roof at Westminster was sent to Farnham, where it was sawn and worked into the component parts of Hugh Herland's elaborate trusses. When ready, the timber was transported by road to Hamme, near Chertsey (Surrey), and then by boat to Westminster.[14] That components (marked up like the timbers of Group 10) could then be delivered to site 'ready for assembling' is clearly stated in a contract to rebuild two water-mills and a wharf at Southwark in 1387–8.[15] This document states that just over six months was allowed for the initial preparation, and two months for the actual erection of the prefabricated structures. The whole sequence of activities associated with wharf construction is admirably illustrated on a somewhat grander scale by the example of the east jetty at Calais, built during the English occupation of the port in the 15th century. In 1440 the clerk of works agreed to purchase 1,400 great oaks 'at ryght lygth price' from the monastic woods in Essex.[16] Having taken the dimensions for the jetty in Calais, the master carpenter returned to England in 1441 and had the timber cut under his direction. In the same way William of Neuburgh in 1367 had spent three weeks in Kent, Surrey and Sussex selecting and organising the felling of the timber for the western jetty.[17] Once felled, the timbers were measured and assembled at the 'Framing Place' at Langley Park in Kent[18] and the component parts of the new jetties transported to Calais ready to be fastened together with iron bolts and clamps supplied by the king's master smith.[19]

It has been suggested that one of the revetments at the Custom House site was the work of John Tottenham, the carpenter sworn to check complaints relating to carpentry in the City from 1325–47. Tottenham is known to have erected a timber fortification on the site at the start of the Hundred Years War in 1339, and the excavator considered that the revetment might have been the foundation for such a superstructure.[20] However, now that more examples of revetments have been found, it is clear that the Cusom House structure in question was a standard type of riverfront revetment (cf. Trig Lane Groups 3 and 4, for example), and need not necessarily be associated with any defensive work. The only carpenter known to have built revetments in the City is Richard Cotterel, who worked at Broken Wharf in 1347.[21]

Although revetment construction incorporated structural features not evident in timber buildings on dry land (the edge-trenched joint on the Group 7, 10 and 11 revetments, for example), there is little evidence to suggest that it was the work of specialist carpenters. Richard Cotterel was employed not only to rebuild the timber-faced wharf, but also to construct the jetty, fence and sheds.[22] The three carpenters engaged to work upon a Southwark wharf in 1389 were required to rebuild two water-mills and the mill-house,[23] while two carpenters employed to work on the roof of Westminster Abbey were also named in a contract for a wharf at Vauxhall in 1476–7.[24] Even Hugh Herland 'the disposer of the King's works touching the art or mistery of carpentry' and architect of the magnificent hammer-beam roof at Westminster, is known to have assisted with the harbour works at Great Yarmouth.[25] He came from a long line of famous carpenters: John Herland his grandfather was possibly

Part III—Analysis

living in Queenhithe, to the east of Trig Lane, in *c*. 1332, while in the 1370s William Herland, Hugh's father, lived on the south side of Upper Thames Street in the parish of St. Peter the Less, of which Trig Lane forms the eastern boundary.[26] However, none of these master craftsmen is likely to have been directly associated with the construction of the humble work found at Trig Lane (although they must presumably have seen it) because they were already fully employed on the King's Works.

It is not known how many carpenters lived in London in the 14th century, although at least thirty are known by name. Out of 107 persons working in the building trade in York in 1381, a total of 52 were engaged in woodworking,[27] and a larger figure for London would not be unreasonable. The City carpenters were certainly numerous enough to form a 'Brotherhood of Carpenters' by 1333.[28]

Although it is not therefore possible on documentary grounds to attribute the design and construction of the revetments found at Trig Lane to a particular carpenter or group of carpenters, it is nevertheless interesting to note that each structure seems to be an improvement upon its predecessor. For example, the Group 11 back-braces were constructed more than a decade later than the Group 10 braces, which were not of course visible when the Group 11 revetment was planned and built. Nevertheless, the latter's back-braces are considered to be a conscious modification of the earlier prototype (*cf.* Figs. 18 and 22), which suggests at least an element of specialisation.

2. Assessment

The revetments constructed during the consolidation of the waterfront at Trig Lane exhibited great structural variety, incorporating both the post-and-plank and stave-building techniques. Nevertheless, all belong to the vertical tradition of revetment construction, in which principal frame members are vertically set, and contrast with the horizontal tradition exemplified by the well-known waterfront structures at Bergen.[29]

Vertical revetments in general may be divided into three types, *unbraced*, *front-braced* and *back-braced*. In the medieval period, the first type is known from a number of sites including Samsø (Denmark)[30] and Schleswig (W. Germany) in the late 11th century.[31] Although none of medieval date has yet been found in the City of London, several Roman examples have been recorded.[32] The Trig Lane revetments were all taller than these and were therefore supported either by front- or back-braces, or, in the case of the Group 3 structure, by both. Front-braced revetments are well known from the 12th century onwards.[33] In most instances the diagonal brace (or shore) supports the head of the vertical post, but in an example from Stretham, near Henfield in West Sussex, only the base-plate was braced by shores set at a lower level.[34] The use of back-braces with horizontally laid tie-backs is known from 13th- to 14th-century contexts in King's Lynn,[35] Dublin[36] and possibly also Lincoln,[37] while diagonally disposed back-braces were found on the Mermaid Theatre site in the City of London,[38] and also at Hull.[39]

The excavated sequence at Trig Lane shows how the front-braced revetment (e.g. Group 3; Group 4; Group 6) was gradually superseded by the development of the back-braced revetment (e.g. Group 7) which was itself further refined by the construction of the Group 10 and Group 11 revetments. These were both built in two distinct levels, separated by a horizontal plate. The reasons for this development are important, and arise from the fact that waterfront timberwork decays rapidly at the level of the contemporary Mean High Water Neap tides (Pl. 72).[40] Timber immediately above this zone is permanently exposed above the fluctuating waterline, while timber below it is subject to submergence twice daily. The wood in the intervening area is thus subjected to regular swelling and shrinking immediately below the zone, but not above it. The physical breakdown of the wood at this point is an inevitable result.

The Trig Lane sequence shows considerable evidence of repairs and often complete replacement of riverfront revetments (e.g. Group 2 with Group 3; Group 4 with Group 6). Some of the extensions themselves may also be seen primarily as a repair or consolidation of the frontage, rather than as a simple reclamation. For example, the Group 10 revetment was seen to supersede a much-repaired and presumably unstable facing comprising sections of the Group 3, Group 4 and Group 6 revetments and, as such, would have proved difficult to repair again *in situ*.

The easier and more stable solution of erecting a new revetment to the south of the dilapidated one was adopted (Fig. 3 and 3f). Parallels for refacing a decayed frontage by reclaiming land on the foreshore in front of the original structure rather than replacing the timber work *in situ* have been found at the Custom House site in the City. Here the second series of timber structures were exactly similar in function with the ones they replaced[41] and survived in excellent condition except for the tops of the posts and planks which had decayed at between +1.20m and +1.50m O.D. All the revetments at Trig Lane also decayed at this level, although timberwork survived elsewhere on the site up to +2m O.D.

At Seal House an earlier frontage was advanced three times between *c.* 1140 and *c.* 1220 and the decayed top of the third medieval revetment was between +0.80m and +1.20m O.D. At Wood Quay in Dublin three successive timber revetments were erected during the 13th century. The second soon collapsed, and was replaced by a third still further out in the river. Subsequently, a stone wall, built in the early 14th century, brought medieval riverfront extension and the contemporary quayside almost to the line of the modern quays.[42] Because the stone wall was not susceptible to the decay which affected timberwork, it did not need to be continually maintained or replaced. As at Trig Lane, the construction of the stone river wall marked a hiatus in the reclamation process.

The development of the form of the Trig Lane revetments themselves is also directly related to the problem of timber decay. Once the heads of the posts of the earlier front-braced type of revetment began to deteriorate, the associated structure would sooner or later have to be replaced completely. However, when the upper level of the Group 10 revetment began to decay, it was only necessary to replace the superstructure above the head of the stave wall with the Group 12 timberwork. The staves themselves remained sound and did not require replacement although the heads of the shores—and therefore the whole

Part III—Analysis 57

of the back-braces—were renewed. The Group 11 revetment incorporated a further refinement. Again, this was a two-storeyed structure, with the plate supporting the upper level of vertical planking laid just below the level of contemporary Mean High Water Neaps,[43] so that the replacement of the decayed higher timberwork could be achieved without affecting the stability of the foundation. But the diagonal shores on the Group 11 back-braces were not joined directly to the second-storey members, as had been the case with the Group 10 back-braces. Instead an additional timber 1.25m long was scarfed to the head of the shore (Figs. 21; 22) and presumably joined to the upper planking which it supported. This extension to the brace could also be replaced if required, and the seven peg holes in the scarf table on the easternmost brace (which was cut from primary timber) demonstrate that this additional member was replaced more than once, as two or three face pegs would have been sufficient to secure the original joint (Figs. 23; 42).[44]

Present-day riverside timberwork, such as jetties and rubbing posts, is often built in two levels, with vertical members incorporating simple edge-halved scarf joints just below the level of the Mean High Water Neaps (Pl. 72). The earliest archaeological evidence for this practice comes from the Chapel Lane Staith excavations in Hull where a revetment incorporating two distinct levels of timberwork was dated to *c.* 1320 on dendrochronological analysis, some 30 years earlier than the Group 10 example at Trig Lane.[45]

3. Reconstruction

It was clear that none of the revetments had survived to its full height since the tops of the structures which were recorded had all been damaged by decay or later disturbance. A reconstruction of several of the revetments was therefore attempted to determine their complete form and, by implication, help define the level of High Water in the medieval period, as this must be assumed to have been lower than the original top of the structures. Initially, the heights of the Group 3, Group 11, Group 12 and Group 15 structures were deduced by an analysis of the direct evidence derived from the structures themselves. It was subsequently possible to suggest the original heights of the other structures by comparing this information with the height of contemporary surfaces and other related data.

Group 3 (Fig. 40). The south end of the horizontally laid tie-back on the Group 3 back-brace was raised so that the tenon (which had been found broken) passed into the pegged mortise in the north face of the revetment post (cf. Figs. 4; 9). The chase mortise and tenon at the foot of the strut dictated the angle at which that member must rise, and its south end was found by projecting this line until it reached the extended head of the post. This was found to be 0.80m higher than the contemporary surfaces, suggesting that the Group 3 revetment's timber cladding was carried above the ground surface as a parapet. The heads of the back-brace struts must also have been visible when operative, a suggestion perhaps borne out by the siting of the chalk foundation of the 14th-century building (Building C, see Pl. 4)[46] which clearly respected their alignment. An original height of *c.* 3.40m is suggested for the Group 3 revetment.

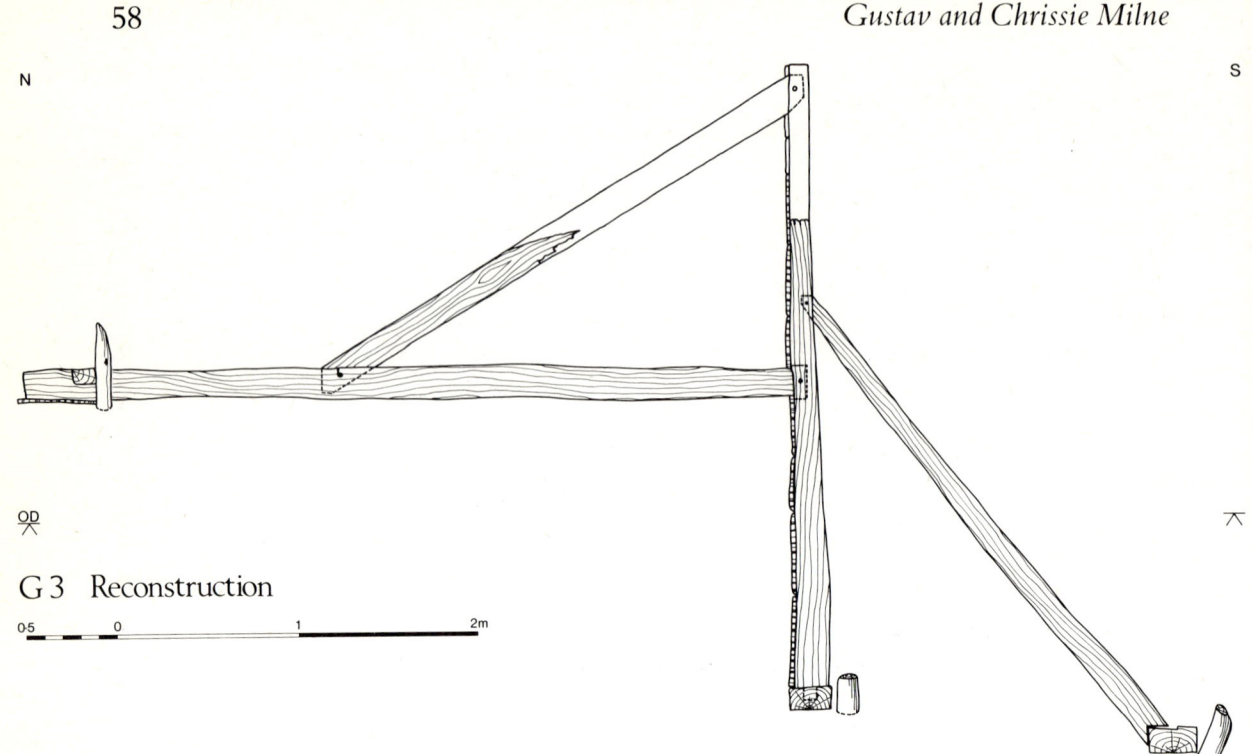

Fig. 40. Trig Lane 1974–76: Reconstructed side elevation of Group 3 revetment: cf. Fig. 9.

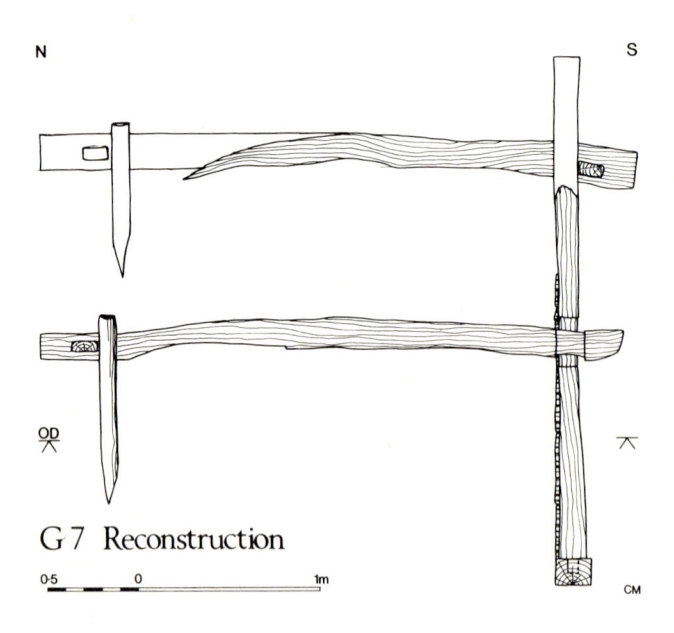

Fig. 41. Trig Lane 1974–76: Reconstructed side elevation of Group 7 revetment: cf. Fig. 13.

Part III—Analysis 59

Group 11 (Fig. 42). Because the heads of the diagonal shores on the Group 11 back-braces passed over the top of the plate laid onto the heads of the revetment's vertical planking (Fig. 22), the structure must originally have carried a second level of timber work. This would have comprised vertical members tenoned into the mortises visible in the decayed plate (Figs. 21b; 23). As these mortises were half the size of those which retained the tenons on the feet of the lower level of vertical planking, it is suggested that the upper level was half the height of the lower. The upper level members may have been braced longitudinally by a top-plate set on their heads. Additional support would have been provided by the member scarfed to the head of the back-brace shore (Fig. 22) which would have been passed between two vertical members, perhaps utilising the same system of edge-trenching as was apparent at the lower level (Fig. 23).

The Group 11 revetment would thus have stood *c.* 2.50m high, with an unparapeted top which was level with the contemporary yard surfaces at *c.* +2.10m O.D. The reconstruction of the scissor-braced trestle (Fig. 38) suggests that its top, and therefore the Group 11 revetment with which it was contemporary, was at the same height.

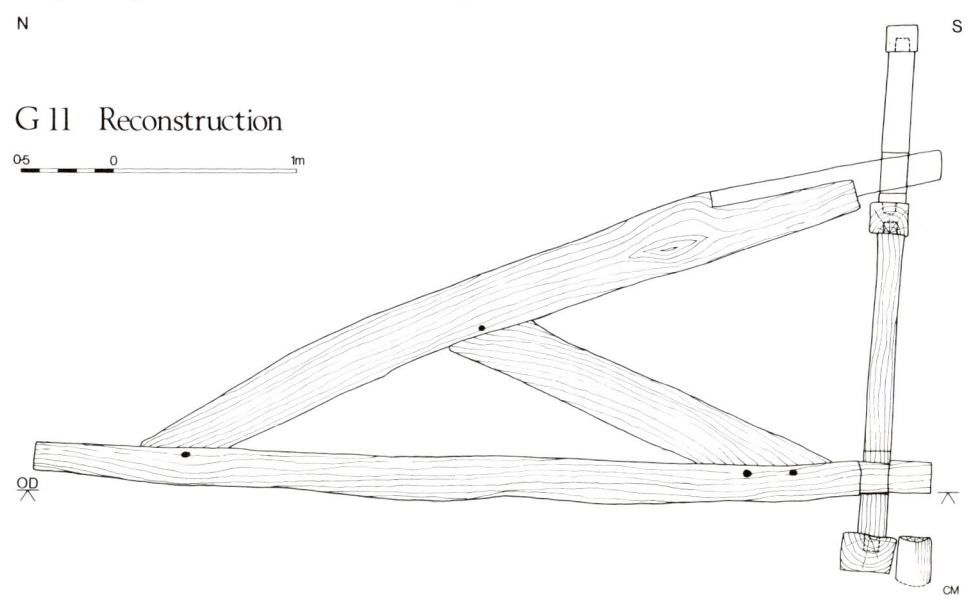

Fig. 42. Trig Lane 1974–76: Reconstructed side elevation of Group 11 revetment: cf. Figs. 22 and 23.

Group 12. It was noted that the north face of the Group 15 wall's western section was not faced at the point at which it butted up against the Group 10/Group 12 frontage (p. 40; Pl. 59). This suggests that the Group 12 vertical planking extended virtually to the same height as the surviving section of the Group 15 wall at that point. A similar height was calculated independently, extrapolating the original form of the eastern Group 12 back-braces by continuing the brace southwards along the line dictated by the angle of the lap joint at its foot to terminate perpendicularly above the revetment face (Fig. 30). A height of *c.* 1m is thus suggested for the Group 12 structure which, combined with the Group 10 stave wall on which it was laid, would have formed a bi-partite revetment *c.* 2.50m tall.

Group 15. The removal of the blocking in the stairhead of the Group 15 river wall revealed the profile of a flight of stairs built into the thickness of the wall (Pl. 61). It was then possible to suggest that the top of the highest stair (and therefore of the wall itself) was at +2.20m O.D. The use of ragstone rather than chalk for the wall's uppermost courses indicated that it originally bore a small parapet (Pl. 56). The southern section of the wall would therefore have stood *c.* 2.70m high (Fig. 48).

The other revetments

The vertical distance from the base of the Group 2 base-plate to the level of the contemporary surfaces was *c.* 2m, which must therefore be the minimum height of that revetment (Fig. 4). The Group 4 and Group 6 structures were probably of a similar height, and the level of the surfaces contemporary with the Group 7 revetment showed that it was also at least 2m tall (Figs. 4; 41). The Group 10 structure was clearly two-storeyed, as the head of the back-brace shores passed over the top of the stave wall (Fig. 18), and would have originally been similar in height to the 2.50m tall Group 10/Group 12 revetment (Fig. 44).

The Trig Lane revetments were therefore assumed to have stood between *c.* 2m and 3.40m high, somewhat shorter than the 3.65m high revetments described in 1347 at Broken Wharf[47] and near Billingsgate in 1404,[48] and the stone wharf at the Tower of London, which was to stand *c.* 5m high.[49]

C. THE MEDIEVAL RIVER LEVELS

The work at Trig Lane has also thrown new light on the nature of the River Thames in the medieval period. It had been evident for some time that the present-day Thames is much deeper than it was in previous centuries, but the problems attendant upon any attempt to establish precise figures for earlier river levels were all too clearly outlined in a recent paper.[50] Attempts at deducing water levels in other medieval ports have included the recording of flood deposits and the actual top of waterfront timberwork at Hull,[51] and of mussel shells on a sealed foreshore deposit in Bergen.[52] An additional problem is that some archaeologists have been reluctant to define the 'river level' which they were attempting to relate to Ordnance Datum. The level of the Thames, like all tidal rivers, fluctuates continuously, changing from high water to low water in just over six hours. Moreover, the level of water at high (and low) tide varies from week to week. For example the highest present-day Astronomical Tide (HAT) would be some 7.7m above the level of the Lowest Astronomical Tide (LAT), but is anticipated only eight times a year, once in March and November, and three times in April and December.[53] The tides which occur after each full or new moon are known as the Spring Tides, and those which follow the moon's first or third quarter are the Neaps. The highest Spring Tides are higher than the highest Neaps. Fig. 43 shows that the level of the present-day Mean High Water Neaps (MHWN) is 1.20m lower than the Mean

Part III—Analysis 61

High Water Springs (MHWS), and 1.27m lower than the Highest Astronomical Tide (HAT). Any attempt to calculate an ancient high water mark must state clearly to which level reference is being made.

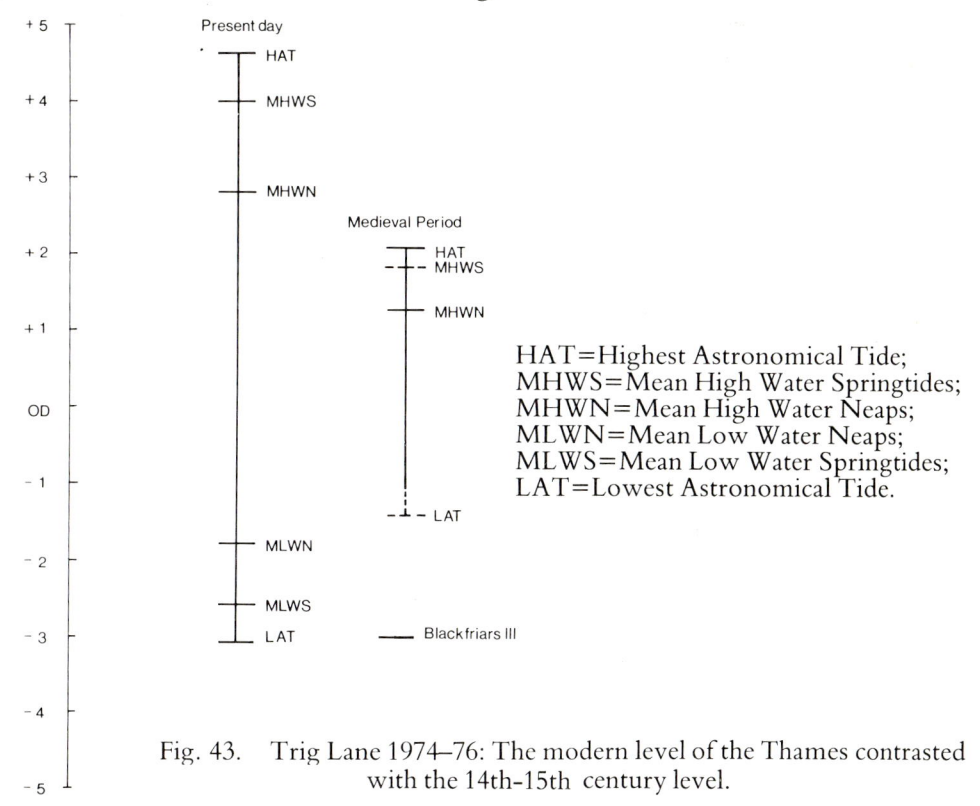

HAT=Highest Astronomical Tide;
MHWS=Mean High Water Springtides;
MHWN=Mean High Water Neaps;
MLWN=Mean Low Water Neaps;
MLWS=Mean Low Water Springtides;
LAT=Lowest Astronomical Tide.

Fig. 43. Trig Lane 1974–76: The modern level of the Thames contrasted with the 14th-15th century level.

Waterfront occupation is normally unlikely to occur at levels below the HAT, for it must be remembered that although the river might rise to this point less than ten times a year, it may rise to or above the MHWS level as many as 228 times *per annum*. The lowest occupation surfaces on the riverfront may thus be used to suggest the highest level to which the river was normally expected to rise, the level of the HAT, once factors such as subsidence and embanking have been taken into consideration. At Trig Lane in the 14th century this level would seem to be at *c.* +2m O.D., 2m lower than the present-day value (Fig. 43). In addition, the medieval revetments decayed at a height of *c.* +1.20m to +1.30m O.D. (see p. 00), and observation of the same phenomenon on the present-day waterfront suggests that the base of the decay zone is coincident with the level of the Mean High Water Neaps, i.e., the lowest high tides. At Trig Lane the difference between the medieval HAT and the MHWN was less than a metre, and may not have been as much as 0.80m.

The difference between the 1978 HAT and the MHWN was about a quarter of the total distance between the highest and lowest astronomical tides (see Fig. 43): if the medieval equivalent represents a similar proportion, then the lowest astronomical tide in the 14th century may have been at about −1.20m O.D.

This figure is supported by two other important sources of evidence. Firstly, none of the principal base-plates of the riverfront revetments was laid below −1.20m O.D., and this level must have been dry for long enough to accommodate the necessary construction work. This included driving in foundation piles, laying sections of base-plate, drilling and pegging the scarf joints, and drilling and pegging the tenons on the feet of the principal posts. These tasks could not be undertaken very easily if the site was permanently under water. Secondly, the wreck of the 15th-century Blackfriars Ship III, found off Trig Stairs in 1970, lay at a depth of between −3m and −4m O.D., some 10m south of the 15th-century river wall. The vessel must have sunk and remained permanently under water in this position, for, had it been visible, it would have formed a substantial impediment to other vessels and to anybody requiring access to and from the common stairs at the foot of Trig Lane.[54] Had it been accessible in the medieval period, it would almost certainly have been salvaged as it seemed to be in good condition, although extensively repaired.

Low tide in the medieval period may therefore have dropped at least as low as −1.20m O.D., to facilitate the construction of the revetments, but not as low as −2m or −3m O.D. to reveal part of the wreck of Blackfriars Ship III.[55]

D. THE DEVELOPMENT AND USE OF THE WATERFRONT

1. Tenement development

The excavations at Trig Lane afforded an opportunity to examine the physical nature and use of the medieval waterfront in the western part of the City. It was shown that the frontage was structurally varied and much indented and, where timber-faced, underwent continuous change through repairs or reclamation. The upkeep of the frontage rested upon the owners or occupiers of the individual waterfront property plots. This point is illustrated, for example, in the London Eyre of 1246, in which the individual citizen's customary encroachments on the waterfront are justified by the need to protect land and tenements from erosion by the river,[56] and by a document dated to 1384, contemporary with the Group 11 revetment. This records that a lessee of a site between Thames Street and the river in the parish of St. Dunstan's was to undertake a comprehensive rebuilding programme which included extending the wharf into the river, '. . . enlarg' strecchyng in the Themesward the seyd wharfe . . . at his owne proper costes'.[57] The development of the Trig Lane frontage also reflects the importance of the role of the occupier, rather than the owner, who need not necessarily be the same person. For example, by 1291, the western, central and eastern properties (labelled A, B, C on p. 9), lying between what were to become Boss Alley and Trig Lane, were all owned by John de London (p. 7). Properties A and B shared the same riverfront revetment, the Group 4 structure, in contrast to property C's Group 3 revetment. By c. 1350, property A had been repaired with the Group 6 revetment, while properties B and C had been advanced with the construction of the Group 7 revetment although the ownership of all three remained the same, suggesting that the development of properties was still actively in the hands of tenants.

Part III—Analysis

Given that the maintenance of the riverfront properties was the occupants' concern, the question of whether individual frontages were advanced separately or in concert would depend on such chance factors as the ability or inability of neighbours to cooperate, or to raise the necessary capital at the same time. Thus, by 1430 all three properties were owned by William Stokke, but were clearly defined archaeologically by three different revetments (Group 12 East and West and Group 11) and three distinct river stairs, supporting the documentary evidence that three different tenants were in occupation (p. 7).[58] However, in c. 1440 when the properties were not owned by a common interest they nevertheless shared a common frontage, the group 15 river wall[59] with a common stair.

Each property was usually served by its own river stair, demonstrating the importance of gaining access to the river and foreshore at a time when the Thames was the major source of water for domestic and industrial purposes, and river transport was by far the most common method of moving men and merchandise. The occupants of the Trig Lane properties appear to have been either dyers or fishmongers (p. 7), both trades which required access to the river or a ready water supply. Archaeological evidence for such exploitation of the river is suggested by the excavation of a possible water tank built as an integral part of the late 14th-century revetment (Fig. 28), which may be compared with the much larger example from the Oyster Street excavations at Portsmouth (Hants),[60] and a post-medieval fishpond set into a starling on London Bridge.[61] A reminder of a more mundane use of the foreshore was provided by the Group 14 feature, which was interpreted as a revetted rubbish dump.[62] There are numerous City records of attempts to curb the illicit dumping of refuse in or around the river,[63] the frequency with which the cases appear demonstrating the inadequacy of the legislation.

Fragmentary remains of medieval buildings were recorded at Trig Lane and are described in a recent report.[46] The excavations exposed only about 10% of the surface area of the medieval properties which extended to Thames Street, some 40–50m to the north. No clear statement on the utilisation of the quayside area based solely on the fragmentary archaeological data could therefore be made.

However, some buildings are specifically mentioned in the documentary references to the properties, and these are discussed by Tony Dyson in Part One (p. 8). This source provides a more evocative indication of the general nature of the surface development than the archaeological evidence on its own. In 1256 the southern portion of the eastern tenement was said to comprise houses, buildings, a quay and a little chamber above the Thames, while the southern part of the western tenement in 1422 featured a messuage and garden with adjacent wharf and the 'stairs of the wharf', as well as facilities for dyeing. A garden is also mentioned with four cottages in the southern portion of the eastern tenement in 1447, and in the central tenement in 1475 a building called 'le dyehous' adjacent to the wharf and two chambers over the great gate of the building were specified.

It was not possible to identify any of these buildings with the fragmentary remains of the excavated structures. Nevertheless, to summarise the report cited above, evidence for timber-framed buildings was recorded, and a storage or semi-commercial function for some of them has been suggested. The topographical relationship of successive buildings to Trig Lane itself, to the river stairs and to the line of the waterfront was clearly never static, although the excavations were not extensive enough for general conclusions to be drawn on this point. However, it is suggested that the riverfront end of the property was perhaps more intensively developed than might have been expected, although there were at least some open yard areas here in the medieval period.

2. Medieval ships and boats

Medieval boat nomenclature is extensive and often somewhat obscure, but it seems there were three main classes of vessel contemporary with the Trig Lane revetments.[64] They are mentioned in a complaint filed in 1356 concerning the building of a stone wharf on the foreshore near Baynard's Castle 'to the nuisance of ships (*navium*), shouts (*shoutarum*), and boats (*battelorum*)'.[65] These terms, although not always used consistently in medieval documentation, refer to sea-going vessels and two sorts of river craft, the cargo and passenger carriers. The relative size of these three classes of vessel is shown in Fig. 45.

Numerous references to *battela* in the London Eyre of 1244 and 1276 show that they were small craft valued at between 2s[66] and 10s.[67] The boats were used principally for the conveyance of one or two passengers along or across the Thames,[68] and in 1372 no boatman was to take more than 2d for hire between London and Westminster, or more than 3d when the boat was full.[69] Although other cargoes such as 28d worth of chalk[70] were occasionally carried, a load of five persons and an excessive weight of faggots was sufficient to sink a boat.[71] Such vessels presumably fulfilled the same function as the 2,000 wherries which John Stow records as serving the needs of the Tudor Londoner.[72] A statute passed in 1555 stipulates that the dimensions of any wherry or boat used for rowing and carrying people upon the Thames should be not less than '22 foote and a half in lengthe, and 4 foot and a half broade in the mydshippe',[73] i.e. about 7m by 1.50m.

Shouts belonged to a larger class of working river boat, usually with a sail, that was specifically designed for the carriage of bulky material.[74] Cargoes known to have been carried on such craft include corn and brushwood in 1244,[75] Purbeck marble in 1348[76] and Reigate stone in 1480–1.[77] A 14th-century 'dong boat', 'the aquatic equivalent of a dung-cart' must have been of a similar type, as it could also carry heavy consignments of stone.[78] The wrecks found by Peter Marsden in 1970 off Trig Stairs[79] belong to this general class of working boat, and have been discussed recently.[80] Blackfriars Ship IV had been carrying a cargo of ragstone and Blackfriars Ship III contained nearly 2,000 cylindrical lead weights, presumably from fishing nets. This wreck may originally have been some 16m long and 3m wide (Fig. 45), twice the size stipulated for a Tudor wherry.

The third class of vessel, *navis*, refers to the even larger sea-going ships. No ship of more than 240 tons is recorded before the middle of the 14th century.[81] By the early 15th century ships over 200 tons were still uncommon, but by 1451 the Crown had been able to hire 34 such vessels.[82] The most famous of the north

Part III—Analysis

European merchant ships in the 13th and 14th centuries was the high-sided deep-draughted cog, portrayed on the seals of Elbing in 1350 and Kiel in 1365.[83] In Bremen in 1962 the wreck of a virtually complete cog was discovered, and it is now dramatically reconstructed in the Maritime Museum at Bremerhaven. She was built in 1380, is some 23.5m long, 7m in breadth, and the deck of her after castle is *c*. 6m above the keel[84] (Fig. 45). Had she ever sailed up the Thames and negotiated London Bridge, she would have dwarfed the contemporary Group 11 revetment at Trig Lane. An earlier vessel from Bergen (Norway), although not a cog, was even larger: 27m long with a beam of *c*. 9m.[85]

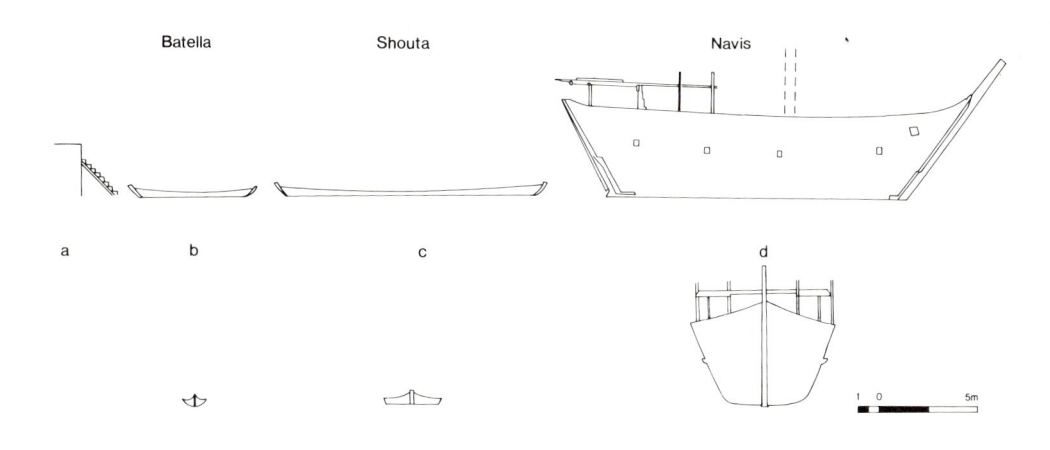

Fig. 45. Trig Lane 1974–76: Diagram to show relative size of three main types of vessel using the late medieval river Thames.
    a) Group 15 river wall
    b) Dimensions of boat taken from 1555 Statute
    c) Blackfriars Ship II (Marsden 1971)
    d) Cog from Bremen (Ellmers 1972)

Other medieval sea-going craft included *balingers* of 20 to 50 tons, used both for fishing and for carrying cargo,[86] *barges* such as the one which brought a cargo of 150 tons of merchandise from Seville to London in 1392[87] and the *hulk*, known from the New Shoreham seal,[88] which gradually replaced the cog. *Farcosta* were another type of heavy cargo vessel, associated with the carrying of stone and timber on the Thames in 1350 and 1380, but also capable of crossing the sea, as a *farcosta* laden with Flemish tiles arrived at the Tower in 1315.[89]

The frequency of the projecting foreshore stairs and the heights of the revetments and river walls at Trig Lane (e.g. Fig. 47) indicate that the sea-going vessels could not have docked against such wharves. However, the smaller shouts and rowing boats would have been able to tie up at the foot of the stairs and operate off the foreshore in tidal conditions.[90]

3. The motivation for riverfront reclamation

From the 7th century onwards medieval land reclamation on, for example, the east coast of England is well known. 'Sea walls' were constructed to keep the sea off salt marsh which in time would dry out to form valuable pasture.[91] The gradual reclamation of land on the banks of a river is a rather different process, but is known to be a feature of medieval ports, both in this country and on the Continent.[92] Several reasons for this extensive reclamation have already been suggested:[93] to win land; to establish a deep-water berth; to overcome the problems of silting and thus facilitate the accommodation of rivercraft.

The need to win land for its own sake is the simplest and most obvious solution, and is the most significant reason advocated by Helen Clarke to explain the 100m wide reclamation at King's Lynn, Norfolk. However, she also suggests that natural silting accentuated by the changing fenland river system was a contributory factor, as was the medieval habit of dumping refuse in or beside the river.[94] Dr Volker Vogel has argued that the 11th-century extensions at Schleswig were directly associated with the need to create a harbour capable of accommodating the deeper draught shipping which was developing at that period,[95] a point made earlier by Dr. Asbjorn Herteig for Bergen.[96] In Holland Dr. Herbert Sarfatij states unequivocally that 'the purpose of the wharves at Amsterdam was to reach the deeper water of the river in its function as a harbour'.[97]

At Trig Lane it is clear that the accommodation of boats was not a major consideration in revetment design, since the small craft which would have operated from the frontage must have tied up at the foot of the projecting stairs rather than directly against the revetments. Nevertheless, the change to back-bracing may well have been partially influenced by a desire to produce a frontage free of obstructive front braces (*cf.* Group 3 and Group 10), to facilitate the easier movement of boats in general. This change also provided more protection from the revetment's bracing system as the back-braces were sealed beneath the dumped deposits behind the revetment, and were no longer exposed to damage on the foreshore.

Below the bridge the very real problem of silting may well have been a crucial consideration, as it was thought to be in Amsterdam.[98] The rate at which the foreshore material accumulated against the medieval revetments at Trig Lane was calculated at between 15mm and 20mm *per annum* (see Fig. 39): for example, some 1.50m had built up against the face of the Group 10 revetment during its life of about 80 years. Since the excavated revetments and river walls were rarely built higher than *c.* 3m, they would have been inundated within *c.* 200 years (assuming that the sedimentation rate has been correctly calculated), unless either the waterfront was advanced southwards over the shelving beach, or substantial dredging took place. There is little evidence for the latter on the medieval London waterfront. In 1481 the Armourers Company asked permission of the Court of Common Council to extend their newly acquired property at Trig Lane southwards (p. 8) and, uniquely, gave their reason for the request. It was not apparently a desire to win more land, but an attempt to overcome one of the problems of silting. This was because neighbouring properties projected further into the river with the result that foul-smelling

Part III—Analysis

refuse was constantly washed up, and retained, against their frontage between tides.

However, the sequence at Trig Lane shows considerable evidence of repairs and of the complete replacement of riverfront revetments caused by the tendency of the timberwork to decay above the level of the Mean High Water Neap tides (see p. 56). Some of these repairs were effected without any physical extension of the property (e.g., Group 2 and Group 3). Others involved the erection of a new revetment to the south of the dilapidated one, and, although the waterfront was thereby advanced, it was often only sufficient to allow for the erection of the new structures (e.g., Groups 7 and 10). This fourth reason for riverfront reclamation, the need to maintain a sound frontage, was first identified as a result of the Trig Lane excavations, and seems to be the most important factor governing waterfront extension on this site. It is suggested that the maintenance of a sound frontage was the principal concern of waterfront property owners,[99] and that the continuous piecemeal reclamation of land at the expense of the river was primarily a by-product of this need. Nevertheless, the value of the extension of the property which sometimes accompanied such work must have been appreciated by its perpetrators, and could have acted as a secondary source of motivation.

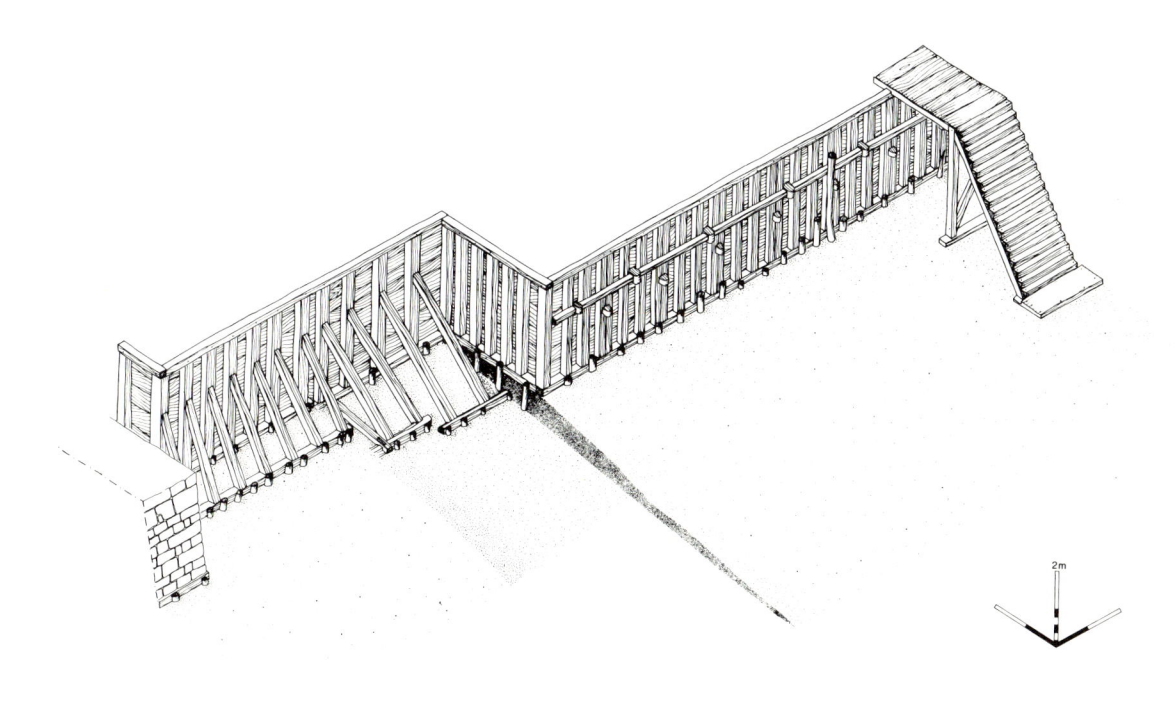

Fig. 46. Trig Lane 1974–76: Period III reconstruction of Trig Lane waterfront in mid-14th century. Note stone wall, back-braced and front-braced revetments all contemporary. Cf. Fig. 3e.

E. CONCLUSIONS

The waterfront excavation at Trig Lane examined a relatively large area over an extended period of time in more detail than had previously been possible on other sites.[100] It encompassed part of at least three medieval property plots, and the sequence of extension and waterfront consolidation on all three was shown to be different (cf. Fig. 4 with Fig. 44). The piecemeal nature of waterfront development shown in Figs. 46, 47 and 48, the indented nature of the frontage, and the variety of structures which could exist contemporaneously (e.g., Fig. 46) were all demonstrated in a way that would not have been possible with a single 3m wide trench.[101] The documentation which is available for the site (p. 4) does not suggest that the Trig Lane properties were any different from any of the other private wharves in the City, so that the pattern of development revealed by the excavators may be taken as the model for most of the London waterfront. By contrast, the waterfronts at Baynard's Castle and the Custom House[102] are known to have had more specialised functions, as the names imply, so could not be regarded as 'typical' sites.

It is suggested that the piecemeal riverfront extensions at the expense of the Thames were not primarily motivated by a desire to win land for its own sake or to accommodate shipping, but were a by-product of the need to maintain a sound frontage. The responsibility for the physical maintenance of the frontage was shown to rest not with a civic authority nor even necessarily with the property owners, but with those who held the individual tenements.

The close dating of the sequence (p. 50) enhanced our understanding of the chronology of waterfront development and provided good groups of dated material for those working on the associated artefacts. For example, the medieval pottery from Trig Lane is the best-dated sequence of its type in the country, and as such has far-reaching implications for medieval archaeologists both in Britain and on the Continent (p. 92).

The examination of the well-preserved timberwork proved to be a particularly valuable exercise, for such revetments had not been studied in detail previously, and it was subsequently possible to classify the structures and suggest reasons for their development (p. 55). The variety of the techniques employed in the construction of this mundane class of structure has relevance for any wider assessment of medieval vernacular timber building, as the carpenters who produced the London revetments seem also to have been responsible for the many other types of timber buildings in the City, no examples of which survive (p. 54). The form and function and development of river stairs was another neglected area of waterfront study on which the present excavations were able to throw some light (p. 43), while the suggested rate of foreshore accumulation, 15m to 20mm *per annum*, needs to be checked against data from elsewhere (p. 52). The method by which the level of the medieval Thames was deduced should be broadly applicable to other waterfront sites, regardless of date or country (p. 61). This should be of value not only to environmentalists but also to nautical archaeologists attempting to evaluate the potential of a port and the nature of the craft which could operate from it.[103]

Part III—Analysis

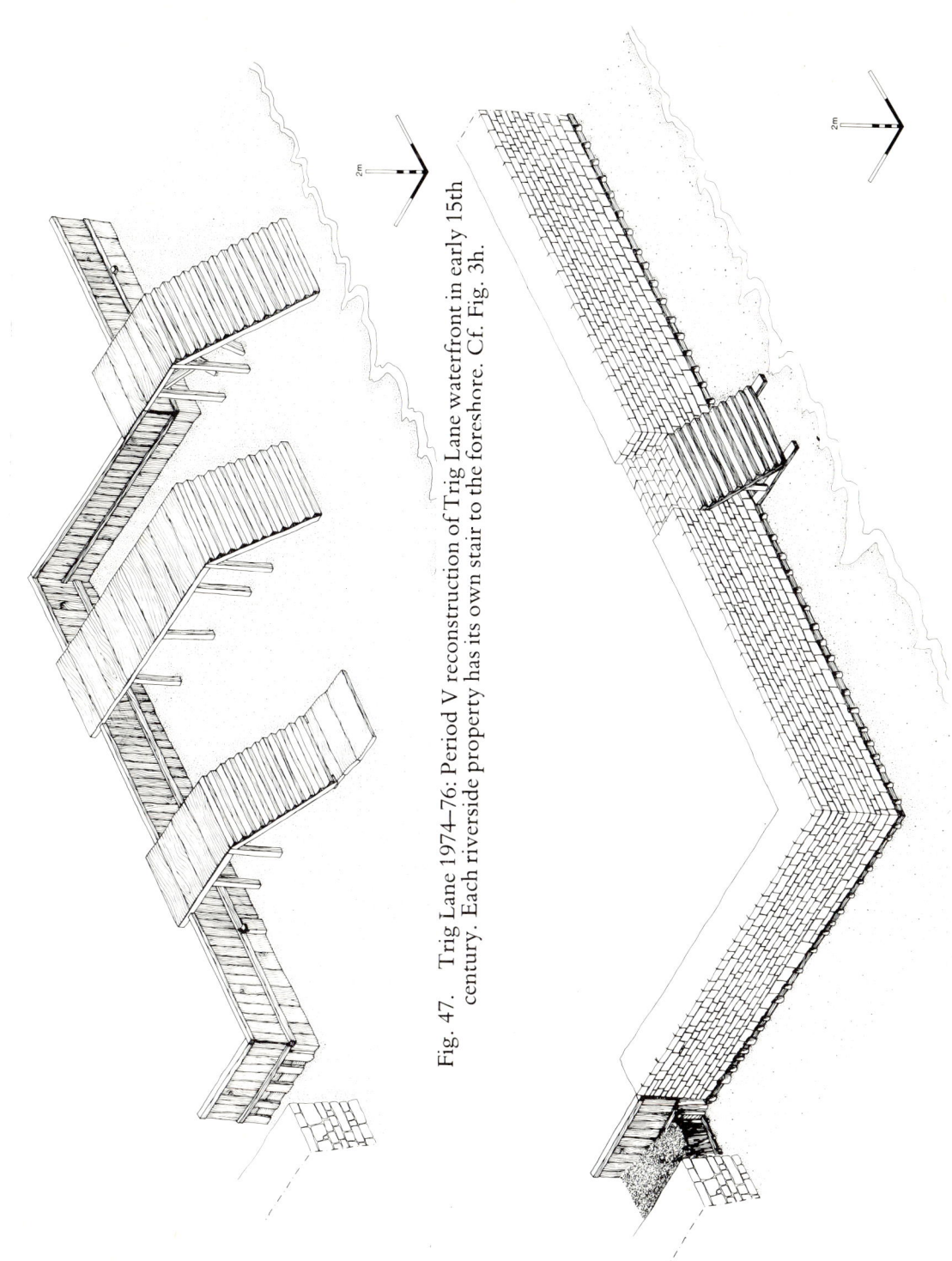

Fig. 47. Trig Lane 1974–76: Period V reconstruction of Trig Lane waterfront in early 15th century. Each riverside property has its own stair to the foreshore. Cf. Fig. 3h.

Fig. 48. Trig Lane 1974–76: Period VI reconstruction of Trig Lane waterfront in mid-15th century. The single stair in the centre of the river wall has replaced the three stairs of the earlier period shown in Fig. 47. Cf. Fig. 3i.

ACKNOWLEDGEMENTS

First and foremost we wish to acknowledge the hard work of all members of the excavation team—both amateur and professional—without which this report would not have been possible, especially Peter Ellis, John and Cathy Maloney, John Burke-Easton and Charlotte Harding (who also assisted with the dendrochronological analysis). We are most grateful to those who prepared the specialist contributions: Donald Brett of Bedford College, University of London on the dendrochronological analysis; R. L. Otlet and A. J. Clark for their work on the radiocarbon determination; Tony Dyson on the documentary evidence; and Michael Rhodes on the finds. Thanks are also due to Trevor Hurst, Jon Bailey and David F. Harrison who undertook most of the photography; Alison Balfour-Lynn for drawing up Figs. 7, 10, 15, 19, 24–8, 43, 45, 66; Peter Ellis and Cathy Maloney for their work on Figs. 23 and 14 respectively; and Diana Twells for the typing. We are also grateful to Cecil Hewett for advice on the carpentry; to Derek Keene for his helpful comments; and to Tony Dyson and Hugh Chapman for guidance and encouragement.

NOTES AND REFERENCES

1. Personal communication.
2. In addition to R. L. Otlet's work, Dr A. J. Clark (Ancient Monuments Laboratory) has calibrated the radiocarbon dates using the new precise curve of Stuiver (*Radiocarbon*, forthcoming). The provisional results confirmed that the radiocarbon measurements are compatible with the suggested tree-ring date.
3. See, for example: J. G. Hurst 'White Castle and the dating of Medieval pottery' *Med. Archaeol.* 6–7 (1962–3) 149; J. Haslam *Medieval Pottery* (Princes Risborough 1978) 9; J. Holdsworth 'Selected pottery groups AD 650–1780' The Archaeology of York 16/1 (1978) 1–2 and cf. 12–15.
4. R. Morgan and J. Schofield 'Tree rings and the archaeology of the Thames waterfront in the City of London' in *Dendrochronology in Europe*, ed. J. Fletcher, B.A.R. 51 (1978) 225–7.
5. O. Rackham *Trees and woodland in the British landscape* (London 1976) 20–2, 66–84.
6. L. F. Salzman *Building in England down to 1540* (Oxford 1952) 418.
7. Many of the tools and techniques employed by medieval carpenters are known from studies of contemporary documentation and illustration, such as the authoritative surveys published by L. F. Salzman *op. cit.* in note 6, 237–52, 340–7; and J. Harvey *Medieval Craftsmen* (London 1975) 99. The study of items in museum collections is equally important (e.g. London Museum *Medieval Catalogue* (London HMSO 1940) 55–9), as is detailed examination of surviving examples of medieval structures. The recent paper by O. Rackham, W. J. Blair and J. T. Munby 'The 13th century roofs and floor of the Blackfriars Priory at Gloucester' *Med. Archaeol.* 22 (1978) 105–22 is an illuminating example of how much can be learned about the medieval carpenter's workmanship, economy of his use of timber and engineering sense from such work.
8. J. Harvey *op. cit.* in note 7, Fig. 42.
9. *Ibid.*, Fig. 7, but called a frame saw in the caption.
10. L. F. Salzman *op. cit.* in note 6, Pl. 19.
11. J. Harvey *op. cit.* in note 7, Figs. 43–5; London Museum *op. cit.* in note 7, 55–9.
12. B. Greenhill *Archaeology of the Boat* (London 1976) Fig. 162.
13. Two sawyers employed at a sawpit at Whitby Abbey (Yorks) in the 1390s were paid 3s 6d for two days' work: J. Harvey *op. cit.* in note 7, 99.
14. *The History of the King's Works. I: The Middle Ages* ed. H. M. Colvin (London 1963) 530.
15. L. F. Salzman *op. cit.* in note 6, 467–9.
16. H. Colvin *op. cit.* in note 14, 439.
17. *Ibid.*, 435.
18. *Ibid.*, 441.
19. *Ibid.*, 442.
20. T. Tatton-Brown 'Excavations at the Custom House site, City of London, 1973' *Trans. London Middlesex Archaeol. Soc.* 25 (1974) 138.
21. L. F. Salzman *op. cit.* in note 6, 435.
22. *Ibid.*
23. *Ibid.*, 467–9.
24. N. Woodward-Smith and J. Schofield 'A late 15th century account for a wharf at Vauxhall, London' *Trans. London Middlesex Archaeol. Soc.* 28 (1977) 284.
25. J. Harvey *op. cit.* in note 7, 127.
26. *Ibid.*, 132.
27. *Ibid.*, 152.
28. C. Welch *The 'Boke' of the ordinances of the Brotherhood of Carpenters of London* (London 1912). A selection of the contracts undertaken by London carpenters is published in L. F. Salzman *op. cit.* in note 6, Appendix B, 417, 418, 433, 434, 441, 467, 483.
29. A. E. Herteig 'The excavation of *Bryggen*, the old Hanseatic Wharf in Bergen' *Med. Archaeol.* 3 (1959) 177–86; E. C. Harris 'Bergen, *Bryggen* 1972—the evolution of a harbour front' *World Archaeology* 5 no. 1 (1973) 61–71.
30. See, for example, D. Ellmers *Frühmittelalterliche Handelsschiffahrt in Mittel- und Nordeuropa* (Kiel 1972) 241; Fig. 170.
31. V. Vogel 'Die Anfange des Schleswiger Hafens' in *Ausgrabungen in Schleswig* (Schleswig 1977) 21–8. The present authors are grateful to Friedrike Hammer for translating this article.
32. D. Jones and M. Rhodes *Excavations at Billingsgate Buildings ('Triangle'), Lower Thames Street, 1974* London Middlesex Archaeol. Soc. Special Paper No. 4 (1980).
33. For example, see T. Tatton-Brown *loc. cit.* in note 20; J. Schofield 'Seal House' *Current Archaeology* 49 (1975) 54–7; G. Milne 'Medieval riverfront revetment construction in London' in *Medieval Ships and Harbours*, ed. S. McGrail, B.A.R. (1979), 145–53.

34. L. Webster and J. Cherry 'Medieval Britain in 1977' *Medieval Archaeol.* 22 (1978) 181–2.
35. H. Clarke and A. Carter *Excavations in King's Lynn 1963–70* Med. Archaeol. monograph No. 7 (London 1977).
36. P. Wallace 'Dublin's waterfront at Woodquay: 900–1317' in *Waterfront Archaeology in Britain and Northern Europe* ed. G. Milne and B. Hobley, Council for Brit. Archaeol. Res. Rep. 41 (1981) 109–118.
37. L. Webster and J. Cherry 'Medieval Britain in 1973' *Medieval Archaeol.* 18 (1974) 201.
38. J. Hillam and P. Herbert 'Tree-ring Dating: Mermaid Theatre, City of London' *London Archaeol.* 3 No. 16 (1980) 439–44.
39. B. Ayers 'Excavations at Chapel Lane Staith, 1978' *East Riding Archaeol.* 5 (1979).
40. For discussion of medieval river levels, see p. 60.
41. T. Tatton-Brown *loc. cit.* in note 20, 132–3.
42. P. Wallace *loc. cit.* in note 36, 115–17.
43. See note 40.
44. But see O. Rackham *et al. loc. cit.* in note 7, 115, Fig. 8.
45. See note 39.
46. G. Milne and C. Milne 'The Medieval buildings at Trig Lane' *London Archaeol.* 4 No. 2 (1981) 31–7.
47. L. F. Salzman *op. cit.* in note 6, 434.
48. *London Assize of Nuisance 1301–1431* ed. H. M. Chew and W. Kellaway, London Record Society, 10 (1973) No. 645.
49. L. F. Salzman *op. cit.* in note 6, 469. This quay was downstream of London Bridge, and was presumably designed to accommodate large sea-going ships, although it is uncertain whether the figure of 5m includes the subsurface foundation of 1m in depth.
50. G. Willcox 'Some problems and possible conclusions related to the history and archaeology of the Thames in the London Region' *Trans. London Middlesex Archaeol. Soc.* 26 (1975) 285–92.
51. See note 39.
52. A. E. Herteig 'The Excavation of Bryggen, Bergen, Norway' in *Recent Archaeological Excavations in Europe* ed. R. Bruce Mitford (London 1975) 72–3, Fig. 30.
53. Port of London Authority *Handbook of Tide Tables* (London 1978) passim.
54. P. Marsden 'Archaeological Finds in the City of London 1967–70' *Trans. London Middlesex Archaeol. Soc.* 23 (1971) 7–9.
55. For a recent assessment of the river level in the Roman period, see. H. Sheldon *Southwark Excavations 1972–74* London Middlesex Archaeol. Soc. and Surrey Archaeol. Soc. Joint Publication No. 1 (1978) 45–7, who suggests that 'the water level in Southwark (the south bank of the Thames) may have been near to +1.00m O.D.'
56. *The London Eyre of 1244* ed. H. W. Chew and M. Weinbaum, London Record Soc. 6 (1970) 343.
57. L. F. Salzman *op. cit.* in note 6, 454.
58. Properties A and B were separate dye-house tenements in 1422, see p. 6.
59. Wrongly attributed to the Armourers' and Brasiers' Company in the interim report, G. Milne and C. Milne 'Excavations on the Thames Waterfront at Trig Lane, London 1974–6' *Medieval Archaeol.* 22 (1978) 98.
60. S. Moorhouse 'Post-medieval Britain in 1970' *Post Med. Archaeol.* 5 (1971) 201, Pl. Xa.
61. *Gentleman's Magazine* 23 (1753) 432. We are indebted to Charlotte Harding for this reference.
62. *Cf.* the Armourers' and Brasiers' extension petition of 1481; see p. 8.
63. For example, see R. R. Sharpe *Calendar of Letter Books, Book A* (London 1899) 218.
64. See also S. McGrail 'Medieval boats, ships and landing places' in Milne and Hobley *op. cit.* in note 36, 17–23.
65. H. M. Chew and W. Kellaway *op. cit.* in note 48, 453.
66. *London Eyre of 1276* ed. M. Weinbaum, London Record Soc. 12 (1976) No. 251.
67. H. M. Chew and M. Weinbaum *op. cit.* in note 56, Nos. 87, 147. M. Weinbaum *op. cit.* in note 66, No. 184. For comparison, a horse was valued at between 5s and £3, M. Weinbaum *op. cit.* in note 66, No. 10.
68. M. Weinbaum *op. cit.* in note 66, Nos. 176, 184.
69. R. R. Sharpe *op. cit.* in note 63, *Book G*, 301.
70. H. M. Chew and M. Weinbaum *op. cit.* in note 56, No. 164.
71. With fatal consequences: M. Weinbaum *op. cit.* in note 66, No. 220.
72. J. Stow *A Survey of London* ed. C. L. Kingsford (Oxford, rev. ed. 1971) i.12.
73. *Statutes of the Realm* 23 (1919) 291.
74. D. Burwash *English Merchant Shipping 1460–1540* (Toronto 1947) 104.
75. H. M. Chew and M. Weinbaum *op. cit.* in note 56, No. 261.
76. L. F. Salzman *op. cit.* in note 6, 350.
77. N. Woodward-Smith and J. Schofield *loc. cit.* in note 24, 282.
78. L. F. Salzman *op. cit.* in note 6, 350.
79. P. Marsden *loc. cit.* in note 54, 1–14.
80. P. Marsden 'The Medieval Ships of London' in *Medieval Ships and Harbours* ed. S. McGrail (Oxford 1979), 83–92.
81. L. F. Salzman *English Industries of the Middle Ages* (1964) 228.
82. D. Burwash *op. cit.* in note 74, 178–9.
83. See D. Ellmers *op. cit.* in note 30, 65, Fig. 42, and B. Greenhill *op. cit.* in note 12, 260, Figs. 175–6.
84. D. Ellmers *op. cit.* in note 30, 66, Fig. 43.
85. A. E. Herteig *loc. cit.* in note 52, 86–7.
86. D. Burwash *op. cit.* in note 74, 104.
87. *Ibid.*, 116.
88. B. Greenhill, *op. cit.* in note 12, 284, Fig. 201.
89. L. F. Salzman *op. cit.* in note 6, 350.
90. The Trig Lane revetments never functioned as part of a major mercantile wharf, but some large ships with, for example, cargoes of wine are known to have off-loaded part of their cargo onto smaller lighters (see, for example, H. T. Riley (ed) *Liber Albus: the White Book of the City of London* (London 1861) 217), and these could have been accommodated at public quays by revetments of the Trig Lane type.
91. W. G. Hoskins *The Making of the English Landscape* (1955) 95–101.
92. G. Milne and C. Milne *loc. cit.* in note 59, 103.
93. G. Milne 'Medieval riverfront reclamation in London' in Milne & Hobley *op. cit.* in note 36, 32–6.
94. H. Clarke and A. Carter *Excavations in King's Lynn 1963–70* Medieval Monograph No. 7 (London 1977) 423–4.
95. V. Vogel *loc. cit.* in note 31, 22–3.
96. A. E. Herteig, *loc. cit.* in note 29, 179.
97. H. Sarfatij 'Archaeology and the Town in the

Netherlands' in *European Towns: their archaeology and early history* ed. M. W. Barley (London 1977) 201.
98. *Ibid.*, 211.
99. The maintenance of a sound frontage was important not only for the security of the riverfront property occupier himself, but also for his neighbour, cf. H. M. Chew and W. Kellaway *op. cit.* in note 48, No. 645.
100. For example, the Custom House site was only open for sixteen weeks: T. Tatton-Brown *loc. cit.* in note 20, 118.
101. B. Hobley and J. Schofield 'Excavations in the City of London—First Interim Report 1974–5' *Antiq. J.* 57 (1977) Fig. 5.
102. P. Marsden 'Early shipping and the waterfronts of London' in Milne and Hobley *op. cit.* in note 36, 14–16; T. Tatton-Brown *loc. cit.* in note 20.
103. S. McGrail *loc. cit.* in note 64.

PART IV

IV. SPECIALIST REPORTS

A. DENDROCHRONOLOGY AND CARBON 14 DATING
by Donald W. Brett with a contribution by R. L. Otlet

Dendrochronological Analysis

Introduction

Before the recovery of the Trig Lane material, timbers from two other medieval London waterfront sites had been studied by Fletcher (Tatton-Brown, 1974) and by Morgan (1977; Morgan and Schofield, 1978). The few samples from the Custom House site were selected with a view to dating the structures by dendrochronological analysis, but most of the timbers were derived from fast-grown trees (with wide rings) and had less than 75 rings, making them of little use for this purpose. A single timber with about 150 rings has since been dated to the mid-12th century, but no sapwood was present to provide the means of exact dating (Morgan and Schofield, 1978). A much larger sampling at the Seal House site resulted in the dating of 20 of the 43 samples by direct comparison with the German reference chronologies or with timbers already dated by this means (Morgan, 1977; Morgan and Schofield, 1978). Only one of the timbers dated in this way had fewer than 80 measured growth rings. Most of the undated primary structural timbers had fewer than 50 measured rings (12 samples) but three had over one hundred rings (details supplied by Dr. Ruth Morgan).

It seems clear from the results of the analysis of the Seal House timbers that the majority of small primary timbers from which the revetments along the River Thames were made will be of little use for *direct* dating by comparison with the available chronologies, and the present study confirms this. However, these small timbers usually have most of the sapwood present and their felling date may therefore be estimated to within a decade—if they are unambiguously associated with a datable timber that itself has sapwood remaining and has not been reused. There is thus the possibility that even small timbers may be indirectly 'dated' and used to 'date' similar timbers by cross-matching their ring-width pattern in a different context, perhaps a different site.

The possibility of using these small timbers in this way obviously depends on the examination of a large number from each structure. In addition, such a large sampling may provide the following information: i) an estimate of the sizes and ages of the trees used by the medieval carpenter, relevant to local supplies and woodland practice (Rackham, 1976); ii) variability of ring-width patterns among trees of these age groups, with possible evidence of woodland practices and sources of the timber; iii) the relative dating by cross-matching between phases of construction, indicating repairs and additions; iv) cross-dating of contemporary or near-contemporary structures between sites, one of which may have been dated independently.

The present aim was to utilize a much larger sample of timbers from the revetments at Trig Lane than had been possible from Seal House, and in the event ninety-four samples were taken from the oak timbers and seventy-seven

Part IV—Specialist Reports

were analysed by the methods described in this report. With hindsight, many more of the 450 timbers revealed at this extensive site should have been sampled in order to provide the necessary replication of the smaller timbers and to gain most information from them, but without additional technical assistance this was impossible. The methods of dendrochronology may demand a different approach from that commonly accorded to other 'finds', because analysis usually needs to proceed along with the excavation to assure replication where necessary and to lessen the risk of loss due to drying-out of the wood as well as to spread the work load in the laboratory. The value of a much larger sampling from any future excavation, and the need for special assignment of staff for the analysis during the course of the excavations, cannot be overstressed.

Methods of sampling and measurement

Samples were cut with a chainsaw from timbers on site while still wet, except in a few instances where timbers exposed during an earlier phase of the excavation had to be cut. After washing to remove mud and other debris, the samples were split or sawn to manageable size and surfaced along one or more edges to expose the growth rings in cross-section. With care, soft sapwood could usually be cut with a new razor blade but in many cases the wood was frozen to consolidate the soft parts before surfacing with a microtome knife or razor.

Ring-widths were measured to 0.05mm using a stero-zoom binocular microscope fitted with an eyepiece graticule. Thus, the initial measurements were done while the wood was wet, after which it was allowed to dry out. Later remeasurement of certain samples was therefore done when the wood was dry. Except where the wood was badly degraded on the exposed edges, the small amount of shrinkage due to drying was of little consequence and new measurements could readily be compared with the initial values obtained from the wet sample. The larger timbers with over one hundred rings have been remeasured two or more times along different radii and the results cross-matched and averaged.

Methods of dendrochronological comparison

Comparison of the series of ring-width measurements derived from each of the Trig Lane samples was made with the data from all the other samples from the site, and several of the Seal House timbers measured by Dr. Ruth Morgan. Similarly, each series was compared with available reference chronologies covering the years AD 1000–1600, including three from Germany (Delorme, 1978; Hollstein, 1965; Huber & Giertz-Siebenlist, 1969), Belfast (Baillie, 1977), west England-Wales (Siebenlist-Kerner, 1978), and southern England (Fletcher, 1977 and by personal communication). The German and Belfast chronologies have been independently constructed and dated by links with the chronologies of living trees from the regions; the English chronologies have been dated in the first instance by reference to the German chronologies. To aid visual comparison, the tree-ring data was plotted on transparent graph paper whilst the reference chronologies were usually plotted on white chart rolls. Computer programs for the following operations were used in the comparisons and cross-matching:

i) Listing data, calculation of mean ring-width, standard deviation and mean sensitivity for each ring-width series. Mean sensitivity is calculated by the equation

$$\text{m.s.} = \frac{1}{n-1} \sum_{t=1}^{n-1} \left| \frac{2(X_{t+1} - X_t)}{X_{t+1} + X_t} \right|$$

This gives a mean estimate of the differences between adjacent growth ring-widths and is therefore a measure of the 'sensitivity' of the tree to changes that affect the growth from year to year. Similar estimates may be calculated by a simplified version of the above equation and are referred to as 'average variation' of 'coefficient of variation'.

ii) Calculation of the agreement percentage (argement coefficient) between pairs of ring-width sequences (generally referred to as pairs of curves), which provides a measure of the similarity of the curves by the coincidence of interannual changes of ring width (Eckstein & Bauch, 1969).

iii) Calculation of correlation coefficient and '*t*' value for the comparison of standardized ring-width sequences (Baillie & Pilcher, 1973).

iv) Calculation of a mean chronology from several sets of data in matching position.

The general characteristics of the timbers studied are tabulated in the archive report housed with the Department of Urban Archaeology, Museum of London.

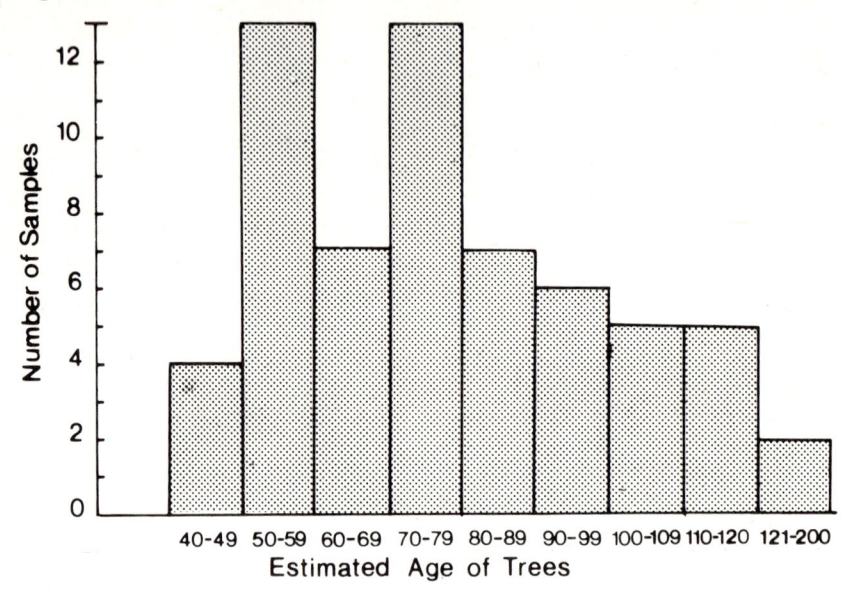

Fig. 49. Trig Lane 1974–76: Frequency distribution of age classes of timber used in revetment construction.

Age and size of the timber samples

Although only a little over 20% of the timbers revealed by excavation has been examined, many of the samples taken give a clear indication of the age of the tree from which the timber was cut, because they still have some sapwood from the outer part of the trunk and include, or closely approach, the centre of the trunk. With the exception of the elm piling (Brett, 1978) and two beech base-plates, the structural timber was exclusively oak and it is this which is the present concern. Thirty-five samples had both the central pith region and some sapwood present; a further thirteen had sapwood and closely approached the centre, as could be determined by the widening rings and the juvenile wood structure. Fourteen others included the central region but had had the sapwood removed; in their case, however, the general similarity to other timbers suggests that they were from similar sized trees and that they fall into the range with 70–100 growth rings. The two largest timbers were both capping beams from beneath stone walls. Both had sapwood present and one closely approached the pith region: these were cut from trees 200–250 years old, much larger than the trees providing the bulk of the timber for the revetments. The frequency distribution of age classes of the other trees is given in Fig. 49. They range in age from 40 to 120 years, those most frequently used being less than 80 years old. These small logs required very little shaping for use; many of the smaller ones were simply squared-off, others were quartered or split in half to provide timber of the required dimensions, procedures which resulted in very little waste and reflect the practice observed in ordinary medieval buildings (Rackham, 1976).

Part IV—Specialist Reports 77

Cross-matching between the Trig Lane timbers

There is no certain match between any of the samples from Groups 1, 4 and 6. Of the twelve samples from Group 3, two braces (1694 and 2874) and a base-plate (1791) agree very well and also match a post from Group 4 (2934). Although the Group 4 timber had no sapwood it resembled other small-tree timbers so that if not contemporary with Group 3 (which it probably was) it is unlikely to be much younger. The relative positions are shown in Fig. 50. The values of '*t*' and agreement percentages are given in Fig. 51 and these can be taken as an indication of the levels which I regard as necessary for a reasonable degree of certainty in matching these small timbers.

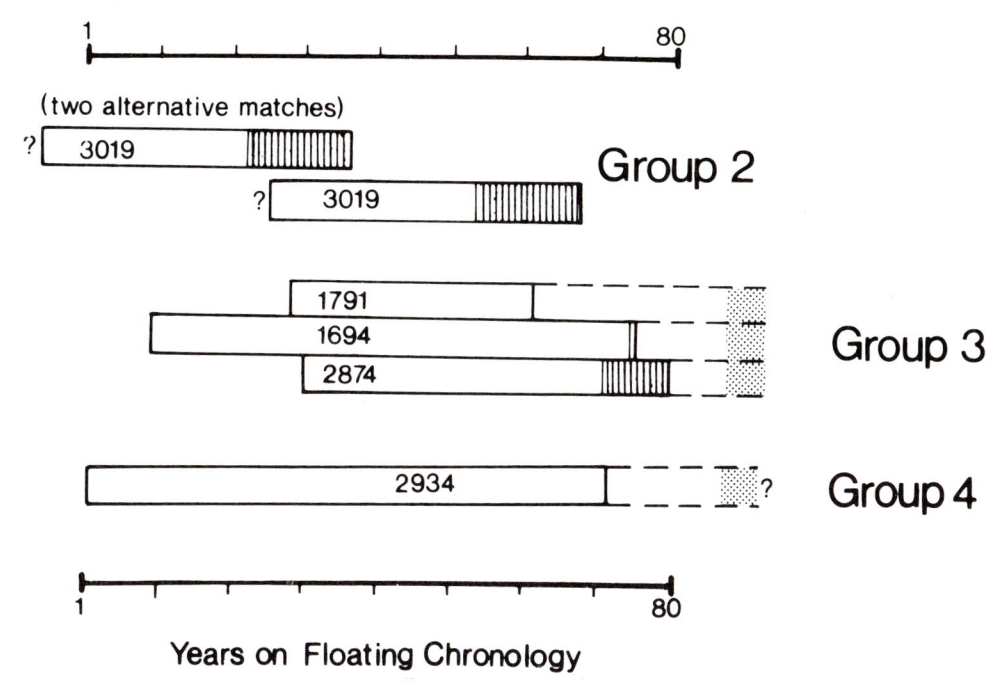

Fig. 50. Trig Lane 1974–76: Matching positions of samples from Groups 2, 3 and 4 indicating relative construction periods.

The single base-plate sample (3019) from the Group 2 revetment gave a low but consistent correlation with these four timbers (values given in Fig. 51) for the match in the position indicated in the diagram, and *t*=4.7 for the corresponding match with the mean chronology of these four samples. In view of the small size of the Group 2 timber (43 rings), however, too much confidence cannot be placed in this possible match and it should be noted that 3019 also correlated with *t*=3.77, 30 years earlier on 2934 (see Fig. 50). (Unfortunately no mutually consistent agreement existed between these early timbers and others from the site.)

Nine samples were taken from the Group 7 structures, but there were no certain matches between any of them. The positions of best fit (including some highly probable matches) were indicated on the bar diagram published by Milne & Milne (1978, p. 100, Fig. 13) but that assumes contemporaneity of the timbers and cannot be substantiated satisfactorily. It is necessary to point out that the diagram referred to was a provisional working hypothesis and although the relationships between Groups 10–15 shown there differ slightly from those given in the present report it will be seen below that the conclusions now rest on a surer footing. There is no such degree of certainty for any match between timbers of Groups 7 and 8 or between these and the higher groups.

The large capping beam (2271) from Group 8 held the promise of a possible link for all the early timbers, but this has not been fulfilled since none of the timbers from Groups 1–7 could be reliably matched to it. Because the sapwood which survives on this timber is well preserved (fifteen rings were measured), it is unlikely that the timber was reused. Two oak piles from below the beam can be visually matched with each other and with the outer portion of the beam, making it reasonably certain that none of these was reused. The relative positions of the three timbers are also shown in Milne & Milne (1978, p. 100, Fig. 13). The possibilities of an overlap between these Group 8 timbers and the inner portion of the Group 10–15 chronology will be considered after discussion of those groups.

		1694	1791	2874	2934
	1694	—	66.7%	76.1%	68.3%
G 3	1791	3.08	—	n.s.	72.7%
	2874	5.03	4.47	—	73.8%
G 4	2934	4.88	4.89	4.68	—
G 2	3019	3.38	3.20	2.97	3.18

Fig. 51. Trig Lane 1974–76: Table showing values obtained with Cross (*t*) and Ringsync (w%) programs for Groups 2, 3 and 4.

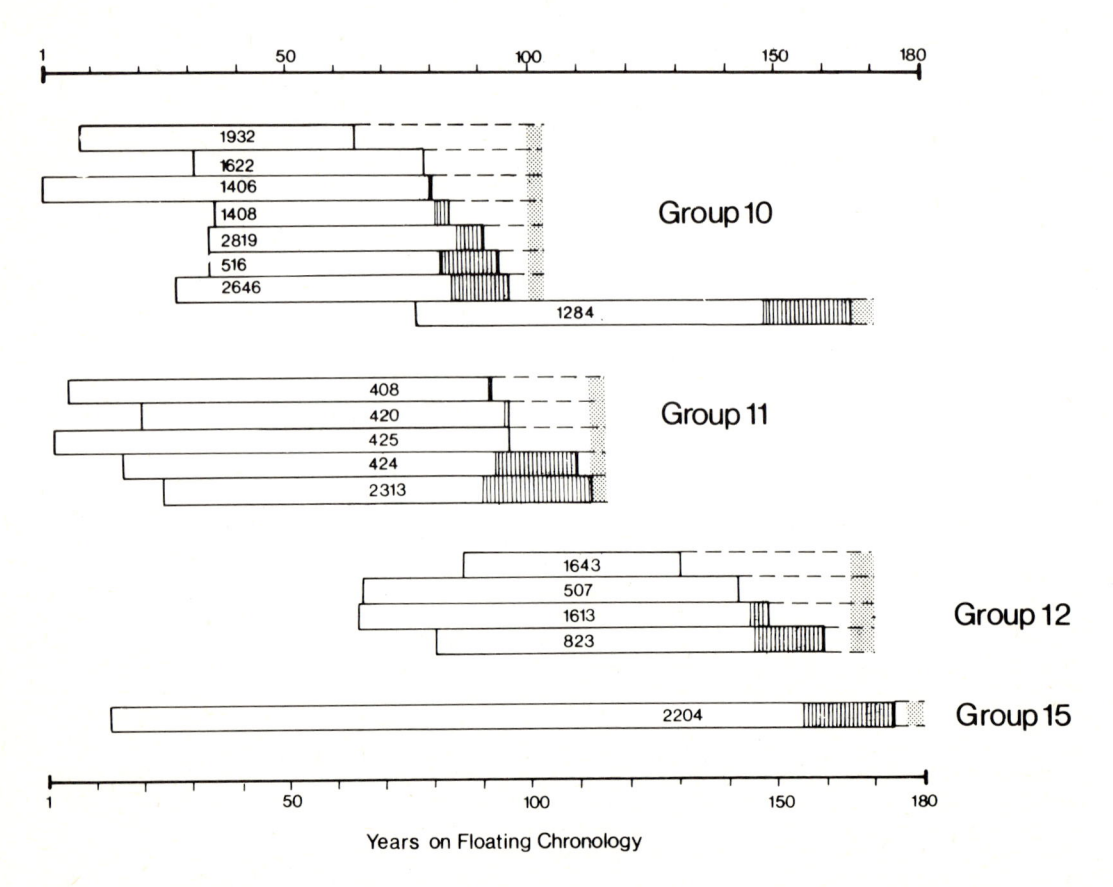

Fig. 52. Trig Lane 1974–76: The major samples of Group 10, 11, 12 and 15 in matching positions.

Part IV—Specialist Reports 79

Fifteen samples represented the Group 10 structures and, although the visual similarity between some of them was sufficient to suggest a match, most of the timbers were small and difficult to place with certainty. Two timbers, both staves (1932 and 2646), could be placed in position against the chronology of the Group 11 timbers and this considerably helped the positioning of some other Group 10 timbers. It is of interest that the matched timbers from Group 10 were all staves; the braces did not show even this degree of matching, and thus demonstrated that they had been reused or were obtained from different sources. The matching of the six staves was therefore largely dependent upon the visual similarity of the graphs, but the match between staves 1406 and 1932, and between staves 1932 and 2646 and the Group 11 chronology, are confirmed by the significant values for t (Fig. 53). A Group 10 average ring-width chronology based on six timbers spans 90 years and cross-dates with the Group 11 chronology with $t=6.44$. This match suggests that the Group 10 revetment was constructed some 10 years before the Group 11 structure was added (Figs. 52 and 53).

	1408	Group 10 1932	2646	2819	Group 11 mean
516a	2.66	2.95	1.94	2.36	2.63
1406	—	4.53★★★	—	—	—
1932	—	—	3.54	2.61	4.30★★★
2646	1.22	—	—	2.02	5.03★★★
2819	2.25	—	—	—	3.16

The values marked thus ★★★ are statistically highly significant ($P<0.001$).

Fig. 53. Trig Lane 1974–76: Table showing values for 't' from the correlations between Group 10 timbers in matched position and for comparisons with Group 11 chronology.

	408 'w'	420	424	425	2313
408 't'		63.2	71.4	81.0	61.0
420	2.77		68.7	73.3	59.9
424	3.63	10.34		74.4	67.4
425	4.85	11.21	9.02		62.0
2313	3.04	3.59	5.12	3.95	

Fig. 54. Trig Lane 1974–76: Table showing agreement (w) and 't' values for comparison of Group 11 timbers.

Cross-matching the individual timbers within Groups 11 and 12 presented the least difficulty; in both there were samples which were so similar that they could only have come from the same tree, and others matched these with high 't' or 'w' values (see Figs. 54 and 55).

The large back-braces of the box-like projection that constituted the Group 11 phase provided some of the best-quality timbers on the whole site, since they were halved tree trunks with centre and sapwood present. The samples 420 and 425 which show such a high level of agreement ($t=11.2$) are clearly two halves of a single trunk about 350mm in diameter from a tree about 110 years old. The large corner post (408), a squared trunk about 2m in length and 400mm–500mm across, also matched these and other braces with high agreement values ($w=81\%$ with 425) and may well have been cut from near the base of the same tree. The ring widths are larger in the corner post (mean width 3.86mm) which is consistent with that

	507 'w'	823	1284	1613	1643
507 't'		66.9	68.8	75.3	70.0
823	7.48		63.9	77.5	72.2
1284	4.73	5.35		69.0	64.4
1613	9.69	10.00	5.32		81.1
1643	6.77	7.73	6.06	9.86	

Fig. 55. Trig Lane 1974–76: Table showing agreement (w) and 't' values for comparison of Group 12 timbers.

possibility. It is of interest that the mean sensitivity for the rings of this post is higher at 0.335 than for the narrower ringed timbers which range between 0.183 and 0.221. The ring-width sequences for five of the Group 11 timbers are plotted in Fig. 56.

The eleven timbers from the Group 12 revetment structure likewise included four (507, 823, 1613, 1643) with a very similar ring-width pattern, evident from the plotted widths in Fig. 57 and from the 't' values and agreement percentages given in Fig. 55. The marked periodicity in this pattern, however, makes it difficult to match with other timbers, but a corner post (1284) excavated with the Group 10 stave revetment matches the plate (507) and back-braces (823, 1613, 1643) from Group 12 as a contemporary timber and thus clearly belonged to that phase of construction. The matching position of the post is shown in Fig. 57 and values for the statistical comparisons are given in Fig. 55.

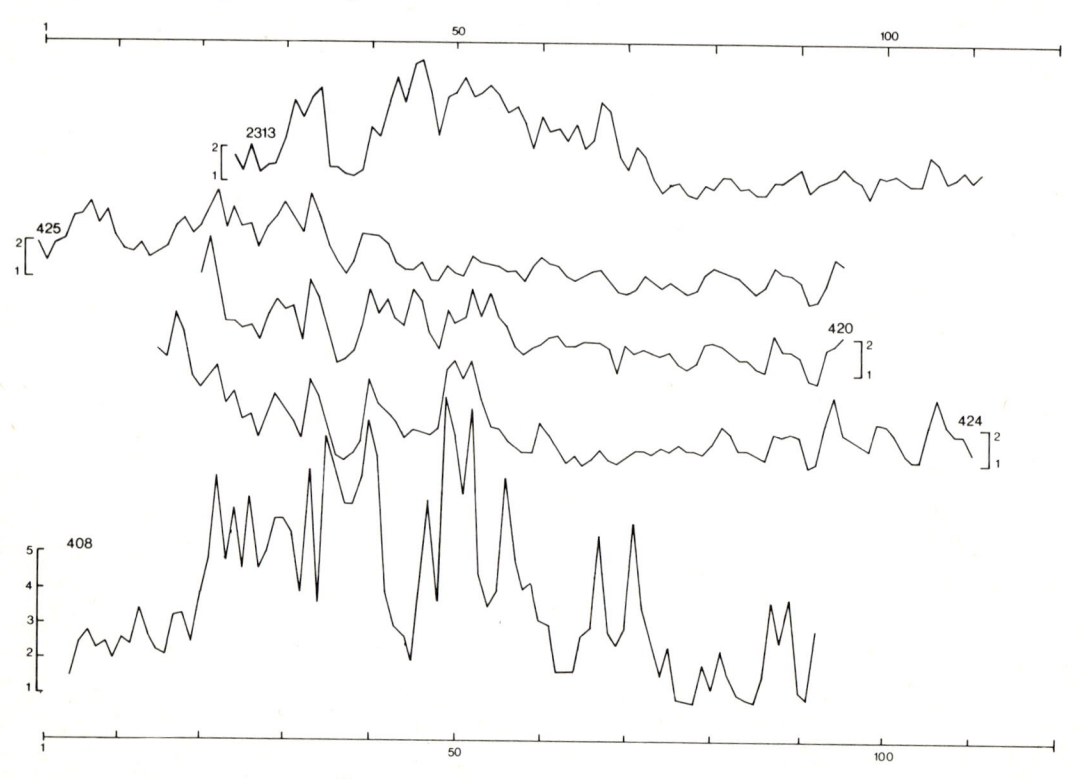

Fig. 56. Trig Lane 1974–76: Ring width sequences of five oak timbers from Group 11 plotted on linear scales: graduations in mm.

Part IV—Specialist Reports   81

No conclusions could be drawn from the four small timbers from Groups 13 and 14. Group 15 was represented by the large capping beam which provided a chronology with 162 rings. Because the sapwood which survived on this timber was well preserved (some 20 rings were present) it is not likely that the timber was reused. This Group 15 chronology almost completely overlaps the 111-year chronology of the Group 11 timbers, matching the braces 420, 424 and 425 with 't' values for the correlations of 4.9, 6.3 and 5.9 respectively. The match between the Group 11 mean chronology and the Group 15 timber with an overlap of 98 years gives a value of $t=5.76$ for the correlation (92 degrees of freedom). The overlapping portions of the chronologies of Groups 10, 11 and 15 are shown in Fig. 58 and their relative positions given in the bar diagram, Fig. 52.

The position of Group 12 in the sequence cannot be as securely fixed because of the difficulties of matching the timbers with regular cyclical fluctuations. The corner post (1284) gives a $t=4.62$ match in the position indicated (Fig. 52) with the Group 11/Group 15 combined average chronology, and a Group 12 chronology averaged from the 5 timbers gives $t=4.67$ for this match (97 degrees of freedom) and a 66.2% agreement of inter-annual trends. This places the Group 12 additions some 70 years after the construction of the main Group 10 revetment, but the Group 15 timber was used only about 10 years after the construction of Group 12.

Dating by comparison with chronologies from other sources
With the possible exception of Group 11, I have not been able to date with certainty any of the individual timbers or group chronologies from Trig Lane by reference to the chronologies that are available either from published sources or by personal communication from others engaged in similar work in dendrochronology. The lack of general similarity to the German chronologies has been a great disappointment and a stumbling block because comparison with the established German chronologies, or with English chronologies derived from timbers dated through such a comparison, has up to now proved to be the only means by which timbers in the south-east of England have been datable. Among the great number of comparisons made, there are, of course, many that can be placed in the category of highly probable. Although it would be pointless to list all of them here, there are a few that are worth discussing, particularly those involving the timbers with over 100 rings which we may confidently predict will at some future time be datable with certainty, following examination of more medieval timbers from the south-east of England.
Group 8 (timber 2271) A statistically highly probable match with the central German chronology occurs at AD 1389 ($t=4.4$, 173 degrees of freedom) but this is not supported by visual comparison and there is no correspondence between trends for the 'signatures' on the German chronology. It seems therefore that this match is purely fortuitous—the once in a millenium chance!
Groups 11 and 15 There is an acceptable level of agreement on the basis of inter-annual trends, $w=69\%$, between the 111 y chronology derived from the Group 11 timbers and the chronology for central Germany of Huber *et al.* with the final ring dated at AD 1373. Agreement is lower for this match on the west German chronology of Hollstein, but consistent matching between these chronologies and the individual timbers of Group 11 supports this dating. Although the Group 11 chronology does not match any of the English chronologies, it shares with some, e.g. Fletcher's Ref 1 (Fletcher, Tapper and Walker, 1974; Fletcher, 1978), the very narrow ring for AD 1353 when dated thus. Such a dating of Group 11 would place the final ring of Group 15 at AD 1436. Cutting dates for the timbers of Groups 11 and 15 would then be about AD 1380±5 and AD 1442±5 respectively.

An earlier dating could be supported by a statistically highly probable ($P<0.1\%$) match on the Belfast Index chronology for the combined 174 y chronology of Groups 11/15 ($t=4.57$, 168 degrees of freedom for the correlation of standardized indices of ring width). This places the final ring of Group 11 at AD 1333 and Group 15 at AD 1396, suggesting cutting dates of about AD 1340±5 and AD 1402±5 respectively. Visual comparison, however, lends no support to this possible match.

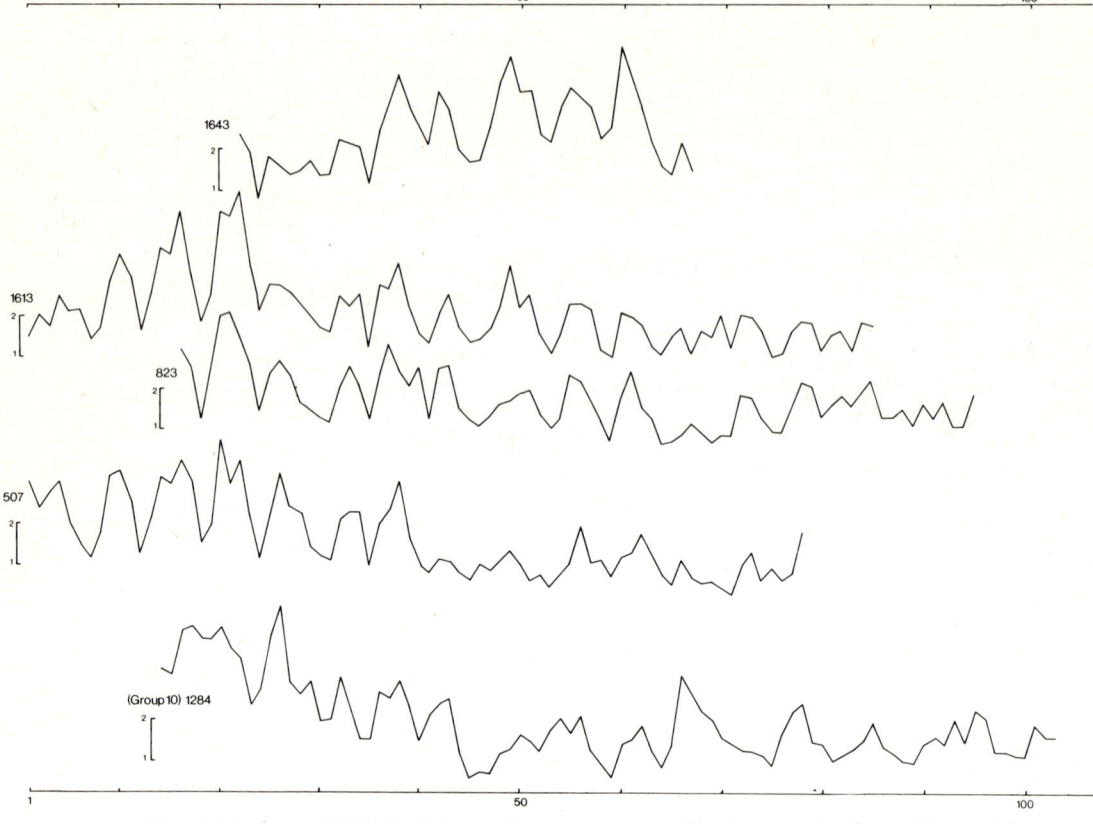

Fig. 57. Trig Lane 1974–76: Ring width sequences of main samples from Group 12: graduations on vertical scales in mm.

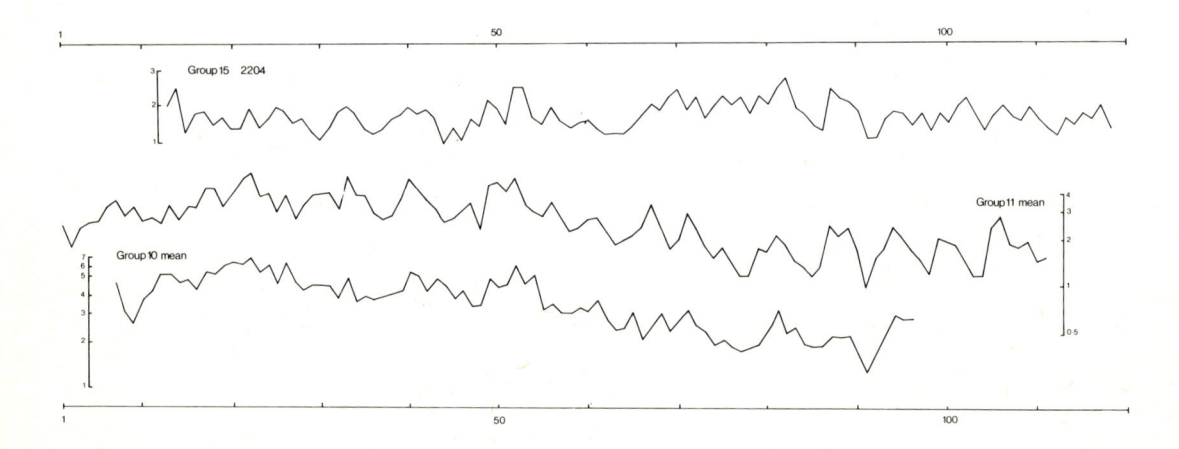

Fig. 58. Trig Lane 1974–76: Overlapping chronologies for Groups 10, 11 and 15. The mean chronologies for Groups 10 and 11 are each based upon average ring widths of five timbers, and are plotted on a logarithmic vertical scale: graduations in mm.

Part IV—Specialist Reports

Carbon 14 dating

Six samples were submitted to the Atomic Energy Research Establishment at Harwell. All had been cut from samples previously used in the dendrochronological analysis, and the positions of the ten to twenty-five annual growth rings which constituted the radiocarbon samples were recorded as shown in Fig. 59. In this, the ring placings given in column 5 are expressed in terms of their alignment to the master dendrochronological curve developed for the site. Using these alignments all results are used to determine a common, albeit arbitrary, datum year with which the placing of the dendrochronological scale can be compared. The hypothetical ring 150, corresponding to the dendro-year AD 1420, was chosen as the datum. Expression of the conventional radiocarbon dates, given in column 6, in terms of the datum year estimates is achieved first by calibration (using data from MASCA, 1977 and 150 year averaging) and secondly by adding on the appropriate growth allowance, being the difference between the mean ring position of the sample and the datum ring 150.

It is seen that with the exception of one, the results form a fairly close set appropriate to that expected from measurement each of the order of ± 60 years to ± 80 years, one sigma, standard deviation. This is confirmed by the T test of Ward and Wilson (T=2.3, X^2 at 5% confidence level=9.49) and enables an overall mean of AD 1390 ± 24 to be determined for the datum ring. Although individual placings of the samples in the dendro scale cannot be assessed by means or radiocarbon measurements of this precision it can be seen that only sample 1 appears to be grossly out of context and that overall the grouped assessment of the datum year is in good agreement with the dendrochronological scale placing within the meaning of the overall standard error of ± 24 years.

Sample Number	Context Number	Group	Harwell Reference	Rings used in Analysis	Radiocarbon Dates (bp)	Carbon-14 Estimate of Datum Ring, 150, with calibration (AD)
1	2271	8	2425	9–28	910±70	1203
2	408	11	2417	18–27	730±60	1379
3	408	11	2416	38–48	670±80	1403
4	425	11	2419	41–60	750±70	1335
5	1764	12	2418	60–84	620±70	1365
6	1613	12	2426	8–28	530±70	1476

NB. Overall (weighted) mean for datum ring is AD 1390 ± 24.

Fig. 59.   Trig Lane 1974–76: Table showing radiocarbon dates for Trig Lane timbers.

B. THE FINDS
Edited by Michael Rhodes
(With contributions by Clive Orton, the late Stuart Rigold, John Clark and Brian Spencer)

1. • Introduction: A discussion of the significance of the waterfront dumps and their contents
by Michael Rhodes

In addition to the valuable sequence of waterfront structures, the Trig Lane excavations produced large quantities of loose finds. This was to be expected since the Thames, its foreshores and its banks have long been recognised as a potential source of well-preserved artifacts. Prior to 1972, however, the area seems to have attracted more attention from mudlarks than from archaeologists (Egan, 1976), a neglect deplored in *The Future of London's Past* (Biddle, Hudson and Heighway, 1973, para. 4.51), which emphasized the importance of obtaining medieval finds from the waterlogged Thamesside deposits for the elucidation of London's trading connections, of her manufacturers and of details of her daily life at this period. The publication of this document coincided with the excavation of a number of large late-medieval rubbish deposits at Baynard's Castle (for site, see Webster and Cherry, 1973, 162–4), the first of a series of waterfront excavations which have now furnished the Museum of London with large collections of well-stratified artifacts, many of which are of remarkable quality. Regrettably, however, only the finds from the Custom House site (which taken alone provide but a small insight into these collections) have received anything approaching a comprehensive analysis (Tatton-Brown, 1974, 189–205; Tatton-Brown, 1975, 118–70), and current resources have permitted the proper analysis of only a few specially selected classes of finds from Trig Lane (see below, pp. 92–108). This introduction attempts to make a preliminary summary of the remaining finds from this site, to outline some of the documentary evidence relating to their possible origins, and to make some general remarks which could be helpful in the future to those wishing to conduct detailed research on these collections and groups of finds from other waterfront sites.

The overwhelming majority of the loose medieval finds from Trig Lane came either from infills behind the successive revetments and river walls or from the foreshore deposits in front of them. The former groups are four times the size of the latter, partly because the infills were greater in volume than the foreshore deposits and partly because hardly any small objects of readily perishable organic materials (i.e. leather, wood, etc.) survived in the foreshores. This could be an indication of the extent to which these materials had deteriorated as a result of exposure prior to burial, or of their relative buoyancy. The strength of the ebb and flow of the river at this period is well documented (see, for example, Chew and Weinbaum (1970, 133–4)). But the deterioration must in great part be due to the relatively unfavourable environment in which they were eventually buried. The infill finds, although generally in good condition, are themselves often not in the optimum state of preservation encountered in London's riverside dumps; for example, organic materials, especially woollen cloth (of which only a few pieces survived at Trig Lane) and ironwork, were generally much better preserved at Baynard's Castle 'dock', where high densities of animal bones, oyster shells and leather waste may, through complex chemical interactions, have contributed to the remarkable survival of materials as delicate as feathers, silk, fur and multi-coloured woollen cloth.

These local inconsistencies of preservation add to the difficulty of interpreting compositional differences between the rubbish dumps, although the surviving evidence suggests that the Trig Lane dumps were rather similar in constitution. For example, there is no indication that different dumps contained primarily domestic or industrial waste or reflected the life-style of different social groups. It is also impossible to say whether the foreshore finds closely reflect activities on the river and along the waterfront or merely illustrate the use of the Thames as a general repository for rubbish. Although the foreshore finds are not inconsistent with the documented use of the area, similar finds have in almost every instance been recovered from the revetment infills, the largest of which, on account of their size, are unlikely to have contained purely local rubbish. The only finds which were not recovered with greater frequency from the infills are the coins, jettons and tokens of Periods IV and V, of which (despite the very much greater volume of the infills) nearly one half (33 items) were found in the foreshores. This is partly explained by a group of 15 lead tokens of a hitherto unrecorded variety (type D4, see Rigold pp. 103–5) from the Period V foreshores, some or all of which must have been mutually associated prior to their loss, which might have resulted from a single action. Otherwise the high proportion of this type of find may simply reflect the relative ease with which such small, often dark (after burial) items were seen against the foreshore material and the greater car with which these deposits were excavated (G. Milne, pers. comm.).

The historical sources, although not fully researched and quite incapable of supplying a satisfactory picture, hint at some of the objects which might be found on the medieval waterfront. The foreshore itself was common soil (Jones, 1954, ix–xiii) to which London's citizens had the right of free access (Riley, 1868, 648–9). Here the common people washed their clothes (*ibid.*) and even entered the water to wash themselves and bathe (Sharpe, 1913, 59, 127 and 256–7). The Thames remained one of London's main supplies of water throughout the medieval period. 13th-century records show that water for domestic purposes was collected in wooden(?) buckets (Chew and Weinbaum, 1970, 42–3) and tubs (Ekwall, 1954, 2). Similarly, 14th-century records refer to earthenware pots (Sharpe, 1913, 252–3), pitchers (*ibid.*, 100) and large earthen vessels (*ibid.*, 178) used for the same purpose. Fishmongers, obliged to dispose of their dirty water in the same place (Riley, 1861, 238), must have used a similar range of vessels. In addition to fragmented pottery, the only find from the Period-III foreshore is what seems to be the iron handle of a bucket, and the Period IV foreshore produced the rim of an iron cauldron(?).

It appears to have been common practice to water horses by the river (Kingsford, 1971, 40–1; Chew and Weinbaum, 1970, 20; Riley, 1868, 549), although access to the foreshore would have been limited to places where there were slopes or ramps in place of stairs at the ends of the common lanes. Horses were also ridden on the foreshore and even in the river itself (Kingsford, 1971, 121; Chew and Weinbaum, 1970, 20 and 27), a hazardous practice in view of hidden obstructions beneath the water (for example, decaying boat remains, see p. 62) and one which cost Peter de Bermondsey, a 'portour', his life in 1340 (Sharpe, 1913, 263–4).

Despite the importance of the Thames as a source of water, it was often difficult to obtain relatively unpolluted supplies because the river was used for the disposal of waste and rubbish (e.g. Riley, 1868, 223). This was more or less tolerated until 1357 (Sabine, 1937, 32–7) when the increasing filthiness of the water gave rise to the need for increasingly strict (if apparently somewhat ineffectual) legislation and the provision of public places for dumping, including riverside laystalls (*ibid.*, 40).

The presence of quantities of dung by the foreshore is often specifically mentioned (see e.g. Riley 1861, 499; Chew and Kellaway 1973, No. 459). Whilst the term 'dong' (in its various spellings) was occasionally used in its broad sense to mean mud, dirt and filth, it usually refers specifically to stable sweepings and manure (Kurath and Kuhn, 1959). References in London sources to dung-heaps (Sharpe 1913, 275–6; Riley 1868, 295) and dung-boats (Riley 1868, 29; Salzman 1952, 350) suggest that dung may have been disposed of separately from other city refuse. If so, this may explain the lack of general rubbish in the 'dark brown organic matter' associated with the Group 14 revetment, which is thought to have been a lay-stall (see pp. 37–38). Literary evidence shows that the value of dung as a fertilizer was widely recognised by the end of the 14th century, if not earlier (see Skeat 1867, pass. IV, lines 129–130; Lodge 1873, lines 274–8; Furnivall 1902, line 527; and for a 13th-century reference, see Clark 1911, 101). Away from the London waterfront, it appears that the usual practice was to pile the manure from streets and stables into dung-hills or muck-hills (e.g. see Harris 1907, 113; and for some M/s refs. see Kurath and Kuhn, 1959). At a later stage the manure would be taken to the fields in 'dong-cartes' (Furnivall 1902, line 4221; Clark 1911, 101). If 'dong-boats' may be regarded as aquatic versions of 'dong-carts' as suggested by Salzman (1952, 350), it would seem reasonable to infer that the dung in London's riverside lay-stalls was destined to be sailed down the river and spread on fields along the banks of the Thames.

Apart from shipping (see pp. 64–65 and Dyson, 1981) there are few readily available documentary references to the industrial use of the foreshore. Hurers (makers of shaggy fur caps) are known to have scoured their caps in the river (Riley, 1868, 549), suggesting that similar types of craftsmen may also have used the waters for this purpose, and boat-building and repair are recorded east of London Bridge, although not along this stretch of waterfront (Tatton-Brown, 1975, 109 and Fig. 2). A few finds indicative of light industry were recovered in the excavations which, although unlikely to have been derived from foreshore activities, could have come from waterside buildings. As has been seen (pp. 4–8), the occupants of the Trig Lane tenements were largely dyers and fishmongers, trades for which ready access to an abundant supply of water and/or the river itself would have been of great importance. Elsewhere along the waterfront references to tilers, metal workers of various kinds, brewers and vintners are also common (Vanessa Harding, pers. comm. and Dyson, 1981), although the extent to which practitioners of these trades congregated specifically by the river is not yet clear. Of the Trig Lane foreshore finds, a bone bodkin may have been associated with the mending of fish-nets, and a crucible (Period IV) and iron and lead waste, the latter consisting of 'runs' and trimmings, must be associated with metal working.

The remaining foreshore finds probably derive from domestic occupation. Domestic industry is represented by pins and needles (Periods I and IV) and a thimble (Period IV), all of copper alloy, and a stone spindle-whorl (Period V). The preparation and consumption of food are portrayed by part of a stone mortar (Period V), a pewter spoon (Period V), part of a pewter vessel (Period IV), eggshell and many animal, fish and bird-bones; and leisurely pursuits by a brass book-clasp, two bone gaming(?) counters and two bone tuning pegs from a musical instrument (all of Period V). Other items of domestic origin include part of an iron box-fitting (Period V) and two personal seal matrices (Periods IV and V). There are also a number of dress fittings and personal ornaments such as a lead pendant (Period V, see No. 121), a copper belt-mount (Period V, see No. 123, buckles (Period IV), pilgrim badges (Period V, see Nos. 118–20, 122 and 125) and a copper-alloy finger-ring (Period IV). The usual scatter of fragmented ceramic building materials is present (all periods), and there are a few small iron knives, a hone and a chalk weight (all from Period IV).

We must now turn our attention towards the rubbish behind the revetments and a consideration of the circumstances which gave rise to these dumps.

The earliest wooden riverside revetments in London date from the mid-12th century (Morgan and Schofield, 1978, 231) and from the first, where they were constructed further into the river than the earlier waterfronts, the spaces behind them were filled with rubbish. Its deposition formed an essential part of their construction (p. 17) and the exclusive use of refuse for this purpose emphasizes how easy it must have been to arrange for sufficient quantities to be dumped in the appropriate places at the appropriate times. They provided an excellent opportunity for waste disposal at a period when London's population was increasing, a trend which was paralleled by an increase in the digging of pits for the disposal of privy and general domestic waste. A recent survey by Peter Marsden and Clive Orton of 143 late Saxon and medieval pits excavated by staff of the Guildhall Museum in the post-war period up to 1973 suggests that pit-digging increased throughout the 10th, 11th and 12th centuries, to reach a peak in the 13th century, after which stone and brick-lined cess-pits came into use and rubbish pits became uncommon (Marsden, forthcoming). This decline in rubbish-pits probably arose because the city was by now so densely built-up that it became difficult to find suitable places for them, as is reflected by the records of disputes between neighbours over the siting of pits (see Chew and Kellaway, 173, xxiv). Records also show that from the beginning of the 14th century, and probably earlier, the city fathers took an active interest in city cleaning and rubbish disposal, for example by appointing special places outside the city where carters and others might dump the city refuse (Sabine, 1937, 21).

Despite the involvement of the city authorities, it appears that refuse disposal at recognised dumps (at least within the city) was anything but free (Sabine, 1937, 38 and 41–2). It is most unlikely that those who constructed the riverside revetments would have been unaware of this and, whilst it would be foolish to overemphasize the possibility of financial gain as a reason for extending successive revetments further into the river, it can certainly not have discouraged major projects such as the filling of the 'dock' at Baynard's Castle where over 900 cubic metres of refuse were accommodated; outside London it might even have been necessary to pay for suitable materials for this purpose (Milne and Milne, 1978, 98).

In addition to general city rubbish, the Baynard's Castle dock contained large dumps of oyster, mussel and cockle shells, many of which, like the oysters from behind the mid-13th century Group 2 revetment at Trig Lane (pp. 17–18), had not been opened prior to burial. The obvious inference is that they had been discarded because they were unsaleable. An Ordinance of Edward I shows that fishermen were only permitted to sell shellfish from their boats for 'one tide and two ebbs' after which they were to be forfeited (Riley, 1861, 214, but see also 329); presumably the measure was intended to guarantee that all shellfish sold on the quay were as fresh as the practice seemed to imply.

The growth of organised rubbish-collection did not eliminate the problem of waste disposal for private individuals and there are a number of orders of the first half of the 14th century which ban rubbish-dumping in the streets and, in particular, in the lanes leading from Thames Street to the Thames (e.g. Riley, 1868, 239 and Riley, 1861, 500). This rubbish could have been left by persons on their way to throw refuse illicitly into the Thames (Sabine, 1937, 32) but some of it is perhaps just as likely to have been placed there by the occupants of the tenements, where there would have been little space for pit-digging (no medieval rubbish pits or cess pits were identified within the excavated area). That refuse from the waterfront area was included in the dumps may be demonstrated by the presence of objects unmistakably associated with fishing from behind the Group 7, Group 11 and Group 15 revetments (the documentary evidence shows that the fishermen congregated mostly, if not exclusively, in the area south of Thames Street). These consist of an iron fish-hook (Group 11), the sawn-off rostrum of a lesser rorqual, *Balaenoptera aucutorostera* (Group 15), a lead net(?) sinker (Group 11), two bone bodkins (Groups 7–11 and Group 15) and two wooden bodkins (Group 11) possibly for net-mending, and three long netting needles with special split eyes at both ends which could be opened by prising the sides apart in order to insert the thread (Group 15). There is also a 70mm long flat wooden stick, pointed at each end (Group 15), which is thought to have been used for insertion between the fish's open jaws as it was hung for drying (inf. from B. Weber).

Fishing is by no means the only trade indicated by the refuse; at least twelve other occupations are represented by their waste-products, tools and accessories. Cobblers' waste and the refuse of other leather-workers are present in quantity and the Group 7 dump produced an iron leatherworker's punch. There are also a number of bronze needles with triangular points thought to have been used for sewing leather. Apart from the timber structures themselves, carpenters are represented by their waste (Groups 11 and 15) and an iron tool-bit (Group 15), and bone-workers' waste was derived from the Groups 7–11, Group 11 and Group 15 dumps. A pot containing traces of red paint was recovered from the Groups 7–11 dump and a small iron-mason's punch from the Group 15 dump. Evidence for the manufacture of amber beads in the form of raw amber, clips, rough-outs, damaged half-finished beads and completed articles, was obtained throughout the sequence, and the Group 2 dump produced some fragments of coral and two coral beads; closely similar material was recovered at Baynard's Castle (Mead, 1977). Scale pans (one each from Groups 11 and 15) and some iron scales (Group 12) are illustrative of trading.

Metal crafts of various kinds are much in evidence. Lead working is illustrated by torn pieces of lead, a cut-up pewter plate (Groups 7–11), off-cuts, 'runs', a stone mould for a brooch(?) (Group 2), and an unfinished cast strap-end (Group 15). Similarly the manufacture of small copper objects is demonstrated by a vessel cut up for reuse (Group 15), trimmings and off-cuts (Groups 7–11) and a fine iron file (Group 15). There is a pair of small blunt-nosed pliers with a small serrated cutting edge at the end of one handle (Group 15), and slags of various kinds were recovered from a number of deposits. In addition, some fragments of crucible were recovered (one from Group 11; two from Group 15) and a number of iron bars may be representative of smithing.

There are also a number of tools and accessories which are as likely to have been used in the home as in the workshop. The most prevalent are items associated with needlework in the form of over one hundred bronze pins, four long bronze needles (one from Group 7, the rest from Group 15), one small bronze needle (Group 12), iron needles (one each from Groups 7–11, 11 and 15), a bone needle (Group 15), and a wooden bobbin (Group 15); three pairs of iron shears were recovered from Group 11 and two pairs from Group 15. Spinning is represented by a stone spindle-whorl (Groups 7–11) and a wooden spindle (Group 15). A small iron hammer-head was recovered from the Group 10 dump and parts of iron flesh-hooks were recovered from the Group 7 and Groups 7–11 dumps; the latter also produced a roughly fashioned bone tool(?) handle. Other items possibly associated with manufacturing include a number of lengths of iron and copper wire, a wooden spatula (Group 15), two wooden pins (Groups 12 and 15), two lengths of string (Group 15), a short length of iron chain (Group 11) and seven struck flint flakes (Group 10). The remains of over 22 iron knives of all sizes, some with bone handles, were recovered throughout the sequence, and are matched by the remains of a range c. 20 hones.

Items of more specifically domestic use are just as numerous. In addition to much of the pottery (see Fig. 60), they comprise nine wooden bowls (one from Group 11, the rest from Group 15), barrel remains (Group 15), an iron bucket handle (Group 15), two fragments of iron cauldron—one with a paw-shaped foot—(Groups 7 and 12), part of a copper cauldron (Group 12), the leg of a copper skillet (Groups 7–11) and part of a copper colander (Group 15). Fragments of three stone mortars were recovered from the Group 11 dump and part of another came from the Group 10 dump. Pieces of eggshell were recovered from the Group 7, Group 10 and Group 15 dumps and the latter produced part of a lava quern and a bronze spoon. Occasional fragments of coal were recovered throughout the sequence. Furnishings are portrayed by the remains of two plaited fibre mats(?) (Groups 7–11 and 11), part of a copper lantern (Group 10), three iron box-fittings (Group 11), an iron box hinge (Group 12), a leaden lid(?) with a hinge (Group 11) and two iron keys (Groups 11 and 15). Recreational pursuits are represented by two bone counters (Groups 7–11 and 10), two wooden counters (Groups 7–11) and a bone die (Group 15).

There are considerable quantities of structural debris and a number of structural fittings. In addition to the usual roof-tiles and iron nails, there are stone roof-slates (Groups 2, 11 and 15), fragments of *c.* 11 ceramic finials (Groups 2, 3, 7, 12 and 15), part of a ceramic louvre (Group 10), a piece of stone moulding (Group 15), four pieces of lead window cames (Group 2), wall-fittings such as iron staples (two each from Groups 10 and 11), an angle bracket (Group 15), three candleholders (one from Group 10, two from Group 15), a large iron door pivot, and two iron keys and two locks suitable for doors (all from Group 15). A number of used ship rivets were obtained from the dumps behind the Group 7 (2 rivets) and Group 11 (12 rivets) revetments and the Group 15 (6 rivets) river wall, which suggest that ships' timbers may have been broken up for re-use in the area from time to time. What appear to be the riveted strakes from a clinker-built boat were used to effect a join between the Group 7 and Group 10 revetments (see p. 26).

The largest category of finds is personal accessories and items of clothing. There are large numbers of shoes, some of which must constitute cobblers' waste; nearly 300 were recovered from the Group 15 dump alone. There are also over 20 pattens (Groups 7–11, 11 and 15), *c.* 85 leather straps and girdles (some with studded decoration), 7 scabbards of various sizes (some embossed), a pouch (Group 11) and some fragments of leather garments (mostly from Group 15). Cloth did not survive well, although fragments of silk cloth and braid were recovered from the Group 2 and Group 10 dumps, and a silk garter(?) from Group 15. Woollen cloth was recovered from the Group 2 and Group 15 dumps; the latter also produced 24 spangles of stamped tinned iron in the form of long leaves or perhaps ferns or feathers. These were suspended from loops at one end which at the time of removal from the earth were seen to be riveted to some finely woven, purple woollen cloth. Unfortunately this was so deteriorated that it could not be preserved. These interesting objects are most likely to have been clothing ornaments, although it is just possible that they were used as horse trappings (Kay Staniland, pers. comm.). The other metal clothing accessories comprise two iron buckles (Group 2), copper buckles (one from Group 2, two from Groups 7–11, two from Group 11, one from Group 12, two from Group 15), a pewter buckle (Group 3), two bronze tag ends (Groups 11 and 15), strap ends (three from Group 11, one from Group 15), a copper sword chape (Groups 7-11), two ampullae (Group 2), pilgrim badges and a number of similar objects (Groups 2, 7–11, 10, 11 and 15). Attention to grooming is illustrated by a hair-net (Group 2), a wooden comb (Group 15) and a bronze ear-pick (Group 15), and there are a number of items of jewellery: two gentlemen's(?) gold finger-rings with red stones (Group 10), a plain gold ring (Group 11), a bronze ring (Group 12), fragments of two jet bracelets (Group 11)

Part IV—Specialist Reports

and a wooden bead (Group 15).

Despite the occasional precious items listed above, the general quality and character of these finds do not match the elevated life-style revealed by the material recovered from the early 16th-century robbing pits at Baynard's Castle 'dock'; there are nonetheless a number of finds which remind us that a proportion of London's inhabitants were not uneducated at this time. These comprise a wooden chessman (Group 2), a bone tuning peg from a musical instrument (Group 15) and bronze strings(?) possibly also from musical instruments (Groups 10 and 11), a bronze stylus for writing on waxed writing tablets (Group 2), four bone parchment-prickers(?) (Groups 7, 7–11, 11 and 15; for identification see Henig, 1977, 163, No. 15) and the bone frames of a pair of reading spectacles (Group 15, see Rhodes, forthcoming).

No items of a specifically ecclesiastical character have been identified. There is slight evidence of military activity in the form of a military crossbow bolt and two quillons (all from Group 15). There are no rustic or gardening tools apart from what may be the left prong of an iron pitchfork (Group 15), although two hunting arrows (Group 15) bring to mind the proximity of the country at this period, and horses are much in evidence. They are represented by nine horse-shoes (one each from Groups 2 and 7–11, two from Group 11, five from Group 15), a bit (Group 3), a cheek-piece (Group 11), four spurs (two each from Groups 11 and 15), a curry comb (Group 15) and six large harness(?) buckles (two from Groups 7–11, one from Group 12 and three from Group 15).

It is noticeable that a high proportion of the smaller finds (excluding manufacturing waste) bear no indication that they were damaged, worn, or were otherwise unusable prior to burial. It is, of course, possible that some were discarded because of superficial damage that is no longer apparent, for example iron objects could have become slightly rusty and other materials could have become discoloured or have lost their paint, but it seems likely that many, such as the coins, jettons and the gold rings, must have been accidentally lost in the rubbish. The frequent discovery of medieval pilgrim badges from Thames-side building sites has led to the suggestion that they could have been used as votive offerings, tossed into the river by thankful Londoners arriving home after their pilgrimage (Hume, 1956, 144–5), but the presence at Trig Lane of so many complete small objects in deposits where a votive significance can be discounted argues against this. Furthermore, of the twelve pilgrim badges and two ampullae recovered at Trig Lane, only five were recovered from the foreshores, which suggests that the majority of previously discovered badges are equally likely to have been removed from rubbish layers.

In addition to contemporary refuse, both the foreshores and the rubbish layers seem to have contained a proportion of earlier material. This is not made particularly clear by the many datable objects discussed below since, excluding three jettons (Nos. 29, 30 and 40) which come from the Group 12 dump thought to contain redeposited material from the Group 10 dump, only four of these items (Nos. 31, 42, 128 and 129) seem to be substantially earlier than the layer from which they were recovered. The best evidence for the inclusion of earlier material comes from the ceramics, not only because residual pottery is often readily distinguishable on typological grounds but, in the dumped deposits at least, because of its battered appearance which contrasts with the freshly broken look of the contemporary material. In addition to sherds of the previous two centuries, it includes pottery of Roman origin (including a PP BR LON tile from the Group 7 dump) as well as late Saxon *Badorf, Pingsdorf* and *Andenne* wares.

The residual material could have been derived from the underlying Roman and late Saxon foreshores, having been brought to the surface in the medieval period during construction work, or foreshore activities such as digging for ships' ballast (Riley, 1868, 589) and mudlarking (the occupation is recorded in the mid-19th century: Mayhew, 1861, II, 136–7 and may have been followed in earlier times). Alternatively it could have been brought to the site in earth removed in the course of digging pits and foundations to the north of Thames Street. Residual pottery has also been recovered at the Custom House site (Tatton-Brown, 1975, 103), where it is said to have been present in large amounts, the 'latest sherds' (the only ones useful for dating) being few in number. At Trig Lane, however, the residual pottery seems to form only about 10% of the whole (pers. comm., Clive Orton), and it is improbable that there has been any significant error in separating it from the contemporary material, since this would probably have caused fluctuations in the graph showing a monotone increase in the use of Surrey ware (Fig. 60).

Although it has not been possible to provide a detailed analysis of all the above-mentioned objects, reports on the most useful objects for dating purposes are appended. These have enabled us to supplement and enhance the dating of the structural sequence, which in turn has corroborated and refined the dating of some of the finds. For the sake of providing a complete account of the numismatic evidence, coins, jettons and tokens from the post-medieval strata, Period VII, are included.

All of the finds are now in the Museum of London and are available for further research. At the present time, however, they have not yet been incorporated into the Museum's E. R. accessioning system; the numbers in brackets are site registration numbers. For ease of reference every individually described object and illustrated pottery form is numbered in sequence.

2. Pottery evidence for the dating of the revetments

by Clive Orton

Introduction

Groups of pottery, some very large, were recovered from a sequence of seven dumped deposits behind the revetments. This note aims to present the results of a preliminary examination of samples of pottery from these groups, and to integrate this additional information into the dating evidence already provided by dendrochronology, coins and sedimentation rates (pp. 50–53). Before this can be done, it is necessary to discuss whether there are likely to be significant differences between the date of construction of a revetment and the date of manufacture of pottery found behind it.

Part IV—Specialist Reports

The interval of time between the date of manufacture of a pot and its final deposition can be broken down into two stages: (i) the 'active life' of the pot, from manufacture to breakage, and (ii) its 'rubbbish life', from breakage to final deposition. During the latter period sherds of the pot presumably form part of a primary rubbish deposit which eventually becomes part of a secondary deposit behind the revetment. The dump itself and the revetment can be regarded as contemporary because neither could survive for long without the other – without a revetment the dump would rapidly erode away, and without a dump the revetment could collapse under the pressure of water at high tide.

With the possible exception of highly decorated vessels, the active life of a medieval pot is likely to have been short. They are of low intrinsic value (Hodges, 1974, 38) and are frequently either unstable (e.g. many jug forms) or subject to stress in the form of repeated heating and cooling (e.g. cooking vessels). Ethnographic parallels (discussed by Vince, 1977, 65–6; see also De Boer and Lathrap, 1979, 126) suggest that an active life of more than five years for any category of domestic vessel made of unglazed earthenware would be unusual. If we assume a maximum active life of five years, or perhaps ten for 'special' vessels, we shall probably be safely over-estimating for all except a very small minority.

It is more difficult to obtain information relevant to (ii), the interval between breakage and final deposition. However, the general condition of much of the dumped pottery—large sherds with freshly broken edges—does not suggest that this interval would have been long. It seems reasonable to assume that the material used was taken from rubbish deposits which, although they may have accumulated over a long period, were still being added to immediately before their use for dumping.

Taking these two points together, it seems that the dating of a revetment, based solely on pottery evidence, is not likely to be more than ten years later than the 'date' of manufacture of the pottery. In practice, therefore, bearing in mind the uncertainties associated with the pottery dating (see below), it seems safe to compare pottery dates with other dating evidence, without the use of adjustments or corrections.

Description
   As a full investigation of the pottery was not possible, a number of standard boxes of pottery from each group (the exact number reflecting the relative size of the groups) were selected for examination. The largest groups studied are from Group 15 (23 boxes examined) and Group 11 (8 boxes examined). About four boxes each from Groups 2, 3 and 7 were investigated, but only three from Group 10 and two from Group 12. The term box here refers to a standard Museum of London storage box, dimensions $c.$ 450mm × 170mm × 120mm.
   By far the most common type of pottery present is *Surrey White Ware* (see, for example, Haslam, 1978, 20–2): a portmanteau term for a number of wares sharing certain physical characteristics, chiefly those of a very pale brown and/or light grey sandy fabric with a partial green (or rarely yellow) glaze (for a more detailed description see Orton, 1977, 82 and Orton and Miller, forthcoming), all of which are thought to have been made in Surrey (although some may have been made in north Hampshire or West Sussex, see Hanworth and Tomalin, 1977, 60).
   Other common types are *London-type Slipped Jugs* (described, but not under this name, by Haslam, 1978, 21; see also Orton, forthcoming), *'West Kent Ware* (Haslam, 1978, 21)—now thought to have at least one source in Essex (E. Sellers, pers. comm.)—*fine splash-glazed wares*

(Orton and Miller, forthcoming), *hard grey ware*, probably from south Hertfordshire (Renn, 1964) but possibly including some *Limpsfield Ware* (Prendergast, 1975) (these are readily distinguished under a low-power microscope, but the Trig Lane material has not yet been sorted to this degree of detail). There are also small quantities of imports (never more than 5% of a group) from Yorkshire or the Midlands (Rutter, 1961), south-west France, Holland and Siegburg.

The composition of the pottery groups from the dumps behind the revetments is shown in Fig. 60. This shows a steady, almost monotone, increase in the percentage of *Surrey White Ware* from 25% in the earliest group (Group 2) to 85% in the latest. There is a rapid decline in the percentage of *fine splash-glazed wares* from more than 15% in Group 2 to less than 5% in Group 7, and a slower decline for *London-type Slipped Jugs*, '*West Kent Ware*' and the grey wares. There is a small proportion of 'Tudor brown' pottery from Group 15, which is similar but not identical to the red fabric at Cheam (Morris, 1970). Imports from Yorkshire/Midlands occur in all but the earliest group, those from France (*Saintonge monochrome* and *polychrome*) occur in the earlier groups and those from Holland are found throughout the sequence. Particularly distinctive are drinking mugs of grey *Siegburg stoneware*—cf. Jacoba (von Bock, 1971, Nos. 156–9) and more globular forms—which constitute about 5% of the latest groups, Groups 11 to 15. Rarer imports include tinglazed ware of Spanish or Islamic origin (Group 3, Group 15).

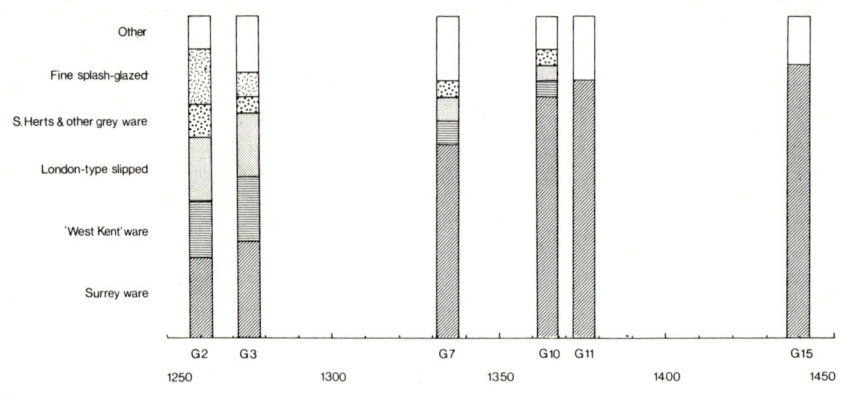

Fig. 60. Trig Lane 1974–76: Proportions of the main types of pottery present in Groups 2, 3, 7, 10, 11 and 15. The horizontal axis shows the suggested dates of the groups.

Surrey White Ware

It was decided, in view of the limited time available for this preliminary study, to concentrate on the dating evidence provided by the *Surrey White Ware*.

The most common types of vessel produced in *Surrey White Ware* are jugs and pitchers, cooking-pots, storage jars, bowls, and small dishes or lids, which are found right through the Trig Lane sequence, accurately reflecting the general preponderance of these forms within the Surrey ware tradition. Other types which occur less frequently, and not consistently in every group (although their absence from some groups may just reflect the smaller size of those groups) are lobed cups, dripping pans, money boxes, skillets and chafing dishes. Distinct chronological trends can be seen in the forms of the more common types (see Fig. 61). Note that Nos. 1 and 9 are based on matching sherds with more complete examples from other sites, and that many forms (especially jugs) represented at Trig Lane have not been drawn.

Three known sources are represented by these forms—Cheam (Marshall, 1924; Morris, 1970; Orton, 1979), Kingston (Canham, 1970), and Farnborough Hill (Holling, 1977). Typical Cheam products are the biconical jug (No. 9) and the barrel-shaped jug (No. 14). Kingston is represented by jugs with stamped decoration (e.g. No. 1, but a much wider range of motifs is present) as well as plainer jugs (e.g. No. 3) including some biconical forms. A typical Farnborough Hill assemblage consists of the large bung-hole pitcher (No. 13), bifid-rimmed cooking-pot (No. 15) and horizontally rimmed bowl (No. 16). The lobed cup in the so-called 'Tudor Green Ware' may also be from Farnborough Hill: examination of the fabric under a low-power microscope strongly suggests a source in Surrey rather than France, and there are no examples of the characteristic French handle (attached to the base of the cup rather than the waist: Nicole Mayer, pers. comm.). Of special interest is a cup from Group 11: a large part of the base has spalled off in firing and the broken surface is completely covered with thick green glaze, indicating a biscuit firing followed by a second firing for the glaze—a technique known at Farnborough Hill (Holling, 1977, 63).

The Dating of Surrey White Ware

The dating of medieval pottery ultimately rests on a series of 'fixed points'—either dated historical events with which groups of pottery can reasonably be associated, or datable objects (e.g. coins) found in association with the pottery. The difficulties of using even apparently certain fixed points have been well presented by Hurst (1962–3). Dates for groups of pottery falling between the fixed points can be interpolated, using as a model the assumptions that changes in pottery styles and sources take place gradually, and that the overall volume of pottery usage does not fluctuate violently.

A distinct Surrey industry was recognised from the discovery of the first Cheam kiln in 1923 (Marshall, 1924). Initially, the terms *Cheam Ware* and *Surrey Ware* were used synonymously: for example, some pots in Kingston Museum, made in the Kingston kiln but added to the collections prior to its discovery, were originally called *Cheam Ware* (Hinton, pers. comm.). Marshall could do little more than guess at the dating of his kiln: one 'vase' (atypical of the production as a whole) was paralleled to a 13th-century specimen in the British Museum, and the characteristic red-painted decoration was dated to the late 13th to early 14th century by comparison with the ornamental margins of manuscripts (Marshall, *loc. cit.*, 90). Later (Marshall, 1941) he seems to have preferred a 13th-century date for *Cheam Ware*.

The first fixed point came from a group of unstratified pottery from Bodiam Castle, Sussex (Myres, 1935). Since the building of the castle started in 1386, Myres argued for a date 'in the century following 1386' for the group (*ibid.*, 223). He commented on the similarity between two biconical jugs (Nos. P.8 and P.9) and the Cheam products, despite his suggestion that P.8 was a waster. No. P.7 now appears to be a Cheam barrel-shaped jug, but this form was not among those recognised as Cheam products at that time. This evidence led to the view that *Cheam Ware* (and, by implication, *Surrey White Ware* as a whole) was predominantly 15th-century in date.

The first attempt to relate this evidence to London was made by Perkins (1940, 226) who used the parallels between Bodiam Castle and Cheam to 'facilitate the identification of 15th century pottery from London'. He identified a Cheam pitcher (Pl. LXIV, No. 2) and three Cheam jugs (Fig. 75, Nos. 3–5) and placed them all in the 15th century, together with a bung-hole pitcher (Pl. LXIV, No. 3), then thought to be from Cheam but probably from Farnborough Hill. He admitted (*ibid.*, 222–3) that the 14th century presented problems, but among the vessels assigned to the 14th century are a *Surrey White Ware* jug (Pl. LXIII, No. 2) and cooking-pot (Fig, 74). Neither is from Cheam and the writer did not identify them as *Surrey White Ware*. Two of his 13th-century decorated jugs (Pl. LXII, Nos. 1 and 2) also seem from their description to be of *Surrey White Ware*. In his introduction (*ibid.*, 210–12) he put forward the view that Surrey produced much of London's pottery from the 13th century onwards, citing kilns at Limpsfield, Earlswood, Cheam and Ashtead, as well as a documentary reference that 'in 1260 the bailiffs of Kingston-on-Thames were ordered to send 1000 pitchers to the king's butler at Westminster' (Salzman, 1923, 170). Of the kilns he mentioned, Limpsfield produced a hard grey ware (see p. 94 above) which is not part of the *Surrey White Ware* tradition, Earlswood products were in an orange-pink fabric and often white-slipped (Turner, 1975) and bear more resemblance to *West Kent Ware* (see p. 94 above), and pottery from Ashtead (Frere, 1941) has yet to be indentified in London.

Significant advances in dating evidence came from two excavations of the 1950s—The Manor of the More, Rickmansworth, Hertfordshire (Biddle, Barfield and Millard, 1959) and Northolt Manor (Hurst, 1961). At the former site, *Surrey White Ware* first occurs in Period II (*c.* 1300–50), the end of which is thought to be contemporary with a change in ownership recorded as having taken place in 1364 (*loc. cit.*, 162), and predominates in Period III (*c.* 1350–1426), which is terminated by a documented rebuilding in 1426 (Period IV), from which *Surrey White Ware* was also found. The writer states that 'Excavations in the City of London produced a great deal of Surrey pottery and by about 1350 it appears to predominate there', citing as evidence an unpublished oven at the Tower of London, dated by coins to *c.* 1350 (*ibid.*, 162). The forms from Period II cannot be related to those from Trig Lane, but those from Period III include a large thumb-pressed base (*cf.* No. 13) and a bowl rim with drooping flange (*cf.* No. 11). Sherds of what appear to be barrel-shaped jugs are illustrated from Period VI, *c.* 1520 (*ibid.*, Fig. 12, No. 11) and Period VII, *c.* 1550–1600 (*ibid.*, Fig. 13, Nos. 4 and 14), but are not commented upon, and we are told that a hard red ware 'appears to replace Surrey wares outside London in the 15th century' (*ibid.*, 162). At Northolt Manor, *Surrey Ware* was divided into *Off-white Surrey Ware* (*loc cit.*, 273) and *Buff Surrey Ware* (*ibid.*, 274), given dates of 1300–1400 and 1350–1425 respectively. Together they provide about one-third of the pottery from Period II, dated by coin evidence to the first half of the 14th century and sealed by the build-up for a rebuilding thought to have taken place shortly after 1346, when the manor changed hands (*ibid.*, 248 and 288). In Period III, which was terminated by the destruction of most of the manor in 1370 (*ibid.*, 220) the *Surrey Ware* constitutes almost half of the pottery, and in Period IV (1370–*c.* 1475) almost all of it. However, the amounts of pottery from Periods III and IV are very small (*ibid.*, 276). There is also a very small percentage of *Surrey Ware* from Ditch 1 (pre *c.* 1300) and Period I–II Grey Layer (*c.* 1300). Forms from Period II are mainly flanged rim cooking-pots (*cf.* No. 5) with one drooping-rim bowl (*cf.* No. 11), while similar cooking-pot rims come from Period III and bifid rims (*cf.* No. 15) from Period IV.

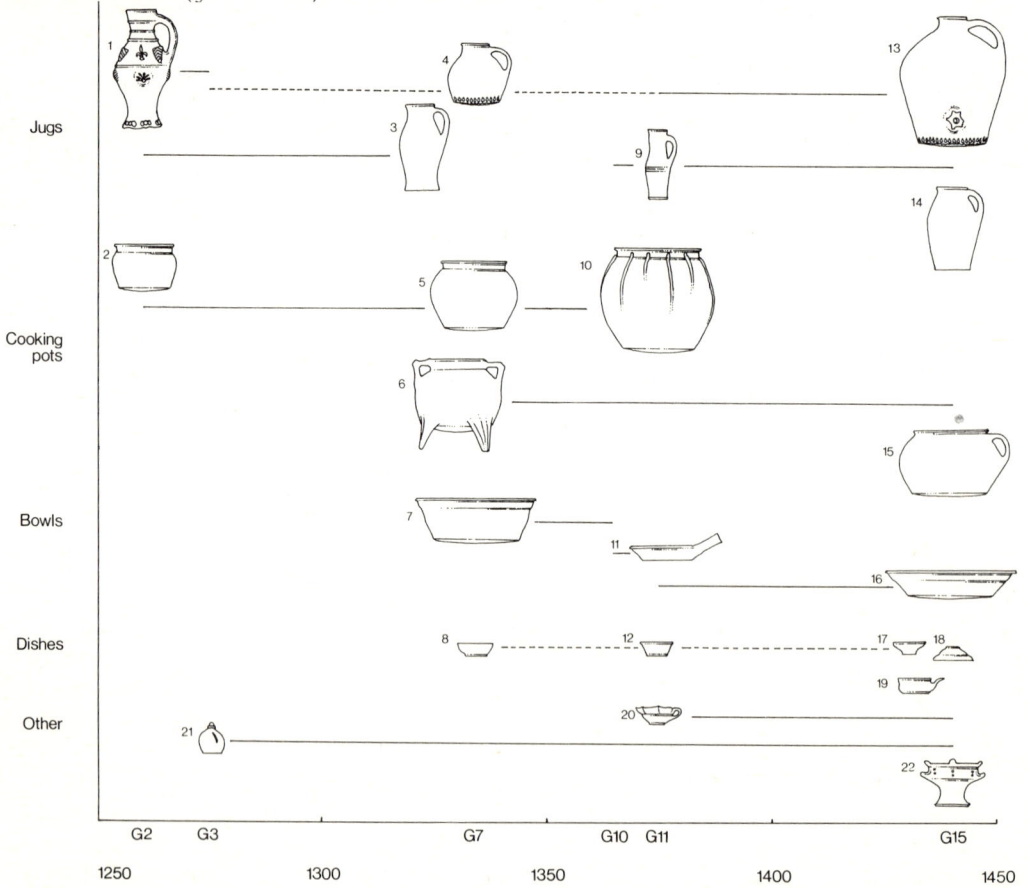

Fig. 61. Trig Lane 1974–76: Diagram illustrating the life-span and evolution of the main *Surrey Ware* pottery forms as evidenced by their presence in Groups 2, 3, 7, 10, 11 and 15. The horizontal axis shows the suggested dates of the groups.

Part IV—Specialist Reports

These two sites, with their fixed points based on documentary and coin evidence, suggest that *Surrey White Ware* arrived in the area north-west of London at or just before 1300. In the absence until recently of more relevant fixed points, this evidence has been extrapolated to London (see, for example, Hammerson, 1975, especially fn. 36) and beyond into Surrey (explicitly but cautiously by Turner (1974, 10) at Merton Priory, and implicitly by Drewett (1974, 10) at Croydon). Such extrapolation appears to the present writer to be unwise. The two manor sites lie within or on the edge of the area producing *South Hertfordshire Grey Ware* (see p. 94), which actually extended into north Middlesex (Sheppard, 1977, Fig. 4). One would not really expect *Surrey White Ware* to make serious inroads into this area until the decline of the local industry in the early 14th century (Hurst, 1961, 267–9), even if it were available in London at an earlier date.

A major advance in our knowledge took place with the discovery of the Kingston kiln in 1969 (Canham, 1970). Turner (*ibid.*) linked this kiln with documentary evidence (Giuseppi, 1937) to revise Hurst's dates for *Off-white Surrey Ware* to *c.* 1250–1350/1400 and to suggest the name *Kingston Ware* for it. Giuseppi's evidence consisted of four then unpublished entries in the Liberate Rolls, for the delivery of successively 1000, 600, 700 and 1000 wine-pitchers made in the Bailiwick of Kingston, to Westminster, over a period of slightly more than two years (1264–6). (These entries had meanwhile been published in Cal. Lib R., 1961, 145, 162, 210 and 252). There is no evidence in these references that the pitchers concerned are of *Kingston Ware*, or even green-glazed at all. However, since several years' excavations in Kingston have failed to produce evidence for the manufacture of medieval pottery other than *Kingston Ware* (Marion Hinton, pers. comm.), it seems reasonable to take the evidence at face value and accept Turner's interpretation. One can then suggest that the Kingston kiln was well established by the 1260s, and a starting date of *c.* 1250 or even a little earlier is realistic. Hurst's *Off-white Surrey Ware* would then include (and possibly equate with) *Kingston Ware* and date to *c.* 1250–1350/1400 and his *Buff Surrey Ware* would include both *Cheam Ware* and *Farnborough Hill Ware* and date to *c.* 1350–1425 or end a little later.

Another fixed point has recently been provided by Dawson (1976) from his excavations at Kennington Palace. Pottery from a group earlier than a building phase dated to *c.* 1353–5 included a Kingston jug with stamped decoration (*ibid.*, Fig 18, No. 1), while pottery from groups after that date included barrel-shaped jugs (*ibid.*, Fig. 18, Nos. 14 and 15), a biconical jug (*ibid.*, Fig. 18, No. 23), a storage jar or cooking pot with applied vertical strips (*ibid.*, Fig. 19, No. 49) and a Farnborough Hill cooking pot (*ibid.*, Fig. 20, No. 74). This evidence strengthens the idea of a 'watershed' between Kingston and Cheam/Farnborough Hill located *c.* 1350.

An assessment of *Surrey White Ware* has recently been provided by Haslam (1978), in the context of a study of English medieval pottery in general. His basic proposition is that the Surrey industry started 'towards the end of the thirteenth century' (*ibid.*, 20), supplied 'most of the London market during the later fourteenth and fifteenth centuries' (*ibid.*, 21) and 'virtually disappeared' after the mid-15th century (*ibid.*, 22), except for the production of Tudor Green Ware. He dates Kingston to the late 14th to early 15th century and Cheam to the 15th century, with the kiln group assigned to the middle of the century. Farnborough Hill is mentioned only as a source of Tudor Green Ware, from the late 15th century onwards. Parallels in his illustrations would suggest the following dating for the Trig Lane examples:

Nos. 5, 7 and 10   early 14th century
No. 4   14th century
Nos. 2 and 19   14th or 15th century
Nos. 1, 3 and 6   late 14th or early 15th century
No. 13   15th century
Nos. 9, 14, 16 and 17   mid-15th century

Discussion

We must now try to use this body of evidence and opinion to obtain pottery dates for the dumped deposits, for comparison with the other dating evidence. Since this body of data is not internally consistent, it is necessary to decide which parts to accept. This amounts to a choice between three postulated chronologies:

(i) 'long' chronology (based on Turner):
   Kingston: *c.* 1250 – 1350/1400,
   Cheam: *c.* 1350 – 1450/1500;
(ii) 'short' chronology (based on Haslam):
   Surrey: *c.* 1300 – 1450/1500,
   Kingston: late 14th – early 15th century,
   Cheam: 15th century;
(iii) 'truncated' chronology (based on Hurst):
   off-white Surrey(= Kingston?): *c.* 1300–1400,
   buff Surrey (= Cheam?): *c.* 1350–1425.

The third seems to be a local variation of the first, adapted to the special circumstances of north Middlesex/south Hertfordshire, i.e., the existence of a flourishing local industry preventing the penetration of *Surrey White Ware* into the area until *c.* 1300. The date of 1425 for the end of *Surrey White Ware* in this area is less securely based. The 'short' chronology seems to be the most difficult to reconcile with the evidence outlined above, or with the sequence demonstrated in Fig. 2. For example, Nos. 5, 7 and 10 which occur in the middle of the sequence (Groups 7, 10 and 11) are dated early 14th century, while No. 1 which only occurs early in the sequence is dated late 14th to early 15th century. It therefore seems most reasonable to use the 'long' chronology for dating the Trig Lane deposits.

The implications are shown in Fig. 39 which compares 'structural' dates for the groups (based on the evidence of dendrochronology, sedimentation, coins, ampullae and tokens) with the dating evidence of the *Surrey White Ware*, using the 'long' chronology. Since *Surrey White Ware* is thought to start *c.* 1250, the Group 2 dump, which contains some 25% *Surrey White Ware*, must date to after *c.* 1250. The earliest recognizable Cheam products are found in Group 10, while Kingston products are common in Groups 2, 3 and 7 but less so in the Group 10 and Group 11 dumps, suggesting that the 'watershed' between Kingston and Cheam products (estimated above at *c.* 1350), lies between Groups 7 and 10.

Group 15 pre-dates the widespread use in London of Tudor brown pottery (although a very small amount is present). The date in London of the change from the coarser *Surrey White Ware* to Tudor brown is currently thought to have occurred *c.* 1475 (Hurst, pers. comm. in Dawson, 1976, 156 and fn. 89), although the analogous change was put rather earlier—*c.* 1425—at Northolt (see p. 96 above). However, since fixed points in the second half of the 15th century are not available, it seems safer to give a looser dating of *c.* 1450/1500.

Comparison of the two columns of dates in Fig. 39 shows considerable agreement between the pottery dates and those based on dendrochronological evidence. The dates of Groups 10, 11, 12 and 15 are reasonably securely fixed by dendrochronology and coin evidence, and the agreement is welcome but not unexpected. The 'structural' dates of the earlier deposits (Groups 2, 3 and 7) are extrapolated from the later dates by argument from sedimentation rates—a new

Part IV—Specialist Reports

and unproven technique—and the agreement is therefore extremely interesting. The pottery evidence, which is in broad agreement with dendrochronological evidence in those groups for which the latter is available, has confirmed the more controversial evidence provided by the study of sedimentation rates (pp. 50–52).

3. English Official Coinage
by John Clark with additional notes by the late Stuart Rigold

23. (2322) Late medieval penny, York. Too corroded for further identification, but not heavily worn. The diameter of the inner ring suggests it is before A.D. 1412, and is therefore most probably Edward III, post treaty, or Richard II. Probably lost in the first generation after 1365. From the Period IV foreshore.
24. (2278) Halfpenny, London. Edward III, treaty coinage, A.D. 1363–9 (North, 1960, No. 1274). Little wear. Provenance as for No. 23.
25. (1097) Penny, York: local die? Henry V or VI; possibly Henry V class C or D, c. 1413–22 (North, 1960, Nos. 1400 and 1401). Moderate wear. From the Group 15 dump (Period VI).
26. (2331) Halfpenny, London. Henry VI(?), possibly rosette-mascle issue 1427–30 (North, 1960, No. 1453). Very little wear. Provenance as for No. 25.
27. (1082) Quarter noble. Henry V, class C (broken annulet to l., mullet to r. of shield on obverse), 1413–22 (North, 1960, No. 1382). *R* initial mark: cross with pellet in centre. No clear obverse initial mark. Rusty and damaged die, moderate wear. Weight 1.695 g (normal weight 1.75 g). Provenance as for No. 25.
28. (674) Halfpenny of George II, 1742. From Context 78 (Period VII).

4. Jettons and Tokens
by the late Stuart Rigold

English 'Sterling' Jettons

29. (2324) *O.* Crown with pellet terminals, or may be three crowns (Berry, 1974, *O.*13) of which the top crown definitely has pellet terminals. *R.* Short-cross moline (Berry, *R.*5) with pellets in quarters; border Berry D/D. Not in Berry (1974). Dia. 19mm. Worn and corroded. Date 1320s or perhaps 1330s. From Context 1457 (Period V, Phase iii) which consists of material probably initially dumped behind the Group 10 revetment (dated to *c.* 1360) and subsequently disturbed and redeposited behind the Group 12 revetment (dated to *c.* 1430).
30. (1390) 'Double reverse' type: Short cross moline (Berry, *R.*5) with pellets in quarters (both sides); border Berry D/D. The cross moline is rather thin, suggesting a date in the late 1290s to early 1330s. Well preserved. From the Group 12 dump; phasing as for No. 29.
31. (552) *O.* Crowned 'sterling' head (unclear), late type (Fox, 1910–14, Classes 10–15). *R.* Long two-strand cross flory (Berry 6E), [LA]TV(?) in quarters; border is Berry F/D strokes and pellets. Not in Berry (1974). Dia. 19.5mm. Suggested date: *c.* 1320s. Residual in the Group 15 dump (Period VI).

English 'Post-Sterling' Jettons
(Fig. 62, Nos. 32–3)

32. (164) *O.* Shield with long cross, pellet in each quarter, as Berry Ed. II Type 17F, but Berry may date this too early. *R.* (Not as Berry) single long-cross flory with cross and/or fleur-de-lys in each quarter. Unofficial, but properly pierced in centre. Dia. 21.5mm. Second half 14th century. From the Group 11 dump (Period V, Phase i and therefore not later than *c.* 1380) (illustrated).
33. (730) Double reverse type. *R.* i Cross flory in cusped quadrilobe, spandrels unclear. *R.* ii Cross crosslet pommée over a diagonal square with three pellets in each quarter; also in each quarter is a shield bearing three pellets. This is related to the reverse that Berry (1974) gives for 'Ed. II Type 17F' and is probably contemporary with this, but later in fact than Ed. II. Dia. 22mm, rather thick (1.3mm), looks unofficial. Provenance and date of deposition as for No. 32 (illustrated).
34. (751) *O.* Standing king and canopy (Berry Obv. Ed. III R.2, Type 4). *R.* Three-strand cross-flory (Berry Rev. Type A), two Rs in each spandrel, lys in quarters, as Berry (1974, Pl. 6, No. 5). Dia. 24mm. Date *c.* 1360s. Provenance as for No. 32.
35. (2388) *O.* Seated king under canopy (Berry Obv. Type 12), trefoils between annulets in border and background. *R.* Short cross with knops, quatrefoils, pellets and RA in quarters; border inscription with saltire stops (unclear); illustration much as Berry (1974, Pl. 6, No. 12). Dia. 23mm. Date *c.* 1360s – 1370s, worn. From the Period V foreshore.

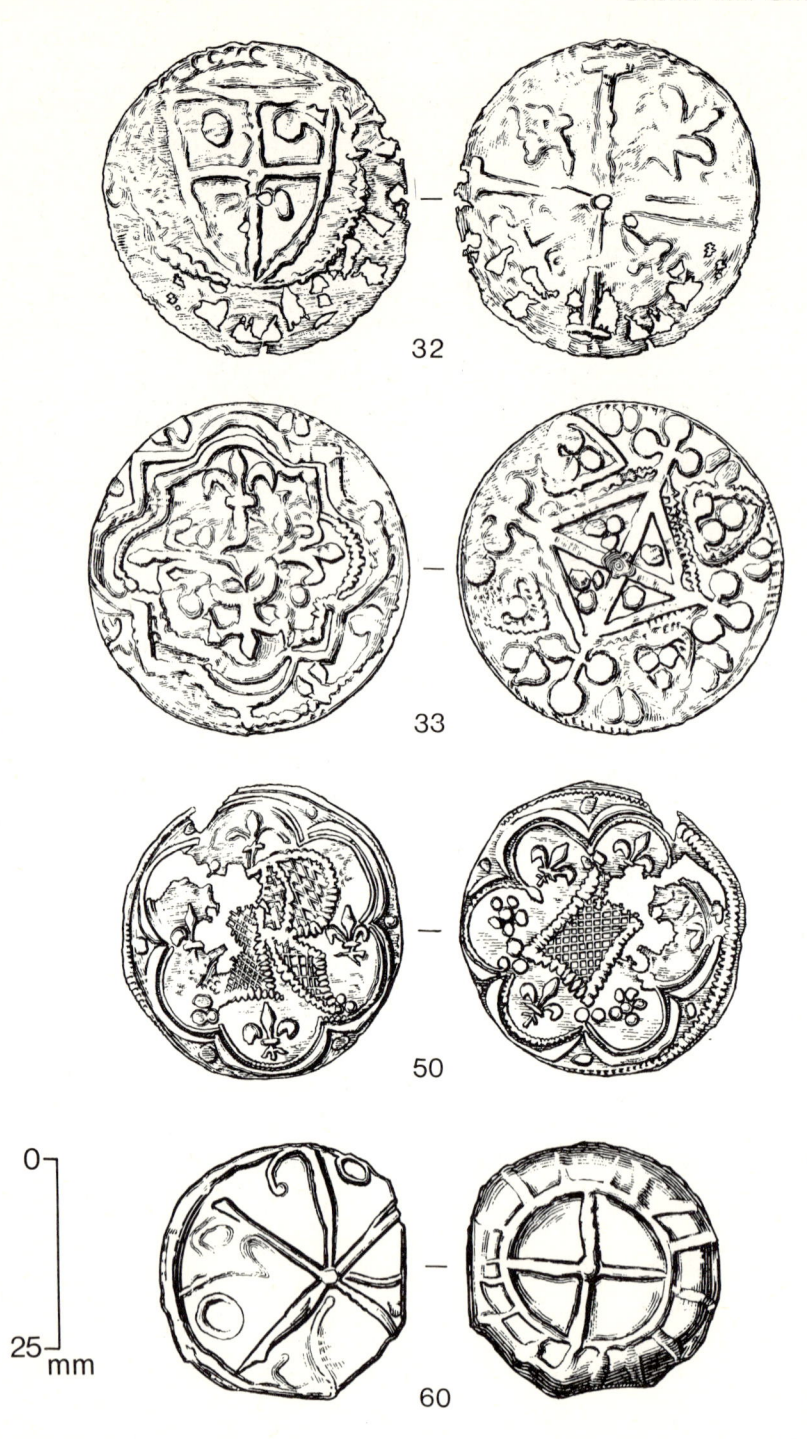

Fig. 62. Trig Lane 1974–76: English 'Post-Sterling' Jettons Nos. 32–33; French Unofficial Jetton No. 50; Lead Token A type No. 60 ($\frac{2}{1}$).

Part IV—Specialist Reports

English 'Sterling – substitute' Jettons
These are blank discs, but pierced at the centre, like proper English jettons.

36. (2186) Dia. 18mm. From the Group 2 dump (Period III, Phase i) dated to *c.* 1250–75; this is early for a 'sterling substitute' and especially early for a small-sized example. It could perhaps be intrusive.
37. (553) Dia. 28mm. Very thick (*c.* 1.9mm). From the Group 11 dump (Period V, Phase i) and therefore not later than *c.* 1380.
38. (2268) Dia. 23mm. From the Period V foreshore and therefore not later than *c.* 1440.
39. (2346) As for No. 38.
40. (2157) Dia. 23.5mm. Small piercing in centre. Thick (1.4mm). 1320s or later. From Context 320 (Period V, Phase iv) a pit-fill (?) associated with occupation contemporary with the Group 12 revetment and therefore datable to *c.* 1430, but may be residual or derived.

French Official Jettons
(Fig. 63, No. 43)

41. (2205) *O.* Shield of France modern with tail of fourth lys at top; legend is 'AVE.... type', but very corroded. *R.* Elaborate three-strand cross-flory in quadrilobe (no surrounding inscription). This is the standard reverse for the large late 14th-century French official jettons that are common in England. Dia. 24.5mm. Date *c.* 1370s–1380s. From the Period V foreshore and therefore not later than *c.* 1380.
42. (2389) *O.* Seated king between branches; inscription is AVE MARIA : GRACIA : PLENA with double crosslet stops. *R.* Short three-strand cross-flory in quadrilobe; legend reads as Obv. except ends with PLEN; pointed trefoil in spandrels. Dia. 28mm. Date *c.* 1340s. Somewhat worn. Possibly residual in the Period V foreshore.
43. (1069) *O.* A crown, AVE on band; inscription with double annulet stops reads AVE : MARIA : GRASIA PLENA DN. *R.* Bowed cross-flory; pierced six-foils in centre and in quarters with a fleur-de-lys and in border (without a circle); there are three six-foils in each quarter. Dia. 26.5mm. The GRASIA spelling occurs on types with English connections and is later than good official ones with GRACIA. *c.* 1420. From Context 1180 (Period VI, Phase iv), an organic deposit related to the final phase of occupation associated with the Group 15 river wall, which was constructed *c.* 1440 (illustrated).
44. (1054) *O.* Shield of France modern. AVE MARIA · GRACIA.... *R.* Standard type, as for No. 41. Dia. 25.5mm. Date *c.* 1380s. Residual in Contexts 1175/1176 (Period VII).

Fig. 63. Trig Lane 1974–76: French Official Jetton No. 43; French 'Derivative' Jetton No. 47 ($\frac{2}{1}$).

Late French Official Jettons

45. (2161) *O.* Shield of France modern, leaves at sides and above; legend garbled. *R.* As for No. 46 but looser. ⋀s in spandrels and Vs in quarters. Dia. 26.5mm. Date *c.* 1430s–1440s. From the Period V foreshore.
46. (970) *O.* Shield of France modern; AVE inscription, corroded, lettering appears to be rather late, but fine work. *R.* Late variation of standard type; plain three-strand cross-flory in quadrilobe. Dia. 27mm. Date *c.* 1420s, under regime of Charles VII (?), but may be a little earlier. Residual in Context 1076 (Period VII).

French 'Derivative' Jettons
(Fig. 63, No. 47)

47. (549) *O.* Shield of France modern with typical recurved sides; saltire initial mark; legend with annulet stops reads AVE MARIA GRACIA. . *R.* Plain three-strand cross-flory in quadrilobe; annulet between pellets in spandrels; As and Ms on cusps. Dia. 27.5mm. From the Group 15 dump (Period VI), and therefore not later than *c.* A.D. 1440 (illustrated).
48. (165) As for No. 47, but no stop after GRACIA on *Obv.* and style generally more slovenly. Dia. 29.5mm. Mid-late 15th century. From Context 126 (Periods VI or VII).
49. (2808) As for No. 48, except double annulet stop on *Obv.* and single annulet in spandrels on *Rev.* Dia. 29.5mm. Mid- to late 15th century. Probably residual in Context 1477 (Period VII).

French Unofficial Jetton
(Fig. 62, No. 50)

50. (759) *O.* Large cross-hatched R between four fleur-de-lys in sexfoil; pellet in each spandrel. *R.* Large cross-hatched I between four fleur-de-lys and two cinqfoils in sexfoil pellet in each spandrel. Good-quality work. Not English because it is not pierced. Not French official. Might be genuinely 'Anglo-Gallic', i.e. Aquitainian. If letters read RI this could stand for RICARDVS, or if IR, could stand for JOHANNES REX. Dia. 19.5mm. Date *c.* 1370–80; in good condition. From the Group 11 dump (Period V, Phase i) (illustrated).

Nuremberg Jettons

51 (3095) Remains of a late 'normal' Nuremberger; H. Krauwinckel or similar. *c.* AD 1600. From Context 78 (Period VII).
52. (1109) Nuremberg counter (probably for gaming) with head of Queen Anne and reverse proper to Charles II. Made by JOHANN JACOB DIETZEL, active 1711–48. Dia. 20mm. Unstratified.

Miscellaneous Copper Coins, Jettons, substitutes or mere discs

53. (237) Very thin copper-alloy disc with two small piercings. Dia. 13mm. From the Group 11 dump (Period V, Phase i), dated to *c.* AD 1380.
54. (565) Probably a mite (24th or 48th part of groat) of a very base billon. Of Flanders in the late 14th century; might be of Louis de Mâle, 1346–84. *R.* Long cross. Reads FLA (for Flanders). *O.* Uncertain design—not a recognizable coat of arms. Apparently reads]ME[(from COMES); M roman not lombardic. Dia. 23mm, inner circle 15mm–16mm. Provenance as for No. 53.
55. (145) Corroded copper-alloy disc. Dia *c.* 20mm. From the Group 15 dump (Period VI) and therefore not later than *c.* 1440.
56. (3) Copper Or of Queen Christina of Sweden, 1645. A thick heavy coin, but not a *platmynt*. From Context 20 (Period VII).
57. (770) Forged halfpenny of George II, very corroded. From Context 1039 (Period VII).
58. (1067) Corroded blank disc. Dia. 25mm. From Context 78 (Period VII).
59. (174) Corroded Sestertius, approx. Flavian–Hadrianic: Domitian or Trajan (?). Dia. 31mm. Thickness *c.* 3mm. Residual in Context 789 (Period VII).

Lead Token, A Type
(Fig. 62, No. 60)

Type A tokens are thick, in high relief, and distantly reflect pennies in their designs, especially on the reverse. They are generally early for lead tokens.

60. (2274) *O.* Three intersecting lines, possibly a crosier and a key or could be a garbled Christogram. *R.* 'Penny' type short cross with strokes in border. Dia. *c.* 17mm—it has a rather polygonal appearance, perhaps as the result of clipping with shears. Quite thick (1.5mm). From the Period V foreshore which is of late 14th to mid-15th century date (illustrated).

Lead Tokens, D1 Type
(Fig. 64, No. 61)

These are thin tokens akin to Smith (1854) No. 772. Tokens of this general kind have been found in Aldersgate Street, London (*ibid.*), Winetavern Street, Dublin (full publication awaited, but see Brit. Numis. Soc., 1972, 203) and Boston, Lincs. (see *ibid.* and Rigold, 1972, 44 and Fig.

Part IV—Specialist Reports

8, No. 4). The designs are consistent with a mid- to late 13th-century date and the Dublin examples, like No. 61 below, have been ascribed to this period on stratigraphic evidence.

61. (2170) O. Double-headed eagle. R. Barry shield. As Smith (1854, Pl. 16, No. 7). Dia 16mm. From the Group 2 dump (Period III, Phase i) which dates to c. 1250–75 (illustrated).

62. (2135) Dia. 17.5mm. Flattened out and design mostly obliterated. Some cross-hatching suggests it is a D1 type. From Context 193 (Period IV: the fill of a drain in use between c. 1345 and 1385).

Lead Tokens, D2 Type
(Plate 73, Nos. 63–8)
These are apparently coarse versions of the D1 type, which seem to date from the mid-14th to mid-15th centuries.

63. (2264) O. Appears to be a curved pentagon surrounded by cross-hatching. R. Unclear. Dia. 15mm. From the Group 10 dump (Period IV) which is dated to c. 1360.
64. (117) O. Cross-hatched lozenge. R. ? Dia. 15.5mm. From the Group 11 dump (Period V, Phase i) which is dated to c. 1380.
65. (327) O. Bird (?). R. Two cross-hatched lozenges. Dia. 16mm. Provenance and date as for No. 64.
66. (735) O. Shield with fess and label on cross-hatched background. R. Rough branched design. Dia. 13.5mm. Thickness c. 1.5mm. Provenance and date as for No. 64.
67. (2276) O. Shield with ∞ design on cross-hatched background. R. Shield with a pale on cross-hatched background. Dia. 13.5mm. From the Period V foreshore of late 14th to mid-15th century date.
68. (2261) O. Grinning leopard face. R. Lozenge bearing a fess. Dia. 13.5mm. Provenance as for No. 67.

Lead Tokens, D3 Type
(Fig. 64, Nos. 70–4)
In design and technique these are apparently related to the D1 type, but are considerably later (late 14th century). They have not been recorded elsewhere.

69. (348) O. Agnus Dei (unclear) right. R. Cusped cruciform design. Dia. 16.5mm. From the Group 11 dump (Period V, Phase i) which dates to c. 1380 (for illustration, see No. 73).
70. (693) O. Six-petalled design with crosses between petals. R. Multi-petalled design. Dia. 17mm. Provenance and date as for No. 69 (illustrated).
71. (733) O. Eight-armed moline design. R. Eight-petalled rosette. Dia. 15.5mm. Provenance and date as for No. 69 (illustrated).
72. (738) O. Lombardic A on cross-hatching within very wide margin. R. Two-petalled design. Dia. c. 21.5mm. Provenance and date as for No. 69 (illustrated).
73. (2275) As No. 69 except Agnus Dei clearer. From the Period V foreshore which dates to the late 14th to early 15th century (illustrated).
74. (2277) O. 'Fern' or 'palm-tree' design. R. Multi-petalled design. Dia. 16.5mm. Provenance as for No. 73 (illustrated).

Lead Tokens, D4 type
(Plate 74, Nos. 75–80)
These are similar to the D3 type but are slightly coarser. They appear to date from the late 14th to mid-15th century.

75. (443) O. Petalled design. R. Star of David containing trefoil. Dia. 13.5mm. From the Group 11 dump (Period V, Phase i) which dates to c. 1380.
76. (586) O. Cross-hatched cruciform design with three pellets between arms. R. Six-petalled design with border of pellets. Dia. 15.5mm. Provenance as for No. 75.
77. (587) O. Cruciform design on cross-hatched background. R. Six-petalled design on cross-hatched background. Dia. 15.5mm. Provenance and date as for No. 75.
78. (734) O. Grinning lion face. R. Bird in tree, with nest and eggs(?). Dia. 16mm. Provenance and date as for No. 75.
79. (2320) O. Six-petalled design. R. Eight-armed moline(?) design. Dia. 16mm. From the Group 10 dump (Period IV) which dates to c. 1360.
80. (1577) O. Unclear. R. Millwheel straight-hatched design. Dia. 13mm. Thickness 1.5mm. From Period V foreshore of the late 14th to mid-15th century.

(Plate 75, Nos. 81–6)

81. (2271) O. Six-petalled design. R. Chequered shield. Dia. 15mm. Provenance and date as for No. 80.
82. (2272) O. Six-petalled design. R. Millwheel straight-hatched design. Dia. 15.5mm. Provenance and date as for No. 80.
83. (2273) O. Cross moline. R. Eight-spoked design. Dia. 15.5mm. Provenance and date as for No. 80.
84. (2279) Sixteen-armed moline design both sides. Dia. 14mm. Provenance and date as for No. 80.
85. (2280) O. Six-petalled design on cross-hatched background. R. Eight-armed moline. Dia. 15.5mm. Provenance and date as for No. 80.
86. (2281) O. Six-petalled design. R. Rosette (?) of pellets. Dia. 16mm. Provenance and date as for No. 80.

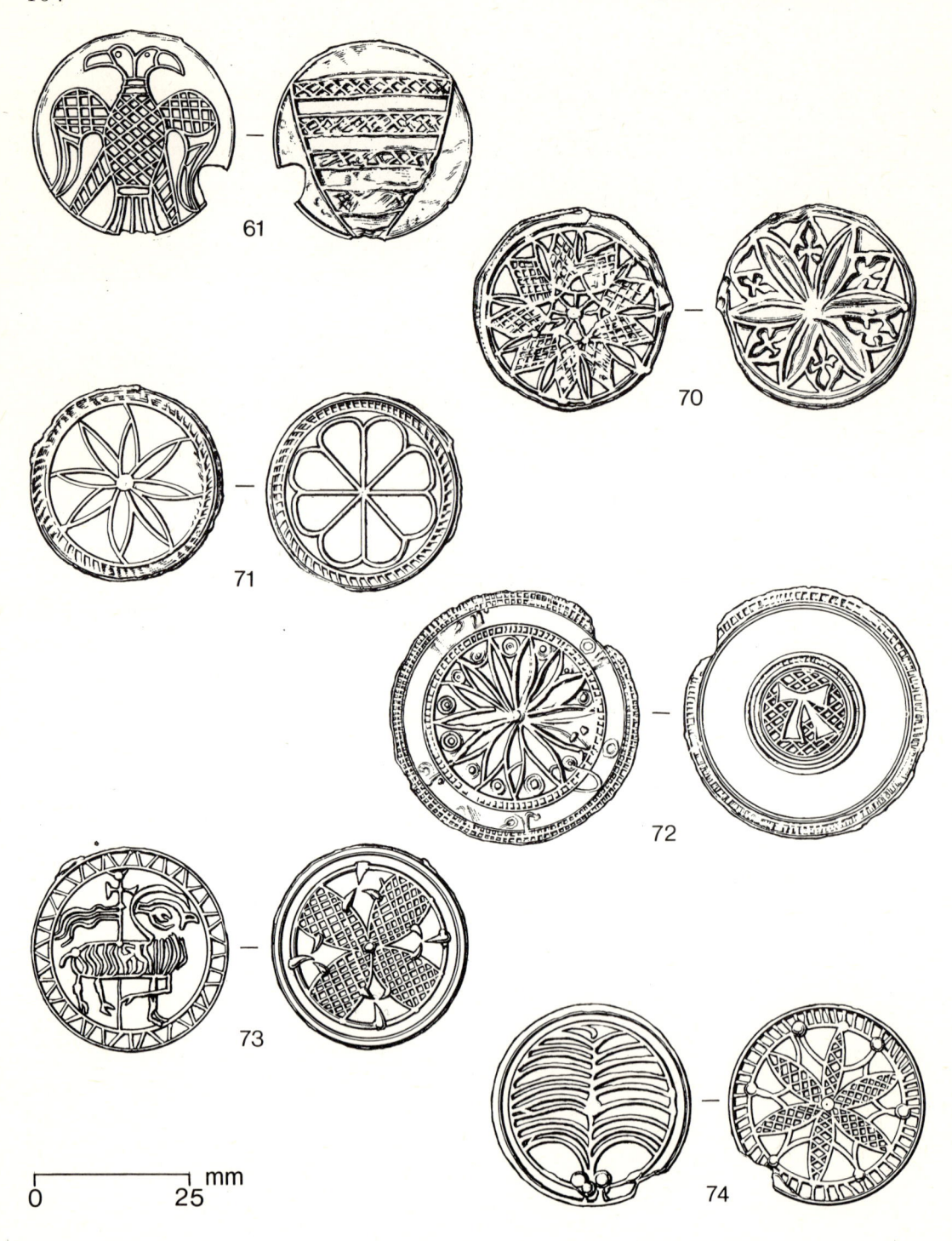

Fig. 64. Trig Lane 1974–76: Lead Token D1 type No. 61; Lead Tokens D3 type Nos. 70–74 ($\frac{2}{1}$).

Part IV—Specialist Reports

(Plate 76, Nos. 87–92)

87. (2282) *O.* Six-petalled design on cross-hatched background. *R.* Cross-hatched cross patée. Dia. 15.5mm. Provenance and date as for No. 80.
88. (1542) *O.* Sixteen-petalled design. *R.* Six-petalled design on cross-hatched background. Dia. 16mm. Provenance as for No. 80.
89. (2270) Whirligig both sides. Dia. 14.5mm. Provenance and date as for No. 80.
90. (1526) *O.* Bird (?). *R.* Six-petalled(?) design. Dia. 16.5mm. Provenance as for No. 80.
91. (2169) *O.* Eight-spoked moline design. *R.* Whirligig. Dia. 15mm. Provenance and date as for No. 80.
92. (2258) Cross-hatched cruciform design, both sides. Dia. 14.5mm. Provenance and date as for No. 80.

(Plate 77, Nos. 93–6)

93. (2260) Six-petalled design on cross-hatched ground both sides. Dia. 14mm. Provenance and date as for No. 80.
94. (2259) As for No. 93.
95. (157) *O.* Petalled star. *R.* Star of David. Dia. 14mm. From the Group 15 dump (Period VI, Phase i) dated to *c.* AD 1440.
96. (158) *O.* Four-petalled design. *R.* Unclear. Dia. 14.5mm. Provenance and date as for No. 95.

Lead Tokens, D5 Type
(Fig. 65, Nos. 97–101)

These are small tokens akin to Smith (1854) No. 773. All of the Trig Lane examples bear an obverse design surrounded by oblique strokes and the reverse shown in the third of Smith's figure, namely a short cross patée with a pellet within an annulet in each quarter. Their date is late 14th to mid-15th century.

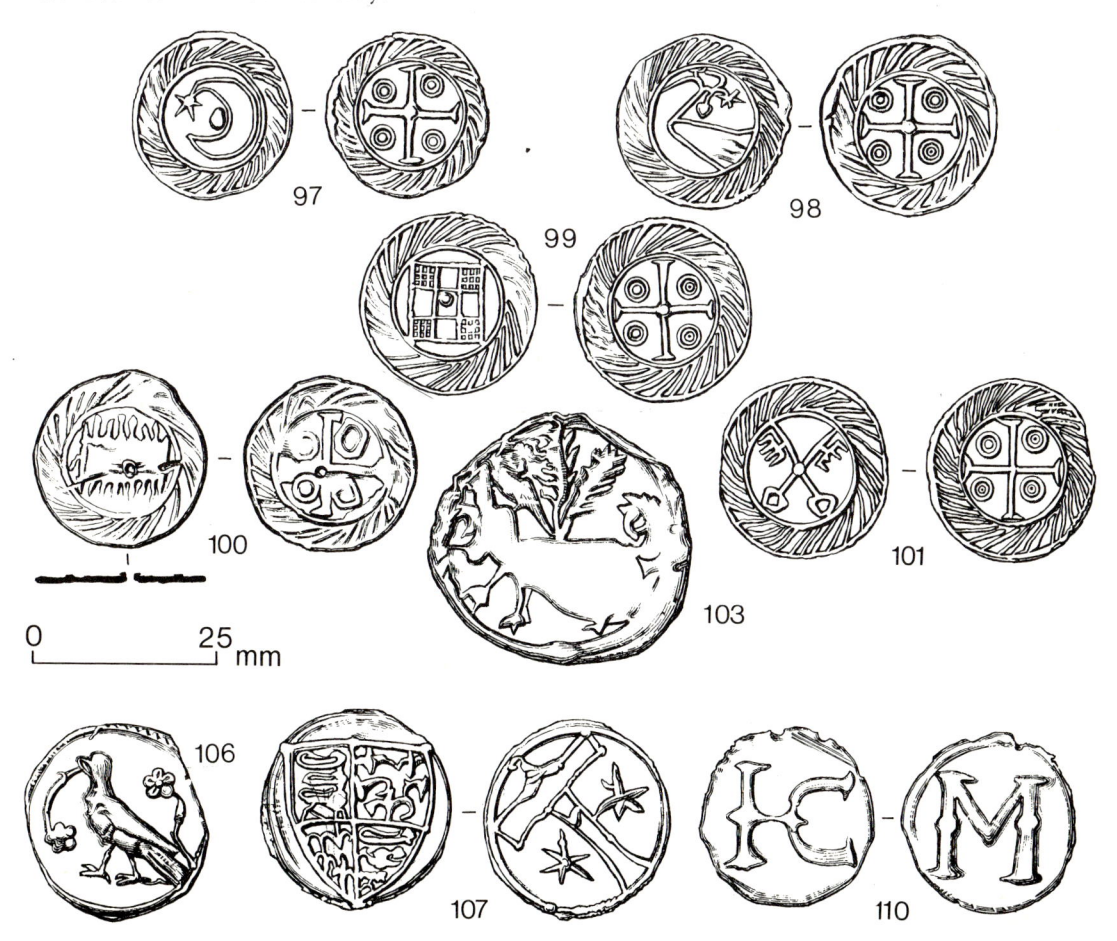

Fig. 65. Trig Lane 1974–76: Lead Tokens D5 type Nos. 97–101; Miscellaneous Lead Tokens Nos. 103–110 ($\frac{2}{1}$).

97. (551) O. Crescent and Star. Dia. 11.5mm. From the Period V foreshore of late 14th to mid-15th century date (illustrated).
98. (2257) O. Swan to right with a star. Dia 12mm. Provenance and date as for No. 97 (illustrated).
99. (2330) O. Square checky or chequer board. Dia. 12mm. From the Group 15 dump (Period VI, Phase i) dated to c. AD 1440 (illustrated).
100. (2332) O. Double-sided comb. Dia. 12mm. Provenance and date as for No. 99 (illustrated).
101. (2563) O. Cross keys (as shown by Smith, *ibid.*) Dia. 12mm. Provenance and date as for No. 99 (illustrated).

Miscellaneous lead tokens and discs
(Fig. 65, Nos. 102–10)

102. (1398) Blank, as far as can be seen. Dia. 15.5mm. From the Group 7 dump (Period IV, Phase i) which is dated to c. 1350.
103. (2347) Uniface. Creature, jaws unclear but not conspicuously long, beside a palm tree design. Perhaps a remote reflection of the COL. NEM. Roman coinage of Nîmes, which has a crocodile beside a palm tree. Might well be foreign but is certainly medieval. Dia. 17mm, thickness 1.5mm. From the Group 10 dump (Period IV, Phase iii) which is dated to c. 1360 (illustrated).
104. (2359) Sheared disc. c. 2mm thick. From the Group 12 dump (Period V, Phase iii) which is dated to c.1430 but probably contains redeposited material from behind the Group 10 revetment, which is dated to c. 1360.
105. (2321) Blank, as far as can be seen. Dia c. 16.5mm, thickness c. 1.5mm. From the Period IV foreshore which is dated mid- to late 14th century.
106. (2262) Uniface. Falcon with rose in beak and another by its tail. Dia. 18.5mm, thickness 1.5mm. From the Period V foreshore which is dated late 14th to mid-15th century (illustrated).
107. (2539) O. Shield of England quartering France ancient, and therefore pre c. 1415. R. T between two stars (possibly connected with St. Thomas' Hospital, Southwark). Dia. 13mm. Provenance as for No. 106 (illustrated).
108. (1401) Blank except for centre pellet. Dia. 23mm. Thickness c. 1.5mm. From the infill of a drain contemporary with the Group 12 revetment (Period V, Phase 4) and therefore deposited c. 1430.
109. (2265) Blank, as far as can be seen. Dia. 12mm. From Context 1485 (Period VII) and therefore not later than c. 16th to 17th century.
110. (2120) O. IC R. M; late 16th–17th century lettering. Dia. 12.5mm, thickness 1.5mm. Unstratified (illustrated).

5. Pilgrim Souvenirs and Kindred Objects
by Brian Spencer

Predominant among the pilgrim souvenirs found on the Trig Lane site are those originating from Canterbury, most of them dating from Chaucer's time when the pilgrimage from London to Canterbury appears to have reached its peak. More intriguing, however, are two items entirely unconnected with Thomas Becket, London's particular spiritual champion: an ampulla from Bromholm Priory, Norfolk, and a badge commemorating the Black Prince and his lifelong devotion to the Trinity. Except for Nos. 111 and 121 (which would have been worn suspended round the neck) and Nos. 112, 122 and 123, every object is, or originally was, provided with a pin and clasp. Nos. 121 and 122 were cast in two-piece moulds, the remainder (except No. 123) in three-piece moulds. Excepting No. 123, all these items are of tin or pewter. A full report on these objects will be appearing in *Trans. London Middlesex Archaeol. Soc.* 33 (1982).

111. Ampulla for holding a dose of Canterbury water: on the front is depicted the figure of St. Thomas in the vestments of an archbishop and on the back his martyrdom; encircling the lower parts of the ampulla is a narrow band inscribed O(P)TIMVS EGRORVM MEDICVS FIT THOMA BONOR(VM) – Thomas is the best doctor of the worthy sick; c. 1250, but subjected to considerable wear before being deposited. From the Group 2 dump (Period III, Phase i).
112. Ampulla commemorating a pilgrimage to the relic of the True Cross at Bromholm Priory, Norfolk: on the front is depicted Christ on the Cross and in the space above, the three crosses of the Calvary; the Exaltation of the Cross is represented on the back: c. 1250, but subjected to considerable wear before being deposited (Pl. 78). From the Group 2 dump (Period III, Phase i).
113. Talismanic brooch bearing the names of the Three Kings, CASPER MELCHIOR B(A)PTIS(AR); c. 1350. From the Group 10 dump (Period IV, Phase iii) and therefore not later than c. 1360.
114. Pilgrim sign representing St. Thomas on horseback and probably commemorating his triumphant return to Canterbury from exile shortly before his murder; perhaps made for the fourth jubilee of this event, 2nd December 1370 (Pl. 77). From Group 7–11 dumps (Period IV to Period V, Phase i) and therefore not later than c. 1380.
115. Fragment of a pilgrim badge probably depicting the shrine of St. Thomas of Canterbury; mid 14th century. From the Group 11 dump (Period V, Phase i) and therefore deposited c. 1380.
116. Cabbalistic brooch in the form of a hexagram with the letter E, perhaps the owner's initial, at its centre. Provenance as for No. 115.
117. Fragment of a badge, an angel's wing. Provenance as for No. 115.
118. Pilgrim sign in the form of a sword slotting into a scabbard which, in turn, is cast in one piece with a buckler; probably a memento of the weapon used to murder Thomas Becket and subsequently

Plate 72. Trig Lane 1974–76: Rubbing posts decaying on the line of the Mean High Water Neap tides on present day Thames Foreshore. The timber above and below this level is sound. Note position of scarf joints.

Plate 73. Trig Lane 1974–76: Lead Tokens D2 type Nos. 63–68. The dash by each reverse view indicates the top centre point on the obverse. Scale 1/1.

Plate 74. Trig Lane 1974–76: Lead Tokens D4 type Nos. 75–80. The dash by each reverse view indicates the top centre point on the obverse. Scale 1/1.

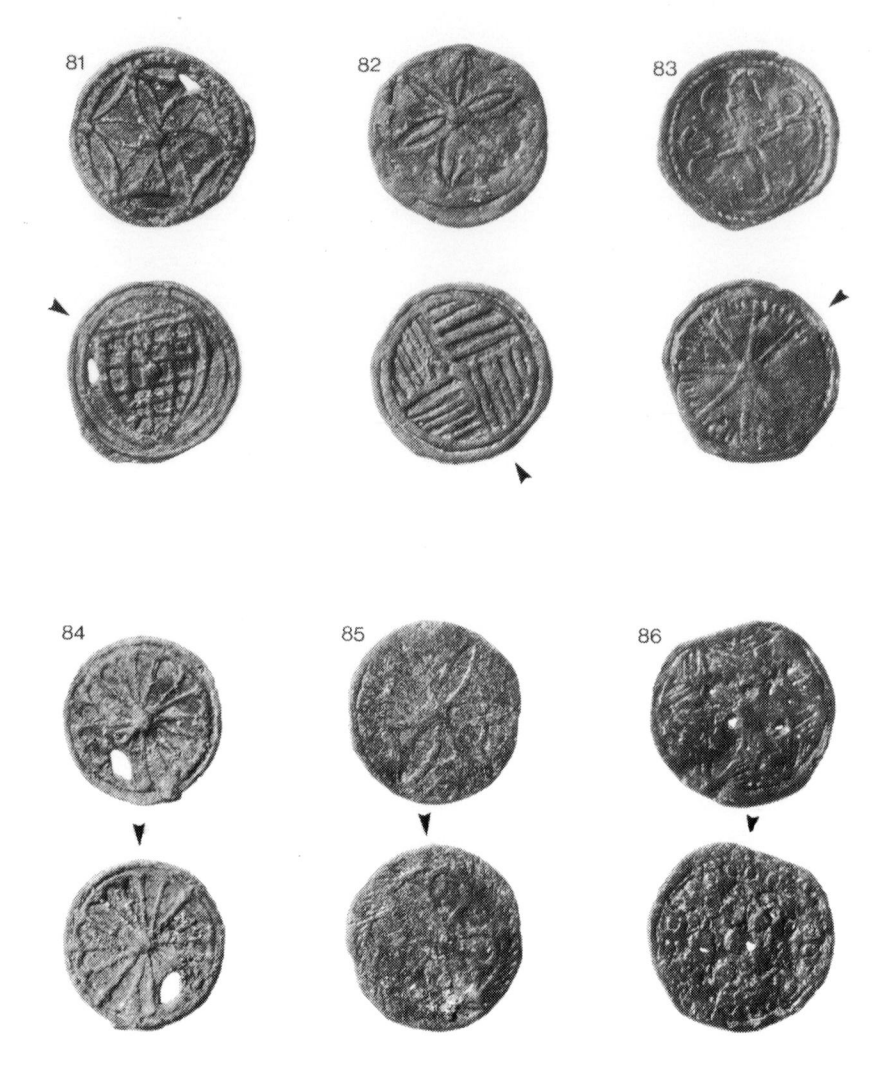

Plate 75. Trig Lane 1974–76: Lead Tokens D4 type Nos. 81–86. The dash by each reverse view indicates the top centre point on the obverse. Scale 1/1.

Plate 76. Trig Lane 1974–76: Lead Tokens D4 type Nos. 87–92. The dash by each reverse view indicates the top centre point on the obverse. Scale 1/1.

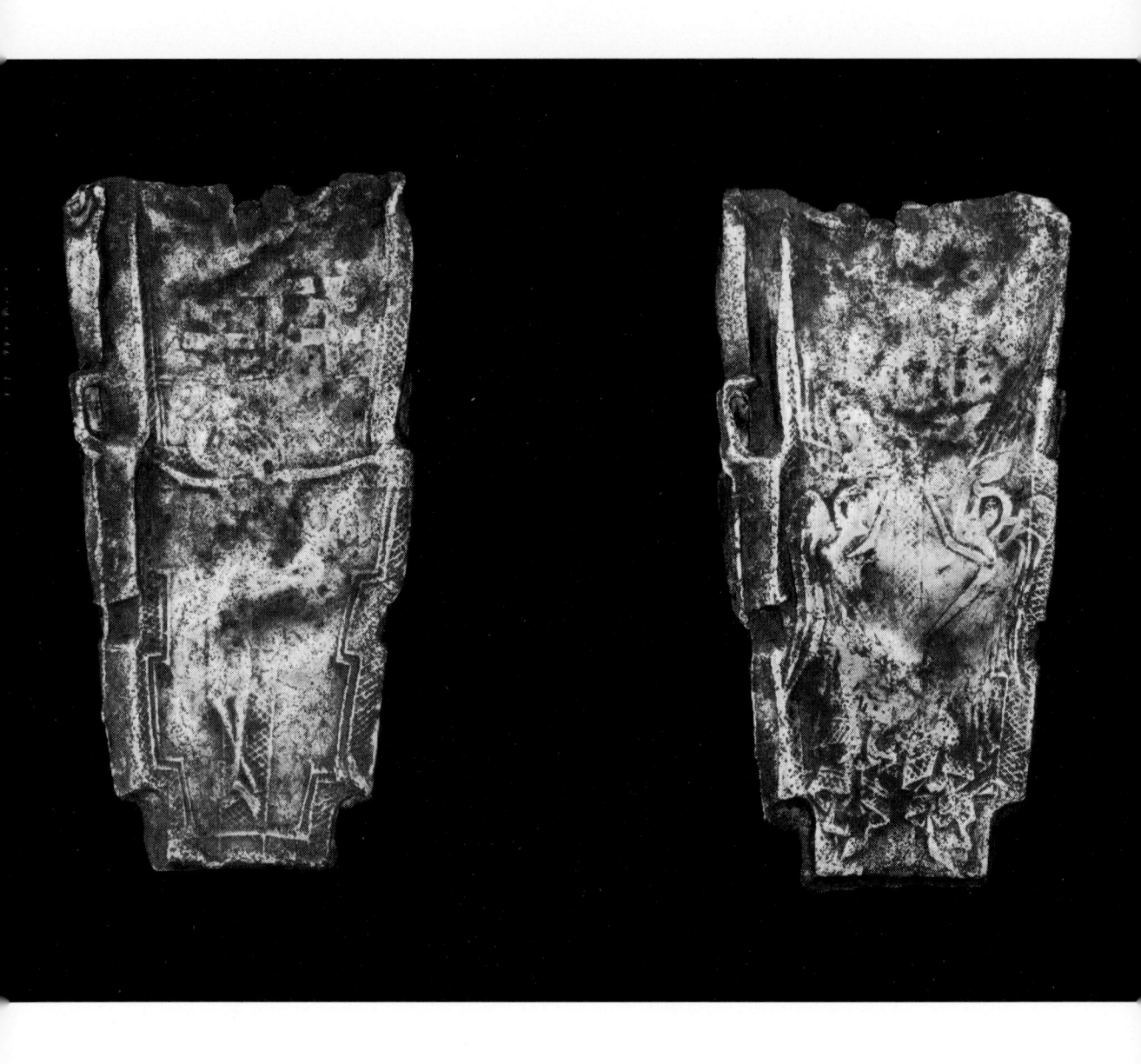

Plate 78. Trig Lane 1974–76: Pilgrim's Ampulla, No. 112 *(left)* front depicting Christ on the Cross; *(right)* back showing the raising up of the Cross by two angels, height 77mm.

Plate 77. Trig Lane 1974–76: *(top)* Lead Tokens D4 type Nos. 93, 95–6. The dash by each reverse view indicates the top centre point on the obverse. Scale 1/1. *(bottom)* Pilgrim badge, No. 114. Depicts St. Thomas of Canterbury on ambling horse, height 81mm.

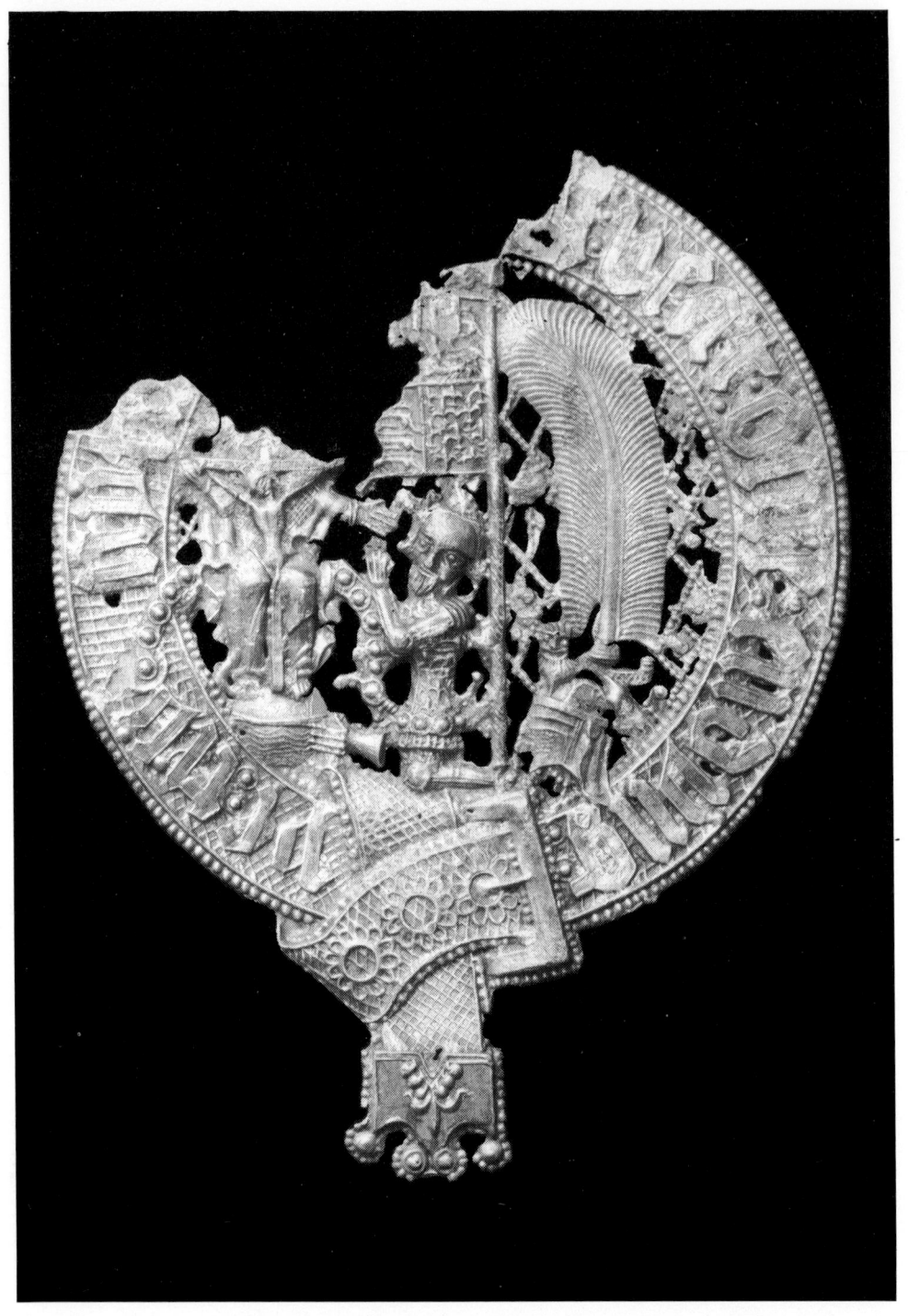

Plate 79. Trig Lane 1974–76: Hat badge depicting the Black Prince kneeling before the Trinity, No. 125, height 83mm; width 61mm.

Part IV—Specialist Reports

PERIOD	III	IV			V			VI
GROUP	G2	G7	G9 foreshore	G10	G11	G12	G13 foreshore	G15
COINS					54 (L14th)		23 (L14th) 24 (1369)	25 (1422) 26 (1430) 27 (1422)
JETTONS	36				32 (L14th) 33 (14th) 34 (1360) 37 50 (1380) 53	29 (L14th) 30 (E14th) 40	35 (1370) 38 39 41 (1380) 42 (1340) 45 (1440)	31 (1320) 47 55
TOKENS								
A							46	
D1	61				62			
D2				63	64 65 66		67 68	
D3					69 70 71 72		73 74	
D4				79	75 76 77 78	80 81 82 83 84 85 86 87 88 89 90 91 92 93 94		95 96
D5								99 100 101
OTHER		102	105	103	104 108		106 107	

Distribution of coins, jettons and tokens.

treasured as a relic at Canterbury; late 14th century. From the Period V foreshore and therefore not later than c. 1440.
119. Part of a pilgrim badge identical to no. 118. Provenance as for No. 118.
120. Sword from a pilgrim badge similar to no. 118. Provenance as for No. 118.
121. Pendant in the form of a sheathed rondel-dagger, with a rectangular loop for suspension; early 15th century. Provenance as for No. 118.
122. Badge depicting the head of a woman within a pierced octofoil and circular frame and backed by a circular plate originally fitted with stitching loops; c. 1370–c. 1420. Provenance as for No. 118.
123. Mount of thin sheet copper alloy stamped in the shape of a scallop-shell, the sign of St. James of Compostella, and pierced for a rivet or stitches. Provenance as for No. 118.
124. Pilgrim sign in the form of a fleur-de-lys within a circular frame, from the lower edge of which protrudes a loop; perhaps associated with the cult of St. Mary Undercroft, Canterbury. From the Group 15 dump (Period VI) and therefore not later than c. 1440.
125. Badge commemorating Edward the Black Prince and perhaps made for his funeral in 1376; identified by a banner of his arms and by his badge of the ostrich feather, the prince kneels before the Trinity, the scene being enclosed by a Garter inscribed 'the trynyty (? & seynt Geor)g be at oure endyng' (Pl. 79). Provenance as for No. 118.
126. Pilgrim badge depicting a bust of St. Thomas of Canterbury (the reliquary containing part of his skull) in a pierced quatrefoil within a square frame. Provenance as for No. 124.
127. Brooch decorated with four fleurs-de-lys in cross and bordered by a band of zig-zags. Provenance as for No. 124.

ACKNOWLEDGEMENTS

I should like to express my appreciation of all those museum staff who assisted in the post-excavation work on the finds and in the production of this finds report. The catalogues were prepared by Caroline Bird, Marija Chapman, Anne Clark, Jon Cotton, Ann Edmondson, Linda Hall, Katherine Hayes, Sue Heaser, Merry Morgan Hill, Vanessa Jones, Margaret Levêque, Alison Balfour-Lynn, Penny MacConnoran, Louise Miller, Janice Moody, Vivienne Pilton, Frances Pritchard, Sandra Rose, Angela Simič, Mary Skalla, Jane Squirrell, Dwayne Sullivan, Andrew Tizzard, Pamela White, Michael Willcox and Margaret Wood. The conservation was carried out by Bill Rector, Andrew Agyrakis, Joyce Andrews and Marilee Parrott, and the radiography of the metal finds was kindly undertaken by John Price of the Department of the Environment. The photographs are by Trevor Hurst and Jon Bailey. Figs. 60 and 61 were prepared by Jacqui Pearce and special thanks are due to Dave Parfitt for illustrating the majority of the jettons and tokens. The jettons depicted in Fig. 63 are by Claire Thorne. Diana Twells, Penny MacConnoran, Katherine Hayes, Vanessa Jones, Claire Thorne and Frances Pritchard were of great assistance in the final preparation of the report for publication.

I should like to express particular gratitude to those who provided the specialist reports. They are John Clark and Brian Spencer of the Museum of London and Clive Orton of the Institute of Archaeology, London. Together with my colleagues in the Department of Urban Archaeology we would like to record our deep gratitude to Stuart Rigold, formerly of the Department of the Environment, who died a short while after completing his contribution to this report. His support and encouragement will be sadly missed.

Clive Orton wishes to thank John Clark for help in finding parallels to the pottery in the collections of the Museum of London and Brian Spencer wishes to thank Dr. J. H. Harvey for his helpful suggestions. I should like, finally, to thank a number of Museum of London colleagues for advice and information given during the course of my own research and the editing of these reports. They are Hugh Chapman, John Clark, Tony Dyson, Vanessa Harding, Peter Marsden, Gustav and Chrissie Milne, Clive Orton, John Schofield, Brian Spencer and Kay Staniland.

C. GLOSSARY OF TERMS USED IN THIS REPORT
Much of the terminology has been taken from Hewett (1969, 9–19)

BARE-FACED a joint with only one shoulder that would normally possess two: *cf.* Fig. 66h and j.

BIRD'S MOUTH defines any joint the profile of which resembles an open beak, as on the foot of the Group 3 revetment brace in Fig. 10b.

BRACE (or shore) diagonally set member supporting a vertical revetment member.

BUTT terminal point.

CLADDING the external covering applied to wall or roof. The most common cladding for the revetments was horizontal planking laid edge to edge.

EDGE AND FACE a dressed timber will usually have two faces wider than its two edges unless it has been literally 'squared'. The 'best face' is the surface most radial to the circle of the log prior to conversion. For example, in Fig. 66a the best face is the upper one. This is the surface first prepared, from which joints are marked and from which pegs are driven.

EDGE-TRENCHING a cut or trench in the edge of a timber into which a similarly edge-trenched member may be set. The examples from the Groups 7, 10 and 11 revetments all incorporated two vertical members with trenches cut in their abutting edges through which an edge-trenched horizontal member was passed. This provided a strong unwithdrawable joint (Figs. 15; 66g).

HEARTWOOD the part of the tree between the pith and sapwood. It contains no living cells, and is often impregnated with substances such as tannins, making it more resistant to decay than the surrounding sapwood (Fig. 67).

GROWTH RINGS concentric rings showing extent of one year's growth, comprising the large earlywood vessels and the small latewood vessels (Fig. 67).

JOISTS framed floor members. The framed feature built in the south-west corner of the Group 11 revetment incorporated three common joists onto which the floor planking was nailed (Fig 28).

JOWL the end of a timber which swells out so that the strength of its end joint may be enhanced, e.g. the Group 11 corner post (Figs. 23; 24; 28).

LAP JOINTS a category of joints in which one part of a timber overlaps another. They could be either face-to-face (Fig. 66a & b) or end-to-face joints (Fig. 66c & d).

Halving the removal of half the depth of two timbers so that they may cross each other at any angle without any variation in thickness. Used on the back-braces of the Group 3 revetment, (Figs 66a; 9).

Notched laps differ from standard squint laps (see below) in that they have a 'V' shaped notch which prevents their withdrawal (Fig. 66d).

A *secret notched-lap* has an additional web of wood on the outer face of the notched member which obscures the notch from view when in position, rendering it 'secret' (Fig. 66c). Such joints were apparently common from the 13th century to the opening of the 14th[1] and have been used in revetment construction to tie the foot of a brace to the base-plate.[2]

Squint laps are laps set at an angle other than 90°. The pair illustrated in Fig. 66e were cut in a timber subsequently reused as a base-plate in the Group I structure, but are seen here in their probable former use (*cf.* Fig. 7). The lap-dovetail illustrated in Fig. 66f is from the Group 4 revetment (*cf.* Fig. 8a).

MORTISE AND TENON Category of joints basic to post-Norman Conquest carpentry and joinery in which a tongue (tenon) at the end of one member is housed in a slot (mortise) in the edge or face of another (Fig. 66h). Commonly used to join the feet of the posts to the principal base-plates.

A *chase-mortise* has one vertical end and one inclined end to accept the tenon of a member designed to run diagonally from the mortised timber, e.g. Fig. 66i. Commonly used in front-braced revetments to join the head of the braces to the head of the posts.

Bare-faced tenons have only one shoulder rather than two (Fig. 66j).
Cut on the feet of the vertically set second storey members of the Group 12 revetment (Fig. 30).

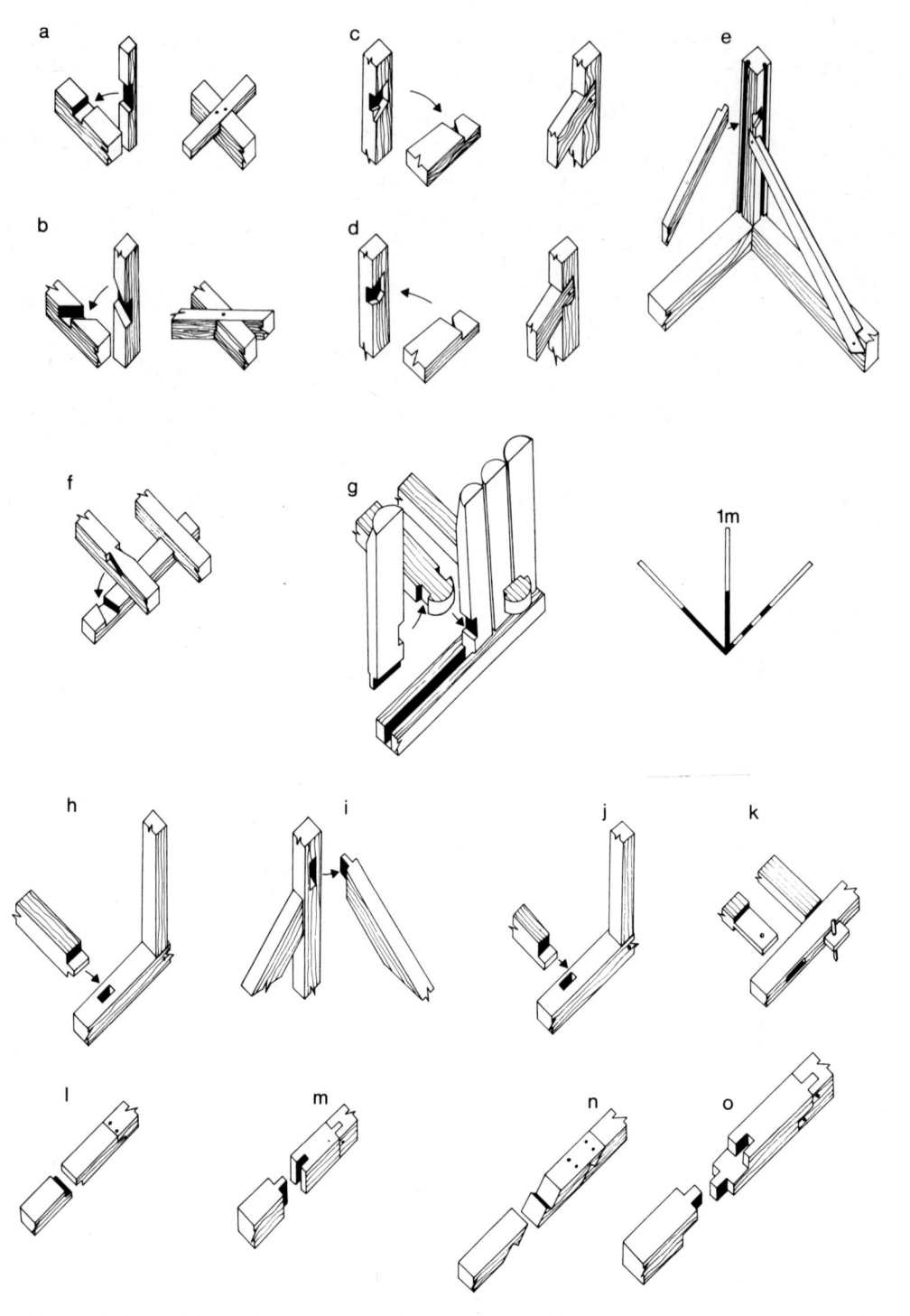

Fig. 66. Trig Lane 1974–76: Joinery details described in Glossary: all examples are from Trig Lane with the exceptions of 'c' and 'd' (Tudor Street) and 'n' (Custom House).

Glossary

A *tusk-tenon* is one which extends beyond the furthest face of the timber it transfixes, after which it is impaled with a peg or key (Fig. 66k). Used on the southern end of the Group 12 tie-backs.

A *free-tenon* is a small piece of wood buried at both ends in mortises cut into adjacent edges of abutting timbers. Used in the Group 10 revetment illustrated in Fig. 26.

PITH the centre of the tree. In living trees its function is concerned with the storage of food substances (Fig. 67).

PLATE horizontal timber at the top or bottom of a framing. The plate into which the principal revetment posts are tenoned in the Group 3 revetment is the *principal base-plate*, while the plate against which the feet of the braces butt is the *subsidiary base-plate* (Fig. 9).

RAYS thin walled cells running radially and horizontally from the centre of the tree outwards.

REVETMENT a facing of masonry, concrete, timber, sods etc. supporting or protecting a bank or embankment. The *'vertical tradition'* of revetment construction incorporates structures in which the principal posts or frame members are vertically set. The majority of the timbers are dressed square and are usually hardwoods, such as oak. This category includes all the Trig Lane revetments. The *'horizontal tradition'* incorporates structures in which the principal frame members are horizontally laid. The timbers could be undressed logs, often of softwoods such as pine.[3]

SAPWOOD the outermost part of the tree beneath the bark, which, in living specimens, contains living cells and assists in water conduction. Because it is prone to decay and to the harbouring of disease etc., it is usually stripped off logs during their conversion into timber (Fig. 67).

SCARF a joint designed to make one long timber from two or more shorter lengths by joining their ends. A scarf is by definition an end-to-end joint. The most common scarf used to join the Trig Lane revetment base-plates was the edge-halved scarf with square vertical butts (Fig. 66l). The plates laid on top of the Group 10 staves were jointed with the scarf shown in Fig. 66m. The through-splayed and tabled scarf shown in Fig. 66n was recorded on the Custom House site[4] and the edge-halved scarf with bridled butts from the Group 11 revetment (Fig. 66o) is shown in detail in Fig. 25.

SOFFIT underside. The lap-dovetail in Fig. 66f is cut on the soffit of the timber which passes over the base-plate.

TIE-BACK horizontally set members tied at one end to the principal vertical members or plates of a frame. See, for example, the Group 7 revetment in Figs. 12; 15.

TIMBER *'meremium'* in medieval Latin was the material of a size suitable for heavy construction work, such as the revetment structures.

WOOD or *'boscus'* was the smaller material such as poles or brushwood suitable for light construction work or firewood.[5]

NOTES AND REFERENCES
1. Hewett (1969, 59).
2. Milne (1979, 148).
3. See, for example, Herteig (1959).
4. Tatton-Brown (1974, 134, Fig. 16)
5. Rackham (1976, 23).

Timber Classification

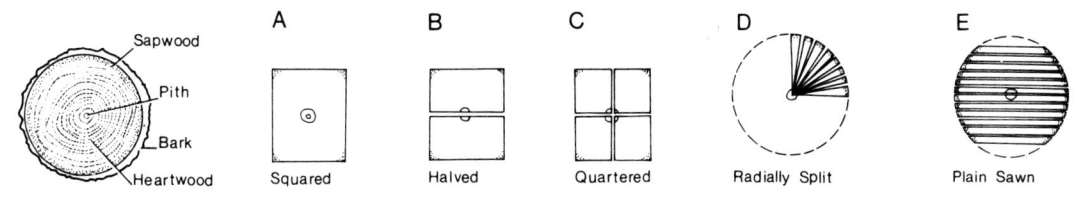

Fig. 67. Trig Lane 1974–76: Some methods of converting wood to timber, shown in diagrammatic transverse sections.

D. BIBLIOGRAPHY

BAILLIE AND PILCHER (1973). M. Baillie and J. R. Pilcher 'A simple cross-dating program for tree-ring research' *Tree Ring Bulletin* 33 (1973) 7–14.

BAILLIE (1977). M. G. L. Baillie 'The Belfast oak chronology to AD 1001' *Tree Ring Bulletin* 37 (1977) 1–12.

BERRY (1974). G. Berry *Medieval English Jettons* (London, 1974).

BIDDLE, BARFIELD AND MILLARD (1959). M. Biddle, L. Barfield and A. Millard 'Excavation of the Manor of the More, Rickmansworth' *Archaeol. J.* 106 (1959) 136–79.

BIDDLE, HUDSON AND HEIGHWAY (1973). M. Biddle and D. Hudson with C. Heighway *The Future of London's Past* (Worcester, 1973).

BRETT (1978). D. W. Brett 'Medieval and Recent Elms in London' in J. Fletcher (ed.) *Dendrochronology in Europe* (Oxford, 1978) 195–9.

BRIT. NUMIS. SOC. (1972). British Numismatic Society 'Proceedings of the . . . Society, 1972' *Brit. Numis. J.* 61 (1972) 199–207.

CAL. LIB. R. (1961). *Calendar of Liberate Rolls, vol. 5: 1260–67* (HMSO, 1961).

CANHAM (1970). M. P. Canham 'Kingston: Medieval Pottery Kiln' *Surrey Archaeol. Collect.* 67 (1970) 102–3.

CHEW AND KELLAWAY (1973). H. M. Chew and W. Kellaway (eds.) *London Assize of Nuisance 1301–1431* London Record Soc. 10 (1973).

CHEW AND WEINBAUM (1970). H. M. Chew and M. Weinbaum (eds.) *The London Eyre of 1244* London Record Soc. 6 (1970).

CLARK (1911). A. Clark (ed.) *The English Register of Gorstow Nunnery* Early English Text Soc. 129, 130, 142 (1911).

CUMING (1868). H. Syer Cuming 'On Signacula Found in London' *J. Brit. Archaeol. Assoc.* 24 (1868) 219–30.

DAWSON (1976). G. J. Dawson *The Black Prince's Palace at Kennington, Surrey* (Oxford, 1976).

DE BOER AND LATHRAP (1979). W. R. De Boer and D. W. Lathrap 'The Making and Breaking of Shipibo-Conibo Ceramics' in C. Kramer (ed.) *Ethnoarchaeology* (New York, 1979) 103–38.

DELORME (1978). A. Delorme 'A Mean curve for the oaks of the southern Weser and Leine Uplands: its usefulness and characteristics' in J. Fletcher (ed.) *Dendrochronology in Europe* (Oxford 1978) 45–53.

DREWETT (1974). P. L. Drewett 'Excavations in Old Town Croydon, 1968/70' *Res. Vol. Surrey Archaeol. Soc.* 1 (1974) 1–46.

DYSON (1981). T. Dyson 'The Terms "Quay" and "Wharf" and the Early Medieval London Waterfront' in G. Milne & B. Hobley (eds.) *Waterfront Archaeology in Britain & Northern Europe* (London, 1981) 37–8.

ECKSTEIN AND BAUCH (1969). D. Eckstein and J. Bauch 'Beitrag zur Rationalisierung eines dendrochronologischen Verfahrens und zur Analyse seiner Aussagesicherheit' *Fortwiss. Centralbl.* 88 (1969) 230–50.

EGAN (1976). G. Egan 'Treasure in the Thames' *London Archaeol.* 3 (1976) 18–20.

EKWALL (1954). E. Ekwall *Street Names of the City of London* (Oxford, 1954).

FOX (1910–14). E. Fox and J. S. Fox 'Numistic History of Edward I, II and III', spread over vols. VI to X of the *British Numis. J.* (not normally cited from the original since the 'Fox Classes' have stood the test of time and are repeated by all subsequent standard works such as North (1960)).

FLETCHER, TAPPER AND WALKER (1974). J. M. Fletcher, M. C. Tapper and F. S. Walker 'Dendrochronology—a reference curve for slow grown oaks, AD 1230 to 1546' *Archaeometry* 16 (1974) 31–40.

FLETCHER (1977). J. M. Fletcher 'Tree-ring chronologies for the 6th to 16th centuries for oak of southern and eastern England' *Journal of Archaeological Science* 4 (1977) 335–52.

FLETCHER (1978). J. M. Fletcher 'Oak chronologies for eastern and southern England' in J. Fletcher (ed.) *Dendrochronology in Europe* (Oxford 1978) 139–56.

FRERE (1941). S. S. Frere 'A Medieval Pottery at Ashtead' *Surrey Archaeol. Collect.* 47 (1941) 58–67.

FURNIVALL (1902). F. J. Furnivall *The Cambridge Ms. Dd. 4.24 of Chaucer's Canterbury Tales* E.E.T.S. 95–6 (1902).

FURNIVALL AND STONE (1909). F. J. Furnivall and W. G. Stone (eds.) *The Tale of Beryn* Early English Text Soc. extra series 105 (London, 1909).

GIUSEPPI (1937). M. S. Giuseppi 'Medieval Pottery in Kingston-upon-Thames' *Surrey Archaeol. Collect.* 45 (1937) 151–2.

HALL (1965). D. J. Hall *English Medieval Pilgrimage* (London, 1965).

HAMMERSON (1975). M. J. Hammerson 'Excavations on the Site of Arundel House in the Strand, W.C.2, in 1972' *Trans. London Middlesex Archaeol. Soc.* 26 (1975) 209–51.

HANWORTH AND TOMALIN (1977). R. Hanworth and D. J. Tomalin 'Brooklands, Weybridge: The Excavation of an Iron Age and Medieval Site 1964–5 and 1970–71' *Res. vol. Surrey Archaeol. Soc.* 4 (1977).

HARDY (1844). T. D. Hardy (ed.) *Rotuli Litterarum Clausarum* 2 (London, 1844).

HARRIS (1907). M. D. Harris (ed.) *The Coventry Lent Book, Part 1* Early Eng. Text Soc. 134–5 (1907).

HARVEY (1975). J. H. Harvey *Medieval Craftsmen* (London, 1975).

HASLAM (1978). J. Haslam *Medieval Pottery* (Aylesbury, 1978).

HENIG (1977). M. Henig 'Objects of Bone, Antler and Shell' in B. Durham, 'Archaeological Investigations in St. Aldates, Oxford' *Oxoniensia* 42 (1977, 83–203) 160–6.

HERTEIG (1959). A. E. Herteig 'The excavations of "Bryggen", the old Hanseatic Wharf in Bergen' *Medieval Archaeol.* 3 (1959) 177–86.

HEWETT (1969). C. Hewett *The Development of Carpentry, 1200–1700* (Newton Abbot, 1969).

HODGES (1974). H. Hodges 'The Medieval Potter: Artisan or Artist?' in V. I. Evison, H. Hodges and J. G. Hurst (eds.) *Medieval Pottery from Excavations* (London, 1974) 33–40.

HOLLING (1977). F. W. Holling 'Reflections on Tudor Green' *Post-Medieval Archaeol.* 11 (1977) 61–6.

HOLLSTEIN (1965). E. Hollstein 'Jahringchronologische Datierung von Eichenhölzern ohne Waldkanta' *Bonner Jahrbuch* 165 (1965) 12–27.

HOPE (1913). Sir W. H. St. John Hope *Heraldry for Craftsmen and Designers* (London, 1913).

HUBER AND GIERTZ-SIEBENLIST (1969). B. Huber and V. Giertz-Siebenlist, 'Unsere tausendjährige

Bibliography

Eichenchronologie durchschnittlich 57 (10–150) fach belegt' *Sitz Osterr Akad Wiss* 178 (1969) 37–42.

HUME (1956). I. Noël Hume *Treasure in the Thames* (London, 1956).

HURST (1961). J. G. Hurst 'The Kitchen Area of Northolt Manor, Middlesex' *Medieval Archaeol.* 5 (1961) 211–99.

HURST (1962–3). J. G. Hurst 'White Castle and the Dating of Medieval Pottery' *Medieval Archaeol.* 6–7 (1962–3) 135–55.

JONES (1976). P. E. Jones *The Butchers of London* (London, 1976).

KINGSFORD (1971). C. L. Kingsford (ed.), J. Stow *A Survey of London* 2nd edn. (Oxford, 1971).

KURATH & KUHN (1959). H. Kurath and S. M. Kuhn *Middle English Dictionary* (Michigan, 1959).

LODGE (1873). B. Lodge (ed.) *Palladins Aemilianus On Husbandry* E.E.T.S. 52, 72 (1873).

MARSDEN (forthcoming). P. V. R. Marsden 'Some Archaeological Evidence for the Post-Roman Development of London'.

MARSHALL (1924). C. J. Marshall 'A Medieval Pottery Kiln discovered at Cheam' *Surrey Archaeol. Collect.* 35 (1924) 79–94.

MARSHALL (1941). C. J. Marshall 'The Sites of Two More Thirteenth Century Pottery Kilns at Cheam' *Surrey Archaeol. Collect.* 47 (1941) 99–100.

MAYHEW (1861). H. Mayhew *London Labour and the London Poor* (London, 1861).

MEAD (1977). V. K. Mead 'Evidence for the Manufacture of Amber Beads in London in 14th-15th Century' *Trans. London Middlesex Archaeol. Soc.* 28 (1977) 211–14.

MILNE (1979). G. Milne 'Medieval riverfront revetment construction in London' in S. McGrail (ed.) *Medieval Ships and Harbours* B.A.R. International Series 66 (Oxford, 1979) 145–53.

MILNE & MILNE (1978). G. Milne and C. Milne 'Excavations on the Thames Waterfront at Trig Lane, London, 1974–76' *Medieval Archaeol.* 22 (1978) 84–104.

MILNE & MILNE (1979). G. Milne and C. Milne 'The Making of the London Waterfront' *Curr. Archaeol.* 66 (1979) 198–204.

MORGAN (1977). R. Morgan 'Tree ring dating of the London Waterfronts' *London Archaeol.* 3, No. 2 (1977) 40–5.

MORGAN AND SCHOFIELD (1978). R. Morgan and J. Schofield 'Tree-Rings and the Archaeology of the Thames Waterfront in the City of London' in J. Fletcher (ed.) *Dendrochronology in Europe* (Oxford, 1978) 223–38.

MORRIS (1970). M. Morris 'Cheam: Medieval Pottery Kiln' *Surrey Archaeol. Collect.* 67 (1970) 116.

MYRES (1935). J. N. L. Myres 'The Medieval Pottery at Bodiam Castle' *Sussex Archaeol. Collect.* 76 (1935) 222–30.

NORTH (1960). J. J. North *English Hammered Coins* (London, 1960).

ORTON (1977). C. R. Orton 'Medieval Pottery' in T. R. Blurton and M. Rhodes 'Excavations at Angel Court, Walbrook, 1974' *Trans. London Middlesex Archaeol. Soc.* 28 (1977, 14–100) 80–6.

ORTON (1979). C. R. Orton 'Medieval Pottery from a Kiln Site at Cheam: Part 1' *London Archaeol.* 3, No. 11 (1979) 300–4.

ORTON & MILLER (forthcoming). C. R. Orton and L. M. B. Miller in J. Schofield and L. Miller *et. al. Excavations at New Fresh Wharf, City of London, 1974–8* (forthcoming).

PERKINS (1940). J. B. Ward Perkins *Medieval Catalogue*, London Museum Catalogue 7 (London, 1940).

PRENDERGAST (1975). M. D. Prendergast 'Limpsfield Medieval Coarseware: Descriptive Analysis' *Surrey Archaeol. Collect.* 70 (1975) 57–77.

RACKHAM (1976). O. Rackham *Trees and Woodland in the English Landscape* (London, 1976).

RENN (1964). D. F. Renn *Potters and Kilns in Medieval Hertfordshire* (Hertfordshire Local History Council, 1964).

RHODES (forthcoming). M Rhodes 'A pair of 15th century Spectacle Frames from the City of London' *Antiq. J.* 62(i) (forthcoming).

RIGOLD (1972). S. E. Rigold 'Numismatica' in S. Moorhouse 'Finds from Excavations in the Refectory at the Dominican Friary, Boston' *Lincolnshire Hist. and Archaeol.* 7 (1972, 21–53) 44–5.

RILEY (1861). H. T. Riley (trans.), J. Carpenter and R. Whitington *Liber Albus* (London, 1861).

RILEY (1868). H. T. Riley *Memorials of London and London Life in the XIIIth, XIVth and XVth Centuries* (London, 1868).

RUTTER (1961). J. G. Rutter 'Medieval Pottery in the Scarborough Museum' *Scarborough Archaeol. Soc. Res. Rep.* 3 (1961).

SABINE (1937). E. L. Sabine 'City Cleaning in Medieval London' *Speculum* 12 (1937) 19–43.

SALZMAN (1923). L. F. Salzman *English Industries of the Middle Ages* (Oxford, 1923).

SALZMAN (1952). L. F. Salzman *Building in England down to 1540* (Oxford, 1952).

SIEBENLIST-KERNER (1978). V. Siebenlist-Kerner 'The chronology, 1341–1636, for certain hillside oaks from western England and Wales' in J. Fletcher (ed.) *Dendrochronology in Europe* (Oxford, 1978) 157–61.

SHARPE (1889). R. R. Sharpe (ed.) *Calendar of Wills Proved and Enrolled in the Court of Husting, London, AD 1258–AD 1688* 1 (London, 1889).

SHARPE (1890). R. R. Sharpe (ed.) *Calendar of Wills Proved and Enrolled in the Court of Husting, London, AD 1258–AD 1688* 2 (London, 1890).

SHARPE (1913). R. R. Sharpe (ed.) *Calendar of Coroners Rolls of the City of London, AD 1300–1378* (London, 1913).

SHEPPARD (1977). D. Sheppard 'A Medieval Pottery Kiln at Pinner, Middlesex' *London Archaeol.* 3, No. 2 (1977) 31–5.

SKEAT (1867). W. W. Skeat (ed.) W. Langland *The vision of William concerning Piers Plowman* E.E.T.S. 28 (1867).

SMITH (1848). C. Roach Smith *Collectanea Antiqua* 1 (London, 1848).

SMITH (1854). C. Roach Smith *Catalogue of the Museum of London Antiquities* (London, 1854).

STOTHARD (1817). C. A. Stothard *The Monumental Effigies of Great Britain . . .* (London, 1817).

TAIT (1955). H. Tait 'Pilgrim-Signs and Thomas, Earl of Lancaster' *Brit. Mus. Quarterly* 20 (1955) 39–46.

TATTON-BROWN (1974). T. Tatton-Brown 'Excavations at the Custom House' *Trans. London Middlesex Archaeol. Soc.* 25 (1974) 117–219.

TATTON-BROWN (1975). T. Tatton-Brown 'Excavations at the Custom House Site, City of London, 1973—Part 2' *Trans. London Middlesex Archaeol. Soc.* 26 (1975) 103–70.

THOMAS (1929). A. H. Thomas (ed.) *Calendar of Plea and Memoranda Rolls 1364–1381* (Cambridge, 1929).

TURNER (1967). D. J. Turner 'Excavations near Merton Priory, 1962–63' *Surrey Archaeol. Collect.* 64 (1967) 35–70.

TURNER (1975). D. J. Turner 'Medieval Pottery Kiln at Bushfield Shaw, Earlswood: Interim Report' *Surrey Archaeol. Collect.* 70 (1975) 47–65.

VINCE (1977). A. G. Vince 'Some Aspects of Pottery Quantification' *Medieval Ceramics* 1 (1977) 63–74.

VON BOCK (1971). G. R. von Bock *Steinzeug, Kataloge des Kunstgewerbemuseums Köln* (Cologne, 1971).

WARD AND WILSON (1978). G. K. Ward and S. R. Wilson 'Procedures for Comparing and Combining Radiocarbon Age Determinations: a Critique' *Archaeometry* 20 (1978) 19–32.

WEBSTER AND CHERRY (1973). L. E. Webster and J. Cherry 'Medieval Britain in 1972' *Medieval Archaeol.* 17 (1973) 138–53.